GRINDHOUSE PURGATORY'S GREATEST HITS

Contents

Cover: ***Codename: Wild Geese*** (1984) © Ascot Film/ Gico Cinematografica

Publisher and Editor-in-Chief: Pete Chiarella. Contributors: Bill Adcock, Dr. Rhonda Baughman, Ken Kish, Dave Kosanke, Robert Morgan, Cory Udler, Douglas Waltz, Mike Watt

THANK YOU

I honestly never expected **Grindhouse Purgatory** to go beyond one issue. The backstory here is that a group of us wanted to start a **Screw**-type of magazine. So I tried to find out who really owned the damned thing. I was given a price, $150K, by the so-called owner. Guys I knew that worked for **Screw** told me to stay away from it, that the name now was poison. So I had to figure something else out.

Andy Copp was a key player in this, he was down for it, but sadly he passed away before we could get this together. So we figured a one-time tribute issue to our friend. After the first issue, people asked when the next one was coming out. I never figured on this happening; so I put the word out that if you wanted to try writing, show me what you have.

So a group of people came on board. Some are still here, others moved on. As with anything new, **GP** had growing pains and had to find a direction. I didn't want to cover the same tired out shit like **Friday the 13th, Elm Street, Halloween** as they have been done to the death. I wanted to go with every genre of grindhouse films there is. I also decided after issue # 3 that I had to stop trying to be the next Al Goldstein.

I had my detractors and enemies as Al did, so I bashed them. This was non-productive, so I stopped. I was dealing with personal attacks that had nothing to do with **GP**, and everything to do with people who felt they should be included. We had to explain to Amazon that a certain party's "reviews" were just personal attacks on yours truly. So it stopped.

 I decided to do this "Greatest Hits Issue" for a couple of reasons. One, we set the cover price too low to fund future issues. Two, to take out the negative stuff I was putting in. Then I wrote some new stuff and had others write some new stuff so you get your money's worth. Right now **GP** has a core group of writers who know their stuff and are passionate about it. When I decided to pay homage to the company that spawned 42nd Street Pete, **Something Weird Video**, the response was huge. Now we are going on fourteen issues.

Right now I would like to thank the writers who contributed articles in the early days, but for whatever reasons, dropped out. Guys, you are always welcome to come back. So to Cory Udler, Dave Kosanke, Annie Riordan, Superfan Rob, and Bill Adcock, thank you, **GP** wouldn't have been a success without your contributions. And a special thanks to Mike Watt, who I have probably driven insane at this point, but Mike is the glue that puts everything together twice a year, and without him, there wouldn't be a **GP**.

Lastly, thanks to you, the readers of **GP**. In a world of electronic, generic media, you made a hardcore printed magazine a success. It is because of your support, **GP** continues and will keep giving you the best we have. I think Andy Copp would be proud of us.

—Stay Sick, but stay safe.
42P

A Totally PC Interview

by Dr. Rhonda Baughman

Well, there's nothing ***really*** all that PC about Grindhouse Purgatory's PC—Pete Chiarella—or 42nd St. Pete as we also call him, but he definitely has a political mindset that is more grounded in logic than literally anyone in our current GOP administration; moreover, he has a more coherent platform than one might think possible for a purveyor of porn and down and dirty loops. OR – maybe that's precisely why Pete's Making America Something That Doesn't Suck Again campaign could win the hearts and minds of all citizens: 42nd St. Pete's actually worked for a living – hard like the rest of us– on the fringes and in the trenches right alongside the people who are the real entrepreneurial backbone and foundation behind the spirit of the capitalism. [1] The masses are part of the reason for capitalism in its current incarnation – and I don't mean that in a nasty way, but imagine, for just a moment, if everyone reading this wanted something, the same thing, so badly they were willing to work en masse, do what's necessary, to get that thing?

> *"That's the trouble with the world [Rhonda] darlin'. People got different ideas*
> *concernin' what they want out of life." - Terry Alexander, Day of the Dead*

We have a lot of power, those of us in that mass, and when we realize it, act upon it, we'll be like the new lead Cenobites ruling over our shared land—but benevolently, empathetically, and intelligently.

> *"We have such sights to show you!" - Doug Bradley, Hellraiser*

---

[1] https://aeon.co/ideas/what-did-max-weber-mean-by-the-spirit-of-capitalism
[2] Rhonda's note: and that sweet, sweet VHS box cover art!
[3] https://spectrum.ieee.org/computing/it/the-lost-picture-show-hollywood-archivists-cant-outpace-obsolescence

"Yeah, like universal healthcare, affordable college tuition, and no more abortion debate—ever—because Roe v. Wade. Also – we have snacks." - Dr. Rhonda Baughman, Hellraiser Ground 0: Let's Do This Shit!

It's a beautiful dream, isn't it? And I asked Pete for his version of the political wet dream. If he could fix the strange times we're in, what's his list of action items? They included:

- Decriminalize marijuana//Offender amnesty, pardons// medical & recreational legal, all levels
- End all aid to Middle East, move troops home and to Mexico/Canada borders
- Russia can fuck right off. We can be civil, but not BFFs
- Tax rate is 10% all individuals, Corporations at 50%
- Current administrative passports revoked/assets frozen, independent investigation to detect extent of damage
- #HealthcareForAll
- #EndStudentDebt, affordable tuition
- UBI revisited
- Women's & LGBTQ rights at forefront
- Short leash on corporations—curb greed: end extravagant bonuses and golden parachutes

There are certainly more we could list, as well as expand on the above, but I think these are bonny swell places to move forward for all mankind, towards an inclusive future – a vision of what's to come, of what could be. One very important step has already happened! Like a God for the rest if is: he created **Grindhouse Purgatory.**

"GP began with … well, to be honest, there was no vision initially. It was a lark, an idea to honor filmmaker Andy Copp. I thought it would be a one-off," Pete says. "I had originally planned to buy **Screw Magazine**, continue in the Al Goldstein tradition but couldn't find out who owned it anymore. Then I heard they wanted $150,000 for the name alone and I was warned away from the deal by a number of people. I had also worked for Goldstein's replacement and it was not a good time; I didn't last a year. So, I obviously decided against the buy in the end. I was fine with the one issue of Screw I was able to contribute to and see my name in, frankly. But there was still the idea a lot of us had—to do something to honor Andy. We missed him. His suicide was tough on a lot of us and to cope, we wanted to do something in his memory, and so that first issue of **GP** was born," Pete says.

"But," he continues, "a few weeks after the first issue, folks came to me to ask when the next one was coming out. That surprised me. So, I started thinking, if issue 1 pays for 2 and 2 pays for 3, well, maybe this is the way we honor Andy. And here we are – six years and many issues later," he says. "As much as I love the magazine and what we write, it's also about giving back. The SWV tribute issue was one of my favorites and many readers let me know they enjoyed it, too. Giving back, paying homage and tribute to the things you love – it's important. You never know where it might lead."

The name 42nd St. Pete scares the fuck out of some people. His thoughts confuse people. He sometimes opens his mouth against injustice and sometimes he just opens his mouth to hear some words come out. He's unpredictable. But I love it when people I don't know personally, people who don't love me unconditionally, find me to say thanks for something I wrote, to tell me how much they loved something I did, appreciated my shit that I poured my heart and soul into. It means a lot to me readers and fans do that. It was an honor, too, to be asked to be a guest at InclusionCon. I've always been a believer in equal rights – and while I'm pretty straight, I don't care who you love or what you do—I think you should have the right to do what makes you happy, do what you please. Not my place to knock any lifestyle. So long as no one's getting hurt, you know? Bans based on sex or gender are complete bullshit. I hope InclusionCon goes well for everyone and all hopes and dreams are realized there. It's one day and one shot; I'm excited to see what happens!"

It was important to both Pete and the magazine's editor Mike Watt that **Grindhouse Purgatory** be available in both print and digital media. Fans requested both and Watt delivered. "Streaming services are great for a lot of people but the love and need for physical media remains," Pete says. "It always will. Physical media is not dead. It's only dead if people want it to be. As great as streaming can be, the problem is there's one company coming to swallow it all: Disney. Mom, smiles, apple pie, and God Bless America and that's all fine, but what's going to happen to all the risqué media? The indie content and media and art with the gore? With controversy? We've seen one purge with no solid reasons given from Amazon already—do we really want to see physical media disappear and risk having things we love taken from us because someone else said so? I know I don't."

"DVDs, VHS, and Blu-Ray, as well as print journalism, isn't just for collectors. It's something everyone should think about it. If you love something, you should own it. If it's extra special to you, own two copies. I'm willing to bet that someone, somewhere, wants to make what you love disappear. And they'll give many reasons why what you love should disappear, but there's only one real reason: because they can."

"*Three on a Meathook* for example—it's not exactly phenomenal. There is that one segment [2] but overall, it's meh. But I know a lot of people who love it. You're probably one of them. Hard to find on VHS, right? No real DVD release unless you count that burnt shit. But because of one scene, or the title, or the cover, or whatever—if you love it, I'm telling you, get a physical copy. VHS and even a shit DVD. When large corporations can make things disappear, get rid of any thing they wish, any time they wish - under the guise of cleansing and morality and religion and…it's about getting rid of the fun…and about sanitizing the world. That day isn't just coming. It's already here. So go buy those physical copies of the things you love – support those men and women who are breaking their backs to make a living and to make sure we have access to all the entertainment we wish. The new content and the old content," Pete says.

Love or hate any genre or industry – the fact remains the smartest, and most creative and capable among us have a real issue with arbitrary authority. I don't think that's just me. If I want to read or watch horror, or porn, or horror porn, or something just plain weird from outside the US, I don't need idiot 'officials' with no knowledge of my tastes and proclivities enforcing their own (or lack thereof on me). It's gross and just plain dumb to think I would ever, EVER, give up my autonomy, my identity, or my freedom of choice.

"The adult entertainment industry may need an overhaul, yes, and there may be some real scumbags," Pete says.

"And what industry is free of those?" I add.

"Exactly. Nothing's perfect and there may need to be protections put into place, but what it doesn't need is sanitized. How much more old material do you want? How much new material do you want? Whichever it is, know that these films deemed "offensive" in any way will be the first to go. It's the reason I have large library and don't jettison much. And film itself holds up – if it's maintained and stored properly. Those horror classics so many of us hold dear: *The Texas Chainsaw Massacre*, *Night of the Living Dead*, *Cannibal Holocaust*, those are examples of the first ones that will go. It pains me that for as much as we digitize, we can't keep up with it all and if technology gets ruined, there may be no way to replace it especially if the original negatives and other original materials has been dumped into an ocean or into a landfill. When that happens – it's only a short matter of time before that media, that art from all genres is gone – and gone forever." [3]

"And who decides what stays - and what goes? Streaming may be great for most people as far as it goes … but not as far as I go." -David J. Schow, The Big Crush

"In terms of new stuff" Pete continues "some of the best art and film and such aren't coming of America. And I want to see them as they are. Not after they're blue-penciled to death. I don't want anything made 'more palatable' by people I don't respect before I even get a chance to see it. I want to make the choice about what I want to see and what I don't want to see. I don't like things shoved down my throat either - that illusion of choice modern cinema gives us, for example. I might get a little excited about the new *King Kong* movies coming out – bi g monsters kicking ass is one of my favorite film eras – but that's it. And I know superheroes are a big deal and that's great if they're your thing, but I still want different choices. I don't want choices taken from me, nor made for me. I see the box office records were 'smashed' and over $350 million was made for the latest superhero caper, and theaters sold out for the opening weeks, but it costs more to go to the theater now [4] So what, I say – I want to see what those

---

[2] Rhonda's note: and that sweet, sweet VHS box cover art!

[3] https://spectrum.ieee.org/computing/it/the-lost-picture-show-hollywood-archivists-cant-outpace-obsolescence

[4] http://money.com/money/5109443/movie-ticket-price-2017/

numbers look like after inflation is taken into account," he says. [5]

"You want it? Own a copy. Support the artist when you can. There's no reason to be bored or complacent. Ever. Go find what you're into. Can't find it – then go create it. " -Dr. Rhonda Baughman, Medium Chill

"I wish could say that I had some idea GP would work, but truthfully, I just didn't," Pete says. "And as much fun as my first three issues were – they were what I'd call growing pains. We didn't want to be just a horror magazine. We're into all of it: art, literature, culture, film. The more obscure the better: we love bringing it into the light. But I do think we've found our groove, a groove at any rate. And we're not saying we know what people want to read either. But they continue to let us know what they enjoy reading and I appreciate that. So, that's one thing we're going to focus on. But those first three issues? They're not part of the current vision we have for the magazine. There will be no more trashing people and we've had to weed out the folks whose hearts just weren't in it, who weren't as excited to create with us anymore. All the writers are hard workers and maybe they came in to fill a certain knowledge gap, but I need to be clear: there are no bad guys here. Just plenty of good people, a few of which I'd like to think I let in, you know, the same way I was let in – if SWV hadn't let me in, if Goldstein's replacement hadn't let me in, then I wouldn't be here and 42nd St. Pete wouldn't exist. I just want to return the favor – and leave the door open for others who'd like to come in."

"What do you think Andy might say if he could see ***Grindhouse Purgatory*** today?" I ask. And I ask because this is just the way I think – and I'm of the mindset Andy would be pleased.

"I hope so," Pete says. "It's still a tribute to him, really. I still miss him. I know a lot of people do. And I don't think the subject of depression should be as difficult to talk about as it is sometimes. Depression is a disease and we can't keep treating it like some unmentionable subject. It shouldn't be taboo.[6] It's insidious and affects millions of people. It affects people I know and love. It affects me. May is Mental Health Awareness month, but that month should be every month. It's part of universal healthcare which this country desperately needs. I find myself often thinking of a quote from ***Lethal Weapon*** where Gibson's character says he thinks about suicide everyday but he also thinks of reasons not to do it – everyday. And I get that. Man, do I get that. I think he'd [Andy] want us to talk about it and to keep fighting."

Pete's not just saying that. Anyone who knows depression understands there are depths that even the hardiest of warriors sometimes sink into and are unable to find a way out. The truth is we might never know if Andy can see us, if he appreciates how many miss him, but if he can, I suspect he'd be amazed at the number of people he touched and encouraged and still continues to inspire today.

"Some readers have requested a sequel to ***Whole Bag of Crazy*** and I've been thinking about it. Some want to hear about the menagerie of pets at my house over the years, and the ones I currently have," Pete says.

"Cuddles is an inspiration, frankly," I say.

"As of today, he's still here. Alert and mobile, taking food through the syringe," Pete says. Cuddles is a cranky-looking iguana who has a tumor. And while we can't all go bankrupt saving our beloved reptiles, we will go as far as we can to ensure they have the highest quality of life while with us. When he's not taking care of pets, he has movie nights—invite only—and can be found creating grindhouse art and writing, if not his own memoirs or GP, then for my own ***Medium Chill*** series. "Aside from, hopefully, more collaboration and expansion with Happy Cloud Media," Pete says, "I'm also hoping there are more filmmakers in the area, creating and inventing new ideas. I'd love to collaborate on projects in the future. What I also have in my head are some behind-the-scenes convention memories I'm thinking about trying to organize in some way. There's so much to recall, though, I'm not sure where to start: promoters, guests, different eras. I'm going to keep thinking in it," he says.

Pete and I both share the same high level of love and respect for Cinema Wasteland – the much-loved fan convention in Strongsville, OH held twice a year by proprietors Ken and Pam Kish. There's never been a bad convention – as a guest or as an attendee, Pete tells me – and I can say the same. Whether I'm sitting at a table or shopping at them – a good time is sure to be there. They get great guests, both regular and new, guests and vendors

---

[5]   https://www.boxofficemojo.com/about/adjuster.htm
[6]   https://adaa.org/about-adaa/press-room/facts-statistics

are in one big room, and the vibe is chill, intimate, and welcoming. An on-site hotel restaurant doesn't suck and if the rooms happen to be sold out and you need to crash, chances are someone knows someone who has a place to rest or lay your head. We're fortunate to have had such a convention for as long as we have and I think Ken and Pam are aware of our gratitude.

"I love seeing my friends at Wasteland. I enjoy meeting new people. I like the variety of personalities in one spot," Pete says.

It's not been easy these last few years for imaginative types, artists, creators, and empaths—while we swim through the trauma of 21ˢᵗ century strange times, looking for artistic islands to visit and rest and catch and draw our collective breath, it feels like we're finally, *finally,* reaching more stable shore. We're not there yet, but we can at least see it through the haze and fog of madness. Although we're told unemployment is low and the economy is bustling, what consumers are, and are not, buying is more telling about the state of the economy than reports from on high. Handshake deals are less likely and risks, if taken at all, are minimal. But many of us out here are still trying, still swimming (even if upstream), still creating – we haven't given up. We're not going to. In the end, that's what will lead us to steadier land – that beautiful beach just waiting for us if we continue to breathe and fight and swim hard for it. [7]

---

[7]   Yes, I'll drown an optimist. I know.

42ND STREET PETE'S
TOP TWENTY GRINDHOUSE HORROR FILMS

1. ***Blood Feast:*** HG Lewis and David F Friedman's gore classic set the bar for on screen violence and gave the movie going public something they had never seen before: Blood & guts in vivid color. TV stations were warned no to pick up this film or ***The Flesh Eaters*** as they were *wayyy* too extreme for even late night viewing.

2. ***The Flesh Eaters:*** black & white classic exploitation/Horror that delivered exactly what it promised, a human being stripped of flesh in minutes. Great score, edited by Radley Metzger, a Nazi mad scientist, and great, for its time, gore effects.

3. ***Night of the Living Dead:*** The first real American horror film and the first real American Monsters, Ghouls, then zombies. This one rebooted the horror film and the floodgates opened. Reviled by critics when it first was released, now considered THE classic horror film

4. ***I Drink Your Blood***: One of the first NOTLD imitations ,Satan worshippers eat meat pies contaminated with rabies and go on a bloody rampage. Released by Jerry Gross as a double bill with a retitled black & white clunker, ***I Eat Your Skin***, the poster and ad. mattes screamed "Two Bloody Horrors to Rip Your Guts Out". Director David Durstun just slapped an R rating on the poster, but got caught by the MPAA. Quick cuts were made and the film attained legendary status. A completely uncut print was finally put out by Grindhouse Releasing.

5. ***Texas Chainsaw Massacre:*** There's nothing I could say about this film that hasn't been said before. A terrifying film with one of the most unique killers in grind house cinema. This is one film that sequels & remakes could never top. Long live Leatherface.

6. ***Bloody Pit of Horror:*** One of the first 'Euro Horrors" to hit these shores. Released by Pacemaker as part of a double bill with Terror Creatures from the Grave, it was my introduction to these type of films. Mickey Hargitay's over the top portrayal as The Crimson Executioner had me mesmerized as he stabbed, cut, burned & tortured a castle of semi naked models. I stayed and saw it twice.

7. ***Zombie:*** Imported right after ***Dawn of the Dead***, ***Zombie*** was first perceived as a rip off, but it was a completely different approach to the genre. Where ***Dawn*** hasn't held up well, ***Zombie*** more than has. Zombie put Lucio Fulci on the map. The NYC area was plastered with posters of a rotting Zombie face with the tag line "We are going to Eat You!!" courtesy of Jerry Gross who originally released the film.

8. ***Maniac***: A tour e Force performance by Joe Spinell, horrific gore effects from Tom Savini, and directed by Bill Lustig, this film was one you either loved or it infuriated you with its violence toward women. Eagerly anticipated by fans, I had a fever of 102, but had to see it. A disturbing film on many levels.
9. ***Halloween:*** Psycho may have been the first mad slasher film, but Halloween was the one who took it and made it a franchise. Too bad it spawned soooo many shitty imitations.

10. ***The Hills Have Eyes:*** Wes Craven's 2nd film and arguably his best. White bread family battles cannibal mutants in the desert. Still packs a punch today and put Michael Berryman on the map.

11.***Grave of the Vampire:*** How can you not love a film that is rated PG and opens with a rape in a grave? A well. crafted, violent film with William Smith & Michael Pataki as father & son vampires. Creepy, bloody and one hell of a battle between the two at the film's climax. One tasteless scene has Mom cutting her breasts to feed the vampire baby. An unheralded sleaze classic.

12. ***Mad Doctor Of Blood Island:*** Second film in what would be known as The Blood Island Trilogy, the first being Brides of Blood. Dr. Lorca' green blooded monster tears up the locals in various gruesome ways. Patrons were give packets of green blood to protect them from becoming green-blooded monsters. The monster came back for another round of carnage in Beast of Blood

13. ***Sssss:*** Sure there are a lot of snake movies, but this one has a guy change into a King Cobra. Veteran character actor Strother Martin is a real sincere but totally made scientist with a penchant for experimenting on his assistants. Real snakes are used and the transformation from man into snake will blow your mind. ***Ssss*** was on a double bill with ***The Boy Who Cried Werewolf*** when I managed a Drive-In during the early 70s.

14. ***Cannibal Holocaust:*** The mother of all cannibal films and the one that really pushed the viewer's envelope. Pulled from several theaters for animal violence, this was the film legends were made of. For years stories persisted as to whether some of the killing were actually real. Also a lot of stories about cut footage surfaced. A grueling viewing experience then and the film will still kick your balls up into your throat when viewed today.

15. ***Last House on the Left***: Here's a film that was supposed to be a hardcore porn film, but turned out to be the ultimate exploitation roughie and put Wes Craven on the map. We all know the story; four scumbags grab two girls, rape & kill them, then the girl's parents extract bloody revenge. The one film that really shook up patrons in the early 70s and opened the door from more depravity to come.

16. ***Suspiria:*** truly terrifying debut film from Argento and the music by Goblin was a first as it blew you away. Tag line '***The only thing more terrifying than the first 89 minutes are the last ten***' was actually true for a change. Still scares the piss out of people today.

17.***The Howling:*** Joe Dante's clever homage to werewolf films and showcasing the SPFX talent of Rob Bottin. Full transformations, gore, in jokes and people changing into werewolves while screwing, how can you not like that?

18. ***Make Them Die Slowly:*** AKA ***Cannibal Ferox***. Debuted at The Liberty Theater on 42nd Street in 1981. A film that promised over 30 acts of cruelty & torture and, for once they weren't kidding. A manipulative and morally bankrupt film, and perhaps the most prophetic title ever slapped on a deuce's marquee as the entire area was dying out slowly.

19. ***Basket Case:*** Frank Henenlotter's timeless midnight show classic about brotherly love, revenge, and "the deuce". ***Basket Case*** played at The Waverly Theater in NYC for a couple of years. Dedicated to HG Lewis, it spawned two sequels and put Frank on the map as perhaps one of the last Grindhouse filmmakers.

20. ***Horror Express:*** Completely underrated film about an alien life force who takes over bodies on the Trans. Siberian express after being trapped in a frozen caveman. Thawed out, it creates a reign of terror on the train. Peter Cushing & Christopher lee star and Telly Savalas is a Russian Cossack who is possessed by the creature.

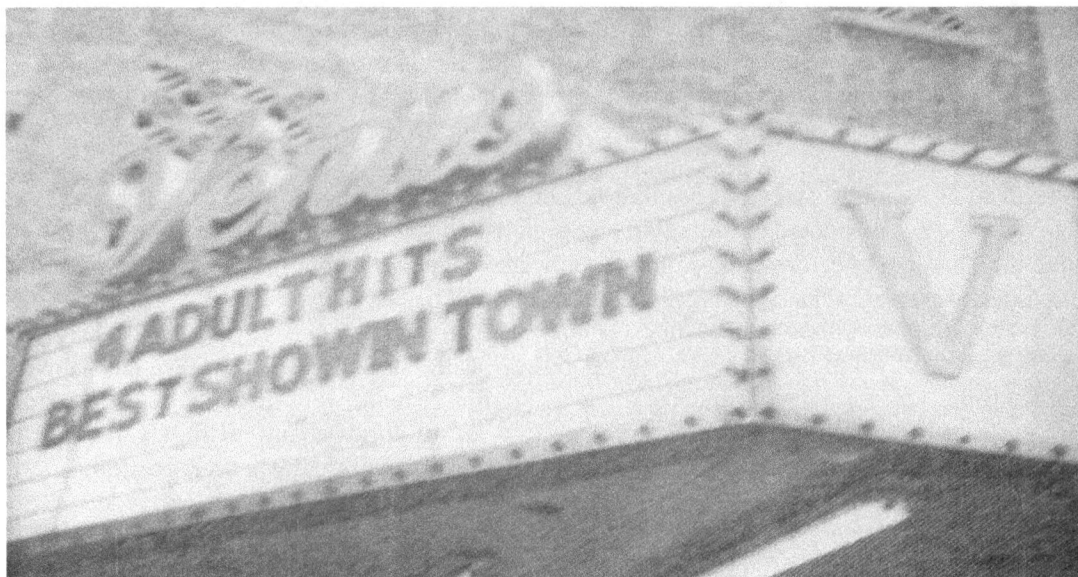

A Lost Saturday Night At The Venus

One of the most notorious porn grindhouse was located on 8th Avenue at 45th Street. It was originally called the Eros 2 as it was practically right next to the Eros 1, a gay porn palace. It was eventually changed to The Venus. The Venus was part of a chain of grindhouse and storefront theaters owned by Chelly Wilson. Wilson controlled most of Times Square's porn theaters and films.

Other theaters under her wing were all the Avon Theaters, The Venus, The Park Miller, The Doll, and many others. Chelly also produced The Avon films like *Taming of Rebecca, Kneel Before Me, Wicked School Girls, Story of Prunella*, and others. It is worth noting that The Avon Films were singled out by the Meese Commission as the "most vile and violent examples of mob produced pornography." Wilson also was a film distributor under the name Variety Films. Strangely enough, the Variety Films library was warehoused in the loft of the Venus.

My first encounter with The Venus was back in 1973 when it was still called The Eros 2. I had found a huge store on 8th Ave called Beeline Books. It was a great place to browse through piles of movie stills, lobby cards, and magazines. It was in spitting distance of The Eros 2. One day after buying a pile of stuff, it started raining heavy.

Now back in the '70s, you took your life in your hands if you rode the subway. A guy with a bunch of stuff like I had was an easy target. Not wanting to get soaked to the skin or get ripped off, I decide to sit out the storm in the Eros 2. I paid the .99-cent admission and entered into the ominous darkness. The place had a funky smell: a combination of spilled malt liquors, piss, smoke, BO, and Pine Sol. As my eyes got accustomed to the gloom, I noticed several sleeping winos. I found a seat away from people and watched something called San Francisco Ball. Sounded innocent enough, but it wasn't. It was a Jack Genero roughie, complete with a kidnapping plot, multiple rapes, and switchblade torture.

A libido killer at best, and soft core. I left after that film as the rain had finally stopped. A few years down the road, The Eros 2 was renamed The Venus. The Venus showed three "features" nonstop from 10am until 7am. Admission during the day was $1.50, then it changed to $3.00 after 8pm. The Marquee said three continuous features, but never said exactly what they were. Sometimes they posted the titles on a hand written piece of paper on the box office window. Most films were on their 3rd run or just some perennial favorites that management knew would draw money. *Black Neighbors, Teenage Fantasies, Ride a Cocked Horse, The Big Man, Ravaged Models* and *The Horny Landlady* ran on and off for years. Mixed combos films (interracial sex) were real popular with the 8th Avenue aboriginals

My night at the Venus was out of necessity, so let me give you a time frame of that enchanting Saturday night. I started out about 9pm at my favorite watering hole, Club 44 on 44th Street. I hung out there with my barmaid/hooker friends, Lisa and Candy. About 11pm I cruised "The Deuce" in search of a movie to check out. *Ilsa, She. Wolf of the*

SS was at The Apollo for the umpteenth time. The last show was at 1:30 am, so I had some time to kill.

I felt a little pussy was in order, so I walked to the corner of 42nd and 8th to a place called the Dating Room. The Dating Room was a massage parlor on the 2nd floor of an old office building. I took and elevator up, then exchanged pleasantries with Leon, the thug/bouncer who was a career sex worker. Leon worked security for a lot of these places and we became friends for a few years.

The place always smelled of Perk, some sweet smelling disinfectant. A few girls were lounging around the waiting area. I picked a petite blonde named Celia, who I spent an enchanted half hour with. After that, I picked up a pint of hooch at Athena liquors, then checked out *Ilsa* for the 5th time. When *Ilsa* ended, the house lights came on and everyone was shooed out of the place. It had just started to rain, so I figured I'd go back to Club 44, then go to Candy and Lisa's place. I was too fucked up to even try to get back home.

As I rounded the corner on 44th street, I saw Nino the bouncer locking up the place. Shit, I thought, now I'm really fucked. The rain got heavier and I had two dry and not so dry choices. I could try to get to an afterhours place on the Lower East Side, or go to The Venus. The Venus won out as I knew I'd be soaked walking cross. town as no cabbie would pick a guy like me up. I drunkenly jogged a couple blocks to The Venus.

I paid the $3 and looked for a seat away from the army of winos, dust heads, faggots, pick pockets and other assorted lowlifes. *Flesh of the Lotus*, the John Holmes private eye film, was ending as I found a seat. I lit my lighter to make sure no one left a deposit on it. On screen was one of the worst Kung Fu fights in the history of western civilization between Holmes and director, Bob Chin. The soundtrack for *The Good, The Bad, and The Ugly* played in the background.

Teenage Fantasies, the pseudo. documentary that put Rene Bond on the map, was up next. Rene was holding a cock and told you she would make it come in a certain amount of time. You could set your watch by this. A big, black hooker plopped in the seat next to me. "Want anything for $10, honey?" she asked. I politely declined. Then she got a tad aggressive and dropped the price to $5. I told her to move on before I put my boot up her fat ass. She cursed me out and bitched about cheap. assed white boys before moving on.

All was quiet for a while, well quite if you don't mind the jungle like cacophony of wheezing, snoring, grunting and farting. Then it happened, a white out. The over used print had snapped, bathing the place in a bright white light. People were caught like deer in the headlights. The big hooker's head popped up from someone's lap with splooge dribbling down her chin. "Fix the fuckin' movie," the now awake crowd screamed. A quick splice and we were back to normal. I went to take a piss as I had just drained what was left of my pint. Some guy was complaining to the box office about having his wallet stolen. Seems he got his pocket picked while he had his pants down. You want to play, sometimes you pay more than you bargained for. I went back to my seat and closed one eye for a bit.

Teenage Fantasies ended and *The Horny Landlady* came on. This one had Vanessa Del Rio, Sharon Mitchell and Bobby Astyr. A NYC one-day wonder. Halfway through the film, the mezzanine lights came on. It was 7am, closing time. A bouncer walked down the aisles with a club, tapping on the seats of the more sedate patrons, rousing them out of their drug and alcohol stupors. As I walked out I noticed the floor was littered with condoms, empty malt liquor cans and pint bottles. I didn't envy the job of the cleanup guy who had a mere three hours to get the place tidied up before opening again at 10am.

The Venus lasted until the bitter end. City Hall was now putting undercover cops in the few remaining theaters to document sex acts between patrons. This was a "health risk" as spreading ground for AIDS. The city has closed virtually all the gay baths and theaters using the AIDS scare. Now they used the same ruse to shut down the straight porn grinders. The story goes that one night the cops just showed up and told everyone to go home. No fanfare, it was over. Variety Photoplays on the Lower East Side suffered the same fate.

The Venus was padlocked, although not before Chelly Wilson had most of the film prints removed when it became apparent the place would be on lock down. The Venus was eventually gutted and became a touristy restaurant. Chelly Wilson lived well into her 90s. After she died her daughter, Bondi, sold off The Venus and other properties. By the time I returned to the city to work at NYC Liquidators, most of 42nd Street and Times Square was a boarded up.

It was eerie seeing that once vibrant strip reduced to a burnt out shell of its former self. Today, it is "Disneyfied." Most of the major players of that era are either deceased or retired. The only thing that remains are the films. Battered, burned and riddled with splices, these films were the lifeblood of the grindhouses and they are all that remain of the wildest era we have ever known.

THE HARLOTS OF 42ND STREET

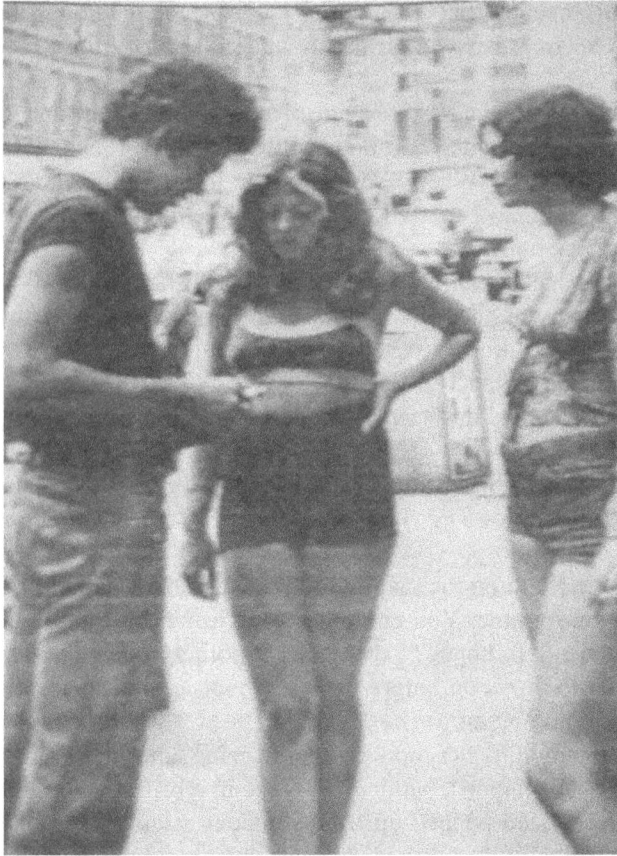

One thing was a given in NYC in the 70s, NYC was a hooker heaven. Be it a lowly drugged out $5 whore on 14th Street or a $200 penthouse call girl, there was something for every taste & price range. Prostitution was rampant, so rampant that in 1967 it was decriminalized by the State of NY from a crime & misdemeanor to an "offense." The maximum sentence dropped from a year to 15 days. This ruling had the unintentional effect of opening up Times Square for all kinds of prostitution.

In the '70s you couldn't stop at a light on 9th Avenue without having your car swarmed by garishly. dressed ladies offering to blow you in your car for as little as $10. Of course, dealing with a street girl was a risky proposition at best. These girls could and would pick your pockets while they sucked your dick. Worse, her pimp could hold you up while your pants were down. Other girls would rent a room in one of the crumbling hotels in the area. They would linger outside and entice potential customers to their rooms. Problem was they might not be alone in that room. Pity the poor guy who just got naked only to have a large black man barge in and demand to know what you are doing with his wife. Ripoffs and muggings were just part of the deal.

My first streetwalker experience took place at *The Green Lantern Motel* on 8th Avenue. The girl propositioned me outside. It was $30 for her and another $25 for the "bridal suite." The girl was nasty and farted a lot. Not a great 1st time, but a learning experience nonetheless. I did better with a bespeckled girl who was hanging outside a bookstore. The store has little "rooms" in the back and this chic slipped a condom on you with her tongue. After talking with her a bit, I found out we both went to the same high school.

In the '70s it was all a hustle. One of the truest films about this era was Andy Milligan's *Fleshpot on 42nd Street*. Everyone was selling their ass in one way, shape or form. You'd be sitting at the bar in the bowling alley in The Port Authority and some guy would offer you his "girlfriend." That same guy might burst into the room when you were in mid stroke too. The safest deal was an apartment brothel, but that was too pricy for the average john.

Then came the massage parlors. It was obvious that Mob would be involved in such a lucrative business. They created a quasi. legal entity with massage parlors, model studios, and photo studios. The first massage parlors were created by Marty Hodas, the hustler who created the peepshows—He took a couple of bookstores that were floundering and turned them into massage parlors. Of course the mob muscled in on this, and Hodas had no choice but to be "partners." This actually helped Hodas as he way able to expand his peep show machine outside of NY.

The mob didn't get into street prostitution as they felt pimps were too stupid to deal with. When a couple of pimps tried to open their own parlors, the places were fired bombed and the operators vanished. Each parlor had an entrance fee, some even had membership cards which gave regular patrons reduced rates.

Of course that fee didn't include the girl's tip. *The Dating Room*, right on 42nd Street, was on the 2nd floor of an office building. It was $13 to get in and tipping was 10 to 20 dollars. After you paid the admission, you were let into a room were at least a dozen girls of various ethnic backgrounds lounged around in lingerie. You would pick a girl, go to room and negotiate the tip. the dating room was pretty cool until it was closed down. It reopened as *Tanfastic*, a pseudo-tanning salon that was barebones & depressing. Not even a bed, just a shag rug on the floor.

There were dozens of these places and *Screw Magazine* reviewed them all and would actually warn patrons of rip off joints, something that didn't sit well with the boys. In fact a hit was put out on the owner, Al Goldstein. The hit was called off when a high ranking Capo pointed out that Goldstein's mag actually helped the mob make money as they owned all the theaters, book stores, strip bars and massage parlors. Each parlor had some kind of hook to get you in. *The Delicate Touch* featured topless shoeshines. *Cupid's Retreat* was a loft with six pup tents set up. Just perfect for the Times Square outdoorsman. *Holiday Hostesses* had three or four girls, of questionable health, sitting around in worn out lingerie. *The Red Ruby* offered 'manicures & pedicures' for men only. the girls dressed in nurse's uniforms. *The Studio* was a dark, small & dingy place that featured 3 unattractive women who, for $15, would let you get dressed in front of them. Anything else was extra. *Her Place* on 45th Street was closed and opened as *The Silver Slipper, Harlow's, The Blue Garter* and the *Lucky Lady*. Nasty place under any name, where the girls felt inclined to give painful VD exams to their customers. This was one of the first place to get the wrecking ball. One place on 14th Street was one flight up. It had no name and the women barely spoke English, but the women & staff there were unusually polite and friendly. This place stayed in operation long after everyone else was shut down.

The higher end "spas" had waterbeds, showers, hot tubs and real attractive girls. They were called *The Harem, The Retreat, the Taj Mahal, Tahiti,* and *Spartacus.* Prices started at $50 and that was '70s money. All of these places advertised in Screw. Massage parlors would hire drunks 7 junkies to hand out fliers on street corners. Independent girls, sick of dealing with pimps, set themselves up in apartments and ran their own ads. By the '80s you had houses of bondage, S&M parlors and Shemale hookers.

The scene still exists today, mostly though the Internet. No longer the "wild west" like everything else was back then, it's rather tame. Gone are 42nd Street and the Massage Parlors, The Spas, and the armies of spandex. clad streetwalkers. Now it is just a chaotic memory, which I actually cherish.

ORIGINS

by Cory J. Udler

When 42nd Street Pete mentioned he was going to put together a fanzine, a REAL honest to God fanzine, I jumped all over the chance to be a part of it. I mean, come on, it's 42nd Street Pete! 42nd Street is a man whom I have a tremendous amount of respect for and a man who IS Grindhouse, a man who was there. The human encyclopedia of everything that is great about cheap, sleazy, insane, bizarre, controversial cinema. And for me to have a small part in this fanzine is a true honor.

For those of you who have no idea who in the blue hell I am, you're not alone. My name is Cory J. Udler. I am a filmmaker and writer out of Wisconsin best known for my *Incest Death Squad* trilogy. I have also made a film called *Mediatrix*, I am wrapping up production on a short titled *Ed Gein: D.D.S.* (I'll give that one a second to sink in), I have written three films for the legendary Ted V Mikels, I have been featured in Lloyd Kaufman's *Produce Your Own Damn Movie* book, I have worked for Charles Band and Full Moon, and I'm also a Three Stooges fanatic and a hell of a good ballroom dancer.

As I mentioned above, I have written three films for Ted V Mikels. I know you guys not only know Ted but probably celebrate every film in the man's catalogue. I know I do. I have since I was 12. years-old and first saw Ted on Jonathan Ross's *The Incredibly Strange Film Show*. I am a fan of all of the heavyweights in the fringe cinema world: Andy Milligan, John Waters, HG Lewis and the list goes on and on. But Ted, there was just something about Ted that struck a chord with me. Was it his Dali mustache? Was it the fact that the first time I'd ever seen the man he was on my TV playing an accordion in the desert? Was it the films? *Astro Zombies, Corpse Grinders, Doll Squad*. Or was it the fact that Ted was, is and forever will be, the most sincere and passionate filmmaker on the planet?

After seeing Ted on the show I made it a point to seek out every single movie of his, and I did just that. My admiration for the man and my love of his films grew the older I got. I loved them for the sensationalism and the fact that these weren't "movies for everyone" when I was younger. It wasn't until I got older that I realized that Ted was a true maverick. He did everything HIS way, whether that was out of ego or necessity is a point I will let you argue. I just know that Ted marches to the beat of his own drummer and his legacy is a testament to how much one man can do with so little. And the fact that Ted is in his mid '80s now and STILL lives, eats, breathes and sleeps his next film is undeniable proof that Ted IS filmmaking.

About eight years ago I was surfing around online and I decided to search out Ted V Mikels. I hadn't heard anything about him in quite a few years and I thought maybe someone out there was as big of a fan of his films as mine. Instead I found the man himself: Ted V. Mikels. I found an e-mail address on his website and decided to shoot off a quick message. I remember writing something to the effect of "I don't know if this will ever reach Ted, but I wanted to thank him for all of the years of entertainment and inspiration." To my shock and delight, Ted himself replied to the message. He still uses that same AOL email address. He gave me his number and told me to call him sometime. I did. That conversation not only forged a friendship that I cherish but it also set in motion a writing partnership between myself and Ted that has spanned three movies to date.

Ted didn't have his next project in mind after his family film departure *Heart of a Boy*. He wanted to return to the horror genre, but not with something grossly exploitative. Instead, we came up with the film *Demon Haunt*, which initially was called *Demon Bloodlust*, but Ted thought that title was a bit too crass. Ted gave me a shot to write that movie. What's funny is that I wrote it knowing Ted's budgetary constraints. It wasn't until a little while into the process that Ted informed me that he was going to do a "CGI extravaganza" with *Demon Haunt*, a process that took over two years to complete. During that time Kevin Sean Michaels (*Vampira: The Movie*) was making his documentary, *The Wild World of Ted V Mikels*, and I met him in Toronto at Fan Expo. I was interviewed for the documentary and was officially and fully immersed forever in that Wild World of Ted V Mikels.

I wrote *Astro Zombies M3: Cloned* with Ted, which is such a fun and bizarre sequel to the franchise. I really felt like I could cut loose on that one. When Dr. DeMarco is reading a children's book to the Astro Zombie, that was me. And Ted must have loved it because he left it in. At one point Ted and I were talking back and forth and he said he wanted to include *The Doll Squad* in this new *Astro Zombies* movie. So, here's Cory not only writing an *Astro Zombies* sequel, but being given the opportunity to write *The Doll Squad* into the story as well! I was writing sequels to two of my favorite Ted V Mikels' movies. Surreal doesn't even begin to describe it. I attended the premiere of *AZM3* at the Palms in Las Vegas with my wife. Ted thanked everyone, by name, including me. If you would have told me 20 years ago that I would be having this experience I would have had you locked up. This is the stuff that dreams are made of, folks.

Ted rode the wave and success of *AZM3* directly into *Astro Zombies M4: Invaders from Cyberspace*. Ted and I talked a bit in the initial writing process of the movie, but he was working with some passionate filmmakers out of Florida who really took the reins on that film. I don't think I ever put pen to paper on part 4.

Then, in 2012, Ted and I started to discuss the next project. That project is *Paranormal Extremes: Text Messages From The Dead*. Nobody comes up with a title quite like Ted. Let's just say *Paranormal Activity* this is not. This is 100% Ted V Mikels and 100% Cory J. Udler. The last part, I don't know if that's good, but the one thing I always tell fans of Ted is that you won't find anyone who loves and respects Ted and his films as much as I do. The integrity, the charm and the fun you've come to expect from Ted's films is not only intact, but maybe it's amped up just a touch when I get my fingers in it.

I make much more subversive and raunchy and controversial films than Ted. My films feature nudity, drug use, tons of blood, and a boatload of bad language. Ted's films were never like that. But Ted still remains my favorite filmmaker and my biggest inspiration. I akin it to Cannibal Corpse being influenced by KISS. I think the highest form of flattery is to take what you learn and gain from a muse and to turn it into something completely your own. Like a parent probably looks at their children, gives them the best tools and advice they can, and then they turn them over to be their own person all while hoping they hold on to the important lessons and gifts you have given them. The gifts that Ted has given me over the years I hold deeply in my heart and soul. I've always said my proudest professional achievement was writing a film for Ted V Mikels. But one of my proudest achievements in my life is becoming good friends with the man I have idolized since I was 12. years. old. The man with the boar's tusk necklace, the handlebar mustache. The man who doesn't know the meaning of the word "quit." So, this weekend, as we celebrate who we are as fans, filmmakers, writers, authors, artists, actors, I thank you for taking a second to hang out with me and read this article. Because without Ted V Mikels, I wouldn't be here.

Theodore Vincent *Mikacevich*; April 29, 1929 – October 16, 2016

Linda Shaw

By Dave Kosanke[8]

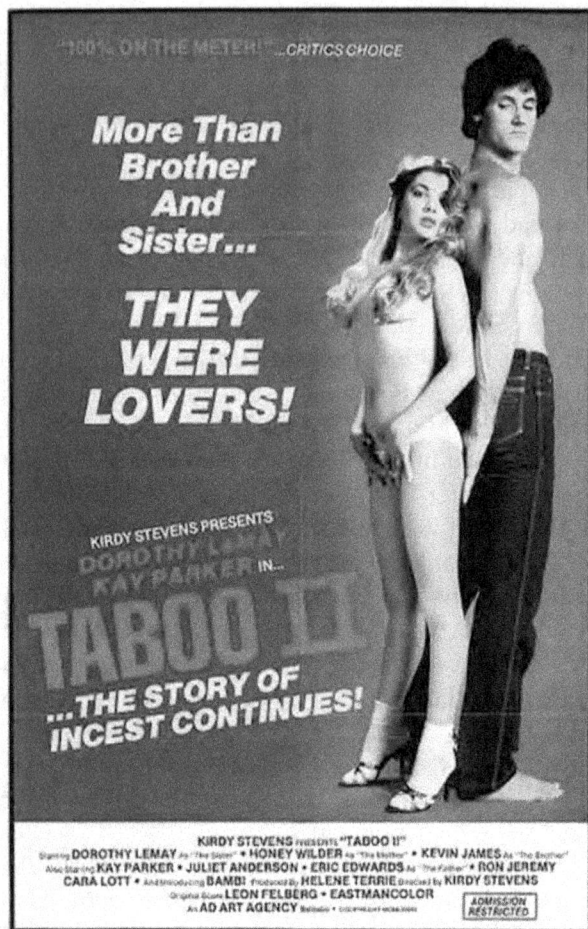

When one thinks about the golden age of pornography, the name Linda Shaw doesn't exactly spring to mind. Actually in the grand scheme of things, if you aren't a drooling porn freak like myself, you probably wouldn't know who she was. Well my intention here isn't to go into an in. depth study of her career, but to point out one oddity that sticks out like a sore thumb from her short lived XXX career...she-male encounters!

Linda Shaw did appear in quite a few high profile films between the years 1981. 1984. Chief among the highlights would be *Taboo II*, where she only gets a small part during an orgy scene conducted by Aunt Peg (Juliet Anderson) but it is one of the most famous porn series of all time so I thought I'd give it a mention. Next up would be *I Like To Watch* which holds a special place in my heart (see sidebar) but also remains a terrific film with (gasp!) good acting, cinematography, music (back when porno's actually had tunes created specifically for the movie and not just rehashed stock junk that you'd hear in nearly every single shot. on. video affair) and a luscious cast willing to ignite the screen on fire with stars like Little Oral Annie and Bridgette Monet. *Sorority Sweethearts* again pairs up Linda with Bridgette Monet, and young stud Marc Wallice (who would go on to become infamous when he tested HIV positive but forgot to tell his co. workers, one of which became infected) gets to appears in a few scenes with Linda. Again, this shot on film affair remains watchable both as a hardcore sex flick, and a lighthearted drama. Her main work is undoubtedly *Bold Obsession* where she gets to highlight nearly every scene as a woman being watched by an unknown dude who instructs her (off camera) to indulge in some wild and wooly sexual behavior, not only for his benefit but for the viewer as well. I guess if you want to see Linda at her all-time best, this would be a good place to start. She made one brief appearance in the mainstream market, playing herself, in Brian De Palma's sleazy *Body Double*. Sandwiched in between the full length flicks were a bevy of 8mm loops and shorts, including rolls in the hay with hall of famers Ron Jeremy and Paul Thomas to name but a few.

Digging up some of the films and shorts wasn't too hard, especially with the internet being such a valuable resource to track down this stuff. Yet the initial discovery of a film entitled *She Male Encounters 3* got my attention due to the involvement of Linda Shaw. When I saw a posting of this on an adult forum, I tried to find some information on it, and that proved futile. The only true source was the movie itself, available on VHS and DVD. The idea of chicks with dicks is *not* my idea of fun, yet the urge to see everything that Linda appeared in was too strong so I had to check it out for myself. This 1982 production directed by Kim Christy (who directed a handful of she. male flicks including *Dude Looks Like A Lady* which, alas, didn't star Steven Tyler) is not so much a movie *per se*, but 3 short vignettes strung together to "resemble" something akin to a film (running time 57 minutes and change). The first segment is entitled *The Seduction of Jennifer* which features Sharon Mitchell, one starlet that had no shame when it came to appearing in cutting edge stuff (for starters check out the similarly named *Violation of*

---

[8] Writer/Publisher *Liquid Cheese: Movies* and *Music To Mangle Your Mind!!!*

Jennifer).

The next romp goes by the title **TV Therapy** and features Linda as Carla Delmar which as far as I can tell was the only time she used that name. That proves to me that she didn't want this to be listed among her "straight" XXX affairs, hence the pseudonym. In this story she appears as Rita, a frustrated housewife chatting with transsexual performer Jaded Jennifer (whose character is called Jennifer, a common name in these here parts don't you think?), When her husband (Mark Walters) comes out dressed in drag, Rita exclaims "he's a queer!" Jennifer retorts with "take my advice and blow this instead" as she whips out her schlong, much to the amusement of Rita! From here we get down to the obligatory sex, which features Linda Shaw's typical gusto as she smokes up the screen. One element that makes this scene stick out is the fact that Linda lets Mr. Walters fuck her in the ass. Hardly groundbreaking by today's standards, but to my knowledge it is the only time she performed the act on camera, which again would maybe explain why she used a different name. Jaded Jennifer can't do much, and she. he. it remains a freak of nature that *only* would appeal to tranny lovers.

Finally the last piece is entitled **Dominant Desires** and has some S & M stuff thrown in, along with porner Craig Roberts who sucks off some she. male, so does that make him gay? The end result here is that this obscure curio from a bygone era of XXX cinema has very limited appeal (probably more shocking to one. handed viewers back then, but with today's love for the bizarre who knows how it would play?), but does this represent a skeleton in the closet for lovely Ms. Shaw? That of course is hard to say, and perhaps only she would know the answer.

The story doesn't end there however. An amazing discovery popped up unexpectedly when I came across a Swedish Erotica magazine entitled **Cross/Dress Stud** (#183) featuring Linda Shaw (referred to as Kitty in the accompanied text) and Mark Walters (dubbed Gabby) still dressed up as a (ugly) woman! What probably transpired was a photo shoot was conducted to incorporate two of the stars from the film. In the early '80s this was more common that you might think, since the smut market was glutted with hardcore magazines of all types. Videotapes had yet to really dent the marketplace, at least not enough so that fans wouldn't need to jerk off to magazines since they had the tape handy in their own home. So to fill that void specialty magazines and books were cranked out to keep those one handed viewers busy when they couldn't frequent their local peep show booth or raincoat theater. Linda Shaw just happened to be featured in numerous publications throughout her brief stint in the XXX business. Some of the more notable folks she worked with under the watchful eye of the photogenic lens were Eric Edwards, Tom Byron and the aforementioned Marc Wallice. The magazine boasts a pictorial that is separate from the film, thus eliminating Jaded Jennifer, which makes sense since I doubt the sales would have been as good had they included a tranny.

Believe it or not Swedish Erotica put out yet *another* mag with the two of 'em dubbed *Mr/Ms*. It is essentially the same pictorial but for some reason this publication has 2 extra pages in the beginning and different front and back covers. The text is also the same except for the aforementioned additional pages. This is #256 in the S. E. series and boasts "ALL NEW" on the cover whereas the **Cross/Dress Stud** mag doesn't bother selling itself as *new*.

In the grand scheme of things I may be the only person writing obsessively about Linda Shaw, but hey *somebody* needs to do it! Digging up and reporting about these obscure artifacts is something I enjoy doing, and I think that all of it remains worthy of some ink, no matter how tasteless or sick some folks think it is. I know my quest to find everything Linda contributed to isn't over yet, so who knows what I'll discover next!

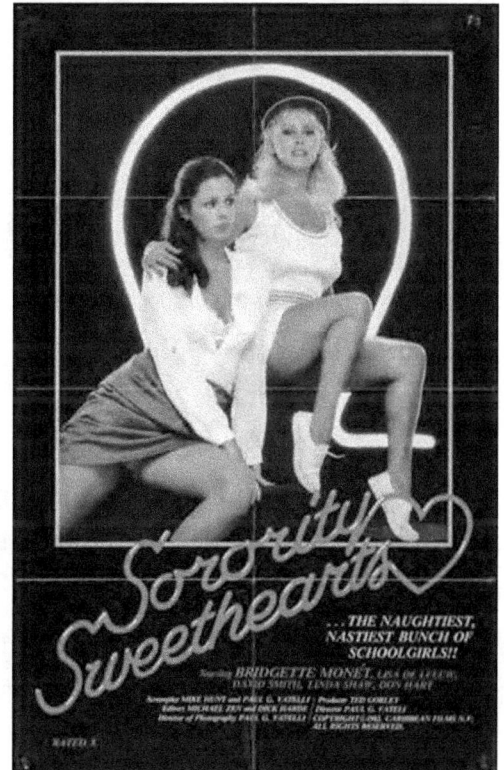

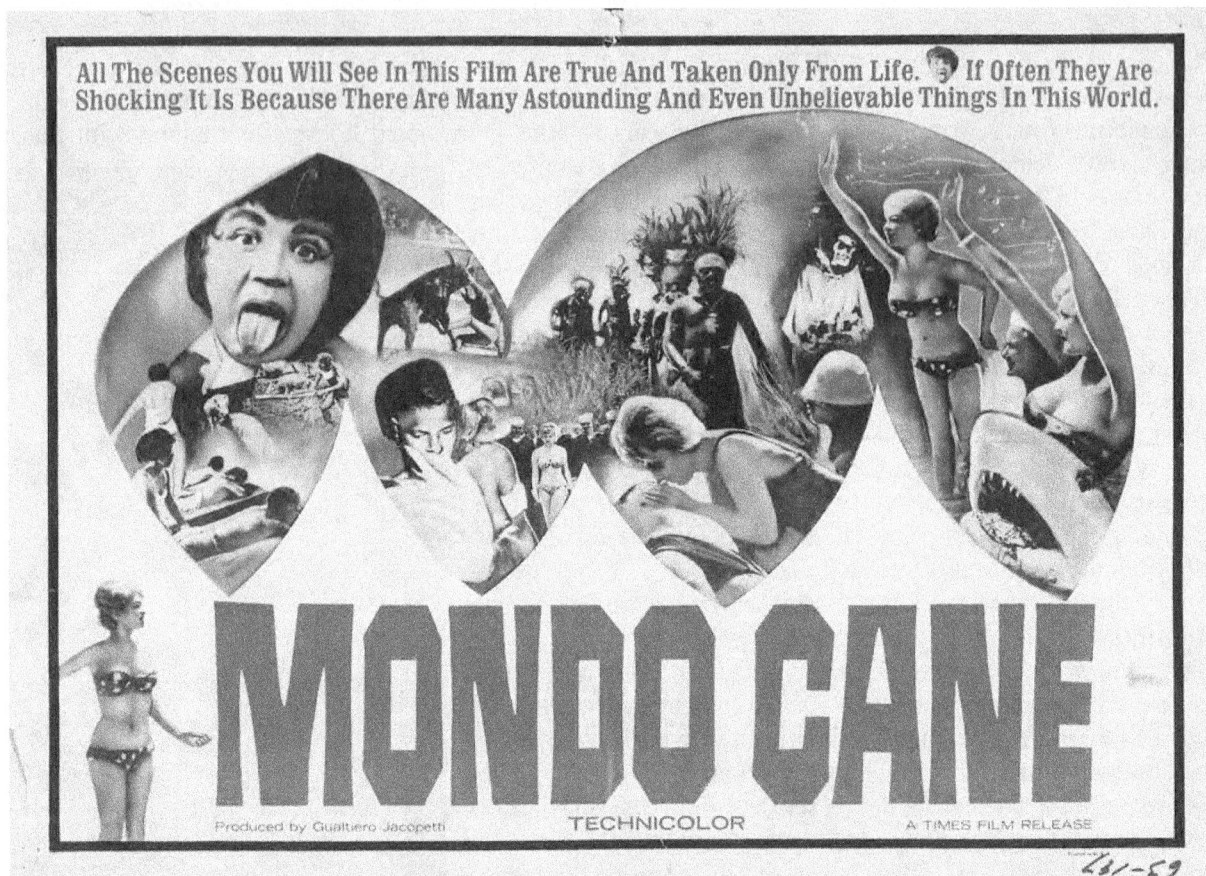

All The Scenes You Will See In This Film Are True And Taken Only From Life. If Often They Are Shocking It Is Because There Are Many Astounding And Even Unbelievable Things In This World.

MONDO CANE

Produced by Gualtiero Jacopetti   TECHNICOLOR   A TIMES FILM RELEASE

THE ROOTS OF MONDO

In 1963 Times Films released an Italian Import, **Mondo Cane**. Shot over a period of three years by documentary filmmakers Gualitero Jacapetti and Franco Properi, the film showcased worldwide weirdness. Arcane rituals, mutations from the Bikini Atoll Atomic Bomb tests, opium dens, victims of shark attacks, animal slaughter, drunken Germans punching each other out in beer gardens, a visit to a Chinese Death house and more. The film was a huge hit both in the States and abroad. The film's title song "More" was a bit hit also. The team of Jacapetti and Prosperi were just warming up.

Mondo Cane 2 was made up of unused footage from the first film. Prosperi, the more mercenary of the two, felt they "owed" the producers and put together another film. Jacapetti however didn't want this released. Prosperi also sold off footage to other producers for more "Mondo" type films. Their next film, **Women Of The World**, is just what it implies, a film shot all over the world featuring women of different cultures. To spice it up, they put in footage of bare breasted native women left over from **Mondo Cane**. This may have been shocking for its time, but now it's just a dated relic of early "Adults Only" cinema.

Africa Addio is the duo's most controversial film. Released in the States by exploitation czar, Jerry Gross, it was heavily edited and re titled as **Africa: Blood And Guts**. The film documented the political upheaval after The French and the British left. The film dwells on violence, death and atrocities of that era. The boys had balls, I'll give them that. They were almost executed by the Rebels. They were also accused of murder as they might have paid of firing squads to get a better shot of the executions. This is really grim stuff, especially the animal slaughter. Footage of mass graves, piles of severed hands, and victims of ethnic cleansing is very unsettling. The animal slaughter is especially appalling as poachers use spears, machine guns and hand grenades to kill elephants for their tusks and leave the carcasses to rot in the heat. The actual cut of this movie runs 11 minutes longer and is more violent.

In 1971, the duo tried something different. They wanted to go back in time and document the slave trade of the

1800s. The result was perhaps the most controversial and inflammatory film ever made. Originally slated to be shot in Brazil, the Brazilian government wanted no part of the guys who filmed *Africa Addio*, so they went to Haiti where they were given carte blanche by Papa Doc to film *Goodbye Uncle Tom*. They created lavish sets and based the content of the film on so called "research" they had dug up. These scenes ranged from brutal to outright disgusting. There were things there that even offended me and that's saying a lot. The film actually played The Cinerama on 47th Street. Critic Pauline Kael was so incensed by it that she raked it over the coals in print. This actually gave the film more attention than it deserved. It was also released by Cannon Films, who later denied any knowledge of the film, as *Farewell Uncle Tom* and was difficult to book as it was rated X, the kiss of death for any film other than a porn film.

Cannon films, fearing a backlash, quickly pulled the film from distribution. The ugly specter of theaters being trashed by angry ghetto audiences weighed heavily in their decision. Although Jacapetti and Prosperi refute claims of racism, I call it like it is. This is one fuckin' racist movie. Aside from the seldom. seen *Mondo Candito,* this was the last time the two worked together. Prosperi made a horror film, *Wild Beasts*, about zoo animals on PCP. Jacapetti got in a lot of trouble after being caught with underage girls. But Mondo kept on coming. West Coast exploitation mavens Lee Frost and Bob Cresse put out *Mondo Bizarro* and *Mondo Freudo* in 1966 and *Witchcraft '70* in 1970. *Slave Trade In The World Today*(1964) was another Italian Import. *Mondo Baloro* was narrated by Boris Karloff as a selling point. Stars like Vincent Price and Peter Ustinov also were used to narrate Mondo films.

And the Mondo Films just kept on coming; *Mondo Mod, Sweden Heaven And Hell, Savage Man, Savage Beast*, and the last Mondo film to play 42nd Street, *Faces of Death*. Then came the video era with more volumes of *Faces of Death. Dying: The Last Seconds of Life*, this one actually lifted scenes from Ruggero Deodato's *Last Cannibal World* and passed them off as "real." Then you had *Death Faces, The Many Taboos of Death* (Ten Volumes), *Traces of Death* and more. The DVD era gave us *Bum Fights, Ghetto Brawls, Street Fights*, and more.

Mondo is still with us today. Reality TV shows, *Survivor*, etc., all have their roots in Mondo. Who would have thought that this weird little film from 1963 would influence entertainment for the last 50 years? The more things change, the more they remain the same.

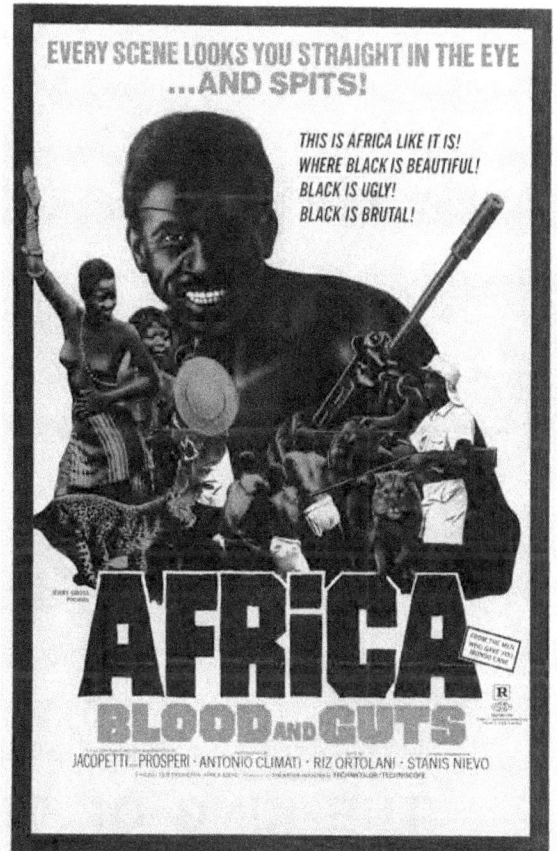

THE KING OF THE SPAGHETTI WESTERNS: THE FALL AND RESURRECTION OF LEE VAN CLEEF

Clarence Leroy Van Cleef was born on January 9, 1925, in Somerville NJ. He served in the US Navy in WWII and dove overboard to rescue a dog, the ship's mascot, during a storm. His post war work consisted of being an accountant, something he and fellow character actor, Jack Elam had in common. He and many other WWII vets, like Lee Marvin, Ernest Borgnine, Jack Palance and Charles Bronson turned to acting. During a performance of Mr. Roberts, he was noticed by director Stanley Kramer, who cast him as Jack Colby in *High Noon*. Lee had no dialogue, but his menacing presence opened the door to many more roles as villains in both westerns and crime dramas. Being that the '50s was the advent of television, there was no lack of work for Lee, Bronson, Elam, Broderick Crawford, RG Armstrong, Warren Oates, and many others.

Lee was involved in a bad car accident in 1959 where he lost his left kneecap and was told by doctors that he would never ride again. Six months later he was back in the saddle. In 1956, Roger Corman took a chance and gave him a leading role in *It Conquered the World*. Corman had also done this with Charles Bronson, casting him as the lead in *Machine Gun Kelly*. Van Cleef played the part well, even though he was talking to a big, rubber monster though out the film. Van Cleef could act and was more than just a villain although he was often quoted as "being born with beady eyes is the best thing that ever happened to me." In the 1958 film, *The Bravados*, he was part of a quartet of killers, Stephen Boyd, Albert Salmi, and Henry Silva, who supposedly killed Gregory Peck's wife. When cornered by Peck, Van Cleef does one hell of a sympathetic turn before Peck shoots him.

As we rolled into the turbulent '60s, Lee did a lot more TV villainy in *Gunsmoke*, *The Rifleman*, *Wanted: Dead or Alive* and many others. Then, in the mid '60s, he gave up acting as he felt he wasn't getting any good parts and was just tired of being the heavy. He turned to painting house for a living. Meanwhile in Italy, a new kind of western, *Fistful of Dollars*, was made starring a virtually unknown Clint Eastwood. Eastwood was known for a TV series called *Rawhide*, where he played second-fiddle Rowdy Yates to Eric Fleming's trail boss, Gil Favor.

Eastwood was the brooding "Man with No Name." ***Fistful of Dollars*** was raw, violent and a lot different than anything ever shot in the US. It was universally panned by the critics as an "exercise in sadism." Never the less, it was a big hit, and director Sergio Leone was asked to do a sequel, ***For a Few Dollars More***.

Leone needed another American actor and Henry Fonda was his first choice. Being that, at that point, Leone was unknown in the states, Fonda wasn't interested. Neither was Charles Bronson, who had been approached to do ***Fistful of Dollars***, but turned it down as he felt the script was crap. Ironically both Fonda and Bronson did do a film for Leone, ***Once Upon a Time in the West***, but it was a commercial flop when first released as American audiences couldn't deal with that Fonda was cast against type as a villain[9].

Other choices were Lee Marvin (who blew it off to do ***Cat Ballou***) Charlton Heston, and James Coburn, who initially agreed, but then wanted a lot more money. Legend has it that Leone was sitting in a bar and Van Cleef walked in. Leone remembered Van Cleef from ***High Noon*** and flew back to Italy with Van Cleef cast as Col. Douglas Mortimer, Bounty Hunter. Eastwood is also a bounty hunter and both men are after psychotic, dope. smoking killer, Indio, played to the hilt by Gian Maria Volente.

More violent than ***Fistful***, it was again shit on by critics, but the lines to see it were around the block. It also boasted a who's. who of actors like Klaus Kinski, Aldo Sambrell, Luigi Pistoli, Mario Brega, and others who would continue to do these films. Interesting footnote is that, when put to the test, Van Cleef was faster on the draw than Eastwood, as someone timed them drawing on the set. Another footnote is that Lee Marvin and Lee Van Cleef did work together twice, ***The Man Who Shot Liberty Valance*** in 1962, and the Twilight Zone episode, ***The Grave*** in 1961. In ***The Grave*** he co-starred with Strother Martin and James Best.

Where ***Fistful of Dollars*** showcased Eastwood, ***For A Few Dollars More*** was Van Cleef's film. At 40 years of age, Lee Van Cleef was on the verge of superstardom. For once he didn't play a villain and his character was a lot more sympathetic than Eastwood's character. Van Cleef's next film with Eastwood was ***The Good, The Bad and The Ugly***, where he returned to his villainous ways. Interesting footnote here is there was a scene in the film he didn't want to do and that was the one where he beat the girl for information. A double was used for that scene. It is also worth noting that this film was the end of Eastwood and Leone's relationship. Half of the cost of the film was Eastwood's salary. If that wasn't enough to cause a rift, the next one ended the relationship for good. Eastwood was going back to Hollywood.

Leone's next project's ***Once Upon a Time in The West*** opening scene was three men waiting for a train carrying Charles Bronson—They were going to gun down Bronson. Leone wanted Eastwood, Van Cleef and Eli Wallach to be the men waiting for the train. The idea was to segue the old west to the new west. Van Cleef and Wallach were in, Eastwood refused. Leone and Eastwood never worked together again.

Lee Van Cleef was now the face of the Spaghetti Western. His next film, ***The Big Gundown***, 1966 directed by Sergio Sollima, is ranked in the top ten Spaghetti Westerns. More "political" than others, the film centered on lawman Jonathan Corbett, who always brought in his man. He is offered the job of state senator if he can unofficially capture Cuchillo, a Mexican who raped a 12. year. old girl, or did he? Tomas Millian excels in the role of Cuchillo and also did quite a few more of these films. ***Gundown*** ran 110 minutes, but Columbia Pictures cut it down to about 90 minutes (a fate another Van Cleef film would suffer down the road). The print ad featured Van Cleef holding a gun and screamed "Mr. Ugly Comes to Town", which was strange as Eli Wallach was "the Ugly" and Van Cleef was "the Bad." US distributors seemed to always do a hack job on any films imported from Europe.

"This is Revenge and There's Nothing sweet About it" so said the print ads for ***Death Rides a Horse***, 1967. A group of robbers massacre an entire family, but a little boy is a witness and vows to track the men down. The little boy is John Phillip Law. Ryan (Van Cleef) is released from jail and has to find his "partners" who put him there. This is the same gang the boy is looking for. Mario Brega, Luigi Pistolli, and Anthony Dawson are the gang and are doing quite well for themselves until Ryan shows up for revenge with Bill, the boy out to avenge his family. Question is, was Ryan there the night of the massacre? The film studies the mentoring relationship between Ryan and Bill, and also the truth that comes out of it.

---

[9] Even though he had played villains in the past—in particular the well. received 1969's ***Fire Creek*** (directed by Vincent McEveety), opposite James Stewart.

"Lee Van Cleef has been dirty, ugly and down right mean, now watch him get violent!" That was the tagline for *Day of Anger*, 1967. This film was cut down from 111 minutes to 95 minutes. Van Cleef is gunfighter, Frank Talby, who takes the town clown, Scott Mary (Giuliano Gemma) under his wing and teaches him to be a man. While Scott gets his confidence back, Talby starts to run roughshod over the town. The climatic battle is teacher against pupil for control of the town.

Beyond the Law, 1967, aka *Blood Silver,* has outlaw Billy Joe Cudlip trying to rob a load of silver. Some how he winds up as Sheriff and not only has to face his former gang, he has another gang after the loot led by former muscle man Gordon Mitchell. As good a film as this is, it fell quickly into the public domain and some really shitty VHS and DVD versions have surfaced along with one legitimate DVD release. Also starring in the film were Antonia Sabato, Lionel Stander and Bud Spencer.

The Commandos, 1968, aka *Sullivan's Marauders*, was also cut from 111 minutes to 82 minutes to squeeze on a double bill. Sgt. Sullivan (Van Cleef), puts together a squad of Italian Americans to infiltrate a camp in North Africa. Basically it was a spaghetti western with tanks instead of horses. Costarring former *Maverick* TV star, Jack Kelly, it came and went quickly in the theaters before falling into the VHS public domain limbo.

"The Man with the Gunsight Eyes Comes to Kill!" was the tagline for *Sabata*, 1969. My fondest memory of Sabata was a huge mock up of Lee Van Cleef on a 42nd Street marquee that read "Lee Van Cleef is Sabata." This is, in my opinion, Van Cleef at his zenith. Dressed in black, with an arsenal of trick weapons, Sabata foils a $100,000 robbery orchestrated by a group of "respectable " businessmen. Sabata is blackmailing the crooks and they send an army of killers after him. Aided by a knife-throwing Carrincha (Pedro Sanchez) and the acrobatic Alley Cat (Nick Jordan) , all the killers wind up dead. So what is Sabata's connection with the man called Banjo (William Berger)? Whose side is he on? Pretty much his own, but he has history with Sabata as Sabata says, "we once played together", after Banjo guns down a group of killers with a cut off rifle in his banjo. Lots of twists, turns, double crosses and great characters make this a fun film to watch. This was Van Cleef's first film for director Frank Kramer (Gianfranco Parolini), it wouldn't be his last.

El Condor, 1970, would be the first of three times Van Cleef costarred with football legend Jim Brown. Brown plays escaped convict, Luke, who is out to rob the fortress, El Condor, of "millions" in gold. Van Cleef plays an unhinged character, Jaroo, a gold prospector, who teams up with Luke to rob the fortress. Costarring Patrick O'Neal, Chief Iron Eyes Cody, Marianna Hill and Elisha Cook , it was action all the way. Script was written by Larry Cohen.

Van Cleef returned to the states to film *Barquero*, 1970, a violent western about a group of outlaws led by Warren Oates, who plunder a town, kill everyone in it, and need to use the Travis's (Van Cleef) raft to cross the river and make their getaway. They also intend to burn the raft so they can't be pursued. Problem is the raft is that Travis isn't going to let that happen. Costarring Mariette Hartley, Kerwin Matthews, John Davis Chandler and Forrest Tucker as Mountain Phil, it was supposed to be directed by Richard Sparr, but Sparr was killed in a helicopter crash while scouting locations. He was replaced Gordon Douglas, who directed the classic sic fi film *Them!*

Return of Sabata, 1971, was the official sequel to Sabata. Another Sabata film, *Adios Sabata*, starring Yul Brynner, was a retitled film originally called *Indio Black*. This was also directed by Gianfranco Parolini and had some of the actors from the original Sabata like Pedro Sanchez and Gianni Rizzo. Interesting thing was that while Brynner was playing Van Cleef's role, Van Cleef was playing Brynner's role as Chris in *The Magnificent Seven*

Ride. **Return of Sabata** had the shootist working in a carnival. The plot is the town is being taxed to death by its founding fathers, who intend to run off with the money. Van Cleef was rejoined by Pedro Sanchez and Nick Jordan from the first film. A lot more gimmicks in this film, but some comedy distracts from the action. **Captain Apache**, 1971, featured a clean. shaven Van Cleef playing a Native American, released on a double bill with **A Town Called Hell,** it was a flop at the box office. Maybe it was because Van Cleef just didn't look like the Van Cleef we were used to as he was clean-shaven. Van Cleef actually sings the title song. Both films fell into the VHS public domain bins.

Bad Man's River, 1971, had Van Cleef playing robber Roy King, who loses his wife to a Mexican revolutionary. But then they collaborate to rob the Mexican government of a million dollars. Costarring James Mason, Gina Lolobrigida, Diana Lorys, Gianni Garko (**Sartana**), and Aldo Sambrell, river had too much comedy for the fans. It, too, wound up in VHS limbo. **The Magnificent Seven Ride**, 1972, was the weakest of the series, probably due to budget. One of the big gun battles took place off camera. Playing the Seven this time around were Luke Askew, James B. Sikking, Pedro Armendariz, Jr., Ed Lauter, Michael Callan and William Lucking (**Sons of Anarchy**). Not exactly Bronson, McQueen, or Coburn, this was the last film in the series.

I was talking to costar Michael Callan at a Chiller Convention. When I asked how it was working with Van Cleef, I was told Van Cleef was very sick during filming. To backtrack into the '50s, Van Cleef was in a film, **The Conqueror**, a John Wayne vehicle (starring The Duke as Genghis Kahn) filmed in Nevada, during the atomic bomb tests. Nearly everyone, including John Wayne, got some kind of cancer. In a Q & A at Cinema Wasteland with Tom Atkins, Atkins told us that he worked with Lee on **Escape from New York** and he was near death from some kind of throat cancer. That was in 1981.

Van Cleef was starting not to look so good on camera in **Take a Hard Ride**. He was a drinker going way back as Beverly Garland, his co-star in **It Conquered The World**, told me he was a wonderful man, but would reek of vodka early in the day. He may have beaten the cancer as he worked steadily up until his death from a heart attack in 1989.

The Grand Duel, 1972, aka **The Big Showdown**, had Van Cleef back in form as an ex sheriff helping a man framed for murder. He also did a crime film, **Mean Frank and Crazy Tony**, 1973, that was released under a couple of different titles on VHS. In 1974 the Kung Fu explosion was in full swing. Why not combine the two genres? **Blood Money**, released in the states by Columbia Pictures as **The Stranger and the Gunfighter**, pair Van Cleef with **Five Fingers of Death** star, Lo Lieh. Directed by Antonio Margheriti, Van Cleef and Lo Lieh are after a treasure. The map for the treasure is tattooed on a couple of whore's ass cheeks. Tagline was 'The Fastest Gun in the West Joins With the Most Brutal Hands in the East." The film was a big hit worldwide. But another film made in 1974 would change the course of Spaghetti Westerns. That film was **Blazing Saddles**.

Blazing Saddles was a huge hit and Italian Cinema was known for copycatting what was big in the USA. More and more westerns started to mix comedy with action. The results were mixed to say the least. Klaus Kinski bitched that the scripts kept getting shittier and shittier, production values fell and these films stopped attracting American stars. 1975 took Van Cleef to the Canary Islands to shoot another hybrid Western/Blaxploitation film, **Take a Hard Ride**. Directed by Antonio Margheriti, it reunited Van Cleef with his costar from **El Condor**, Jim Brown. Rounding out the cast were Fred "The Hammer" Williamson, Jim Kelly, Harry Carey, Jr., Dana Andrews, and Barry Sullivan. Van Cleef looked very haggard in this film.

God's Gun, 1976, and **Kid Vengeance**, 1977, were low points for Van Cleef. **God's Gun** was horrible, casting him as twins, one a priest, one a gunfighter. Ad in an over acting Jack Palance, a near death Richard Boone, and Leif Garrett, it was really bad. Shot in Israel and directed by Gianfranco Parolini it was a dud. Even worse was **Kid Vengeance** with Jim Brown, John Marley and Leif Garrett. looks like someone wanted to give Garrett a push. I saw this film on a double bill with **Assault on Precinct 13**. Van Cleef returned to the states for a TV movie **Nowhere to Hide**, in 1977. It was directed by Jack Starret who did a lot of biker films and was Gabby Johnson in **Blazing Saddles**. Had Van Cleef returned to the states earlier, he could have been as big a star as Eastwood, Bronson and Reynolds. But Van Cleef liked working abroad and continued to bounce back and forth doing films like **The Perfect Killer**, 1977, and **The Squeeze**, 1978, once again for Antonio Marguerite, costarring Lionel Stander and Karen Black. another TV movie, **The Hard Way**, was in 1979.

1980 saw Van Cleef costar with Chuck Norris, who was hot at the time. Then Van Cleef went to work for John Carpenter in **Escape from New York** as Hauk. The film was a huge hit and a new generation of fans discovered Van Cleef. Van Cleef was considered for the role of Garry in **The Thing**. He went to Spain to shoot Goma. 2 in 1984.

In 1984 Van Cleef had his own TV show, *The Master*, in which he was a ninja. The show costarred Timothy Van Patten. Van Cleef's double for the martial arts stunts was none other than Sho Kosugi. Something I remember about the show was that Van Cleef appeared on *The Tonight Show* with Johnny Carson to promote *The Master*. He seemed very ill at ease on *The Tonight Show*. The show lasted one season. Van Cleef went back to do two pictures for Antonio Margheriti, *Code Name Wild Geese*, 1984, and *Jungle Raiders*, 1985. *Code Name Wild Geese* was a cash. in film to capitalize on the hit film *The Wild Geese (*with Richard Harris). Van Cleef is incarcerated helicopter pilot Archie Travers who is recruited by *Escape From NY* and *For a Few Dollars More* costars, Ernest Borgnine and Klaus Kinski. After seeing all three in one scene, I would have loved to have been the fly on the wall during rehearsals. *Jungle Raiders* had Van Cleef playing another helicopter pilot.

Armed Response, aka *The Jade Jungle*, was an action yarn directed by Fred Olen Ray. Costarring a who's-who of character actors: Michael Berryman, David Carradine, Ross Hagen, Mako, Dick Miller, and Laurene Landon, it was about a jade statue stolen from an Asian crime boss. I asked Fred Olen Ray how it was to work with Van Cleef. Fred told me he was a true pro and great to have on the set. But he had to be picked up everyday because of his drinking. He didn't trust himself to drive anymore. He did one more film for Margheriti, *Der Commander* in 1988. Then *Thieves of Fortune,* 1989 , another low budget film. He did a cameo in *Speedzone*, a *Canonball Run* rip-off, in 1989.

On December 16th, 1989, I received a call from a friend telling me that Lee Van Cleef had just died of a heart attack at age 64. I honestly felt a great sense of loss. Here was a guy who I watched growing up. First in a million TV westerns, then in the Grindhouses and Drive-Ins of the '70s. "Mr. Ugly" was gone, but never forgotten. His legacy is the great films he made. When *The Good, the Bad and The Ugly* was restored, a voice over expert recreated Van Cleef's distinctive voice. One could almost wonder what would have happened if that fate changing meeting with Van Cleef and Leone never took place. Rest in Peace, Lee Van Cleef and thanks for all the memories I have of your work. Adios, Sabata.

CODE NAME: WILD GEESE

**Lee Van Cleef Ernest Borgnine & Klaus Kinski Couldn't Give
Lewis Collins The Rub**

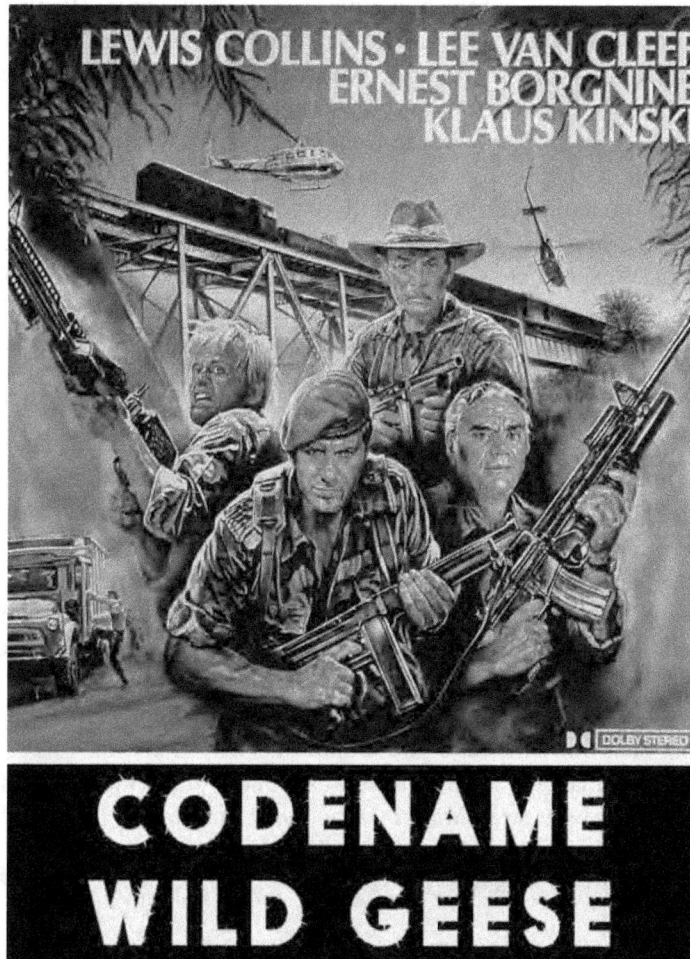

Talk about a blah leading man. Watching Lewis Collins act is like watching the lemon pie go sour at your local grocer. Maybe it's me, but this guy has zero charisma. He was a big British TV star on a show called *The Professionals*. He did four feature films, all his other work was British Television. Three of the films he did were were mercenary/commando films directed by Antonia Margheriti (aka Anthony Dawson). *Der Commander* (1988) paired him with Lee Van Cleef and Donald Pleasance. *Kommado Leopard* (1985) paired him with Klaus Kinski. Both films followed this one.

   This would be Lee Van Cleef's fourth film for Antonio; he would do two more before his death in 1989. Kinski worked for Margheriti on several films, most notably the excellent gothic western *And God Said to Cain* (1970). There was footage ,that a friend had , showing Kinski going bat shit crazy on the set of *Code Name: Wild Geese* (1984). Ernest Borgnine seemed out of place here and didn't mention this film in his autobiography, Ernie.

   Wesley (Collins) leads his men on a covert mission. Something goes wrong and he loses his helicopter pilot. He gets a new mission: go to The Golden Triangle to destroy an opium processing facility. They also have to kill The General, who is the local despot. The General is a big bald Asian guy with a Fu Manchu mustache. Fletcher (Borgnine) is head of the DEA in that area. He hires Wesley's team. Charlton (Kinski) is a shady 'operative" who is not above murder and lining his own pockets.

   Needing a pilot, Wesley finds a prolific smuggler, China (Van Cleef) in jail with two years to serve. Wesley makes China an offer; two days work and he walks away from serving his last two years. Charlton is against hiring

China for an undisclosed reason. China wants a cash payoff on top of him walking. Wesley tell Charlton to "take care of it." Continuity problem here as we don't know the heat between China and Charlton, nor what deal was worked out between them.

To keep things from getting boring, Wesley and Fletcher get chased though a construction tunnel by bad guys. The stunt driving here is really good. Turns out the bad guys are Charlton's men. Being that The General has eyes all around, they decide to steal one of his helicopters. They capture the small outpost and fly in. They blow up the processing plant and free the prisoners. One is a reporter, Kathy (Mimsy Farmer) who tried to interview the General.

She says they decided to hold her for ransom and make her a heroin addict to control her. One merc gets shot and China leaves the helicopter to save him. One of the General's men blows the 'copter up, stranding the team. They trek though the jungle and come to a mission that takes in the General's victims. They leave Kathy and the wounded merc there while the rest go blow up a train carrying opium.

Fletcher and Charlton have a meeting. Charlton is going in after Wesley. Fletcher tells him that either way, you'll get what's coming to you. Wesley's crew blows up the train and a bridge. One wounded merc rides the train to his death. They go back to the mission, which the General attacked. The find everyone dead and the priest crucified. Before the priest dies, he gives them the location of another opium facility, and guess who owns it?

Charlton and his crew attack Wesley. More mercs are killed. China finds a helicopter. Wesley finds a flamethrower. They take off and Wesley burns down the factory and fries Charlton. The three return to Fletcher's hotel, but Wesley isn't done. One of the higher ups was Charlton's partner. He was also responsible for the death of Wesley's son. Wesley shoots him. The film ends with Wesley and Fletcher arguing. Wesley asks Fletcher is anyone here honestly doing any good. Fletcher has no answer.

There are huge continuity problems with this film. Seems Wesley's son's death isn't mentioned until the end. We never see the evil General get killed and the looping of the dialog is all messed up. The words don't match the emotions the actors are showing. Especially with Ernest Borgnine. Maybe he was disgusted with the whole thing as most of his scenes are with Kinski. Kinski is voiced over by someone with a British accent. The film's only saving grace is lots of explosions and the bridge-blowing-up scene is spectacular. Lee is good, but it becomes obvious that he is there to give Collins the rub.

The film is not really that bad, but will leave you wondering why it couldn't have been better. The title was a cash in on the highly successful *Wild Geese* (1978). There was a bunch these mercenary films out of Italy. This genre was short lived and most of the films went straight to the home video market.

REMEMBERING ANDY COPP: QUIET NIGHTS OF BLOOD AND PAIN (2008)

By Mike Watt

The late Andy Copp was an indie director who wasn't afraid to ask hard questions. He didn't make horror movies for cheap thrills or even any sort of emotional catharsis. You actually got the impression that his movies haunted him after he finished them. From his surrealistic masterpiece *The Mutilation Man* to the emotional agony of *The Atrocity Circle,* Copp took a hard look at the world and the people crawling over it and didn't see a lot of up. side. He saw a civilization of tortured souls who can only increase their own misery while increasing the misery of those around them. Andy Copp's movies are rife with unanswered questions. He wasn't about comforting the viewer; he wasn't about hand. holding. Regardless of how you view his films, you cannot say he ever took the easy way out.

In *Quiet Nights of Blood and Pain*, Copp tackled the question of our ongoing war with the Middle East by viewing it through the eyes of two former soldiers. Adrienne (Amanda Delotelle) suffers from PTSD and fights with the government every day just to get her pay and assistance. Every night, she relives the horrors she experienced in Iraq and her only friend is a Viet Nam Vet who still bears his own scars from both that war and his "welcome" home. Elsewhere in the city, William (Loren S. Goins) is walking around in an unending nightmare. Responsible for interrogating terror suspects, William was in charge of extracting information by "any means necessary." In the state of panic that was the early days of a Post 9/11 world, torture and aggression was deemed a necessary evil because there could be other attacks planned. All of America was in danger. To protect the American people, William was told to do "anything", and in doing so, something inside of him broke permanently. Now he's home, abandoned by veterans administrators, off of his medication, alone, desperate. He views every person he meets as an enemy sympathiser, taking war protests very, very personally.

Quiet Nights of Blood and Pain takes the empty Conservative cry of "If you don't support the war, you don't support the troops" and treats it very seriously. Burdened by the knowledge that they were fighting an unjust war but still conditioned to believe they were doing it for our protection, both Adrienne and William chose their paths and were rewarded with derision. Damaged by the war, they were discarded by the military and confronted with either disinterest or disdain by the rest of us. At the same time, Adrienne, at least, understands the protestors' point of view more deeply than they ever could because she was there. William, on the other hand, can't stop killing. The agression builds up inside of him and he reverse. justifies his murderous actions by rationalizing that he's still fighting for the American way of life and that anyone around him *could* be a terrorist.

That the paths of these two soldiers will collide is inevitable and ideology won't matter at that juncture. And Copp didn't ask anyone to take sides. He wasn't saying that this is a "pro" or "anti" war movie. All he was asking is that we, the viewers, think about what he's presenting. Regardless of which political stance you want to take, war is a fucked up thing and we're living in a fucked up world. And what will it take to un. fuck it? The creator was begging for answers as much as his creations. If these questions seem heavy. handed, maybe that's what it takes to get through to the disaffected, desensitized culture of today.

Like his other films, the theme is more powerful than the presentation. Delotelle is fine as Adrienne and Goins is so understated as William that you feel his monotone delivery is another by. product of his mental breakdown. The majority of the supporting players are flat and the movie has a number of technical problems, but if you're paying attention to those things, you're missing the point entirely. Every independent film suffers from budget limitations—it's the nature of the game—but Copp was trying to say something with his films. He shot primal screams and wondered why nobody else seemed to care. Slasher films and vampires keep independent horror alive. But these monsters pale in comparison to what's really out there.

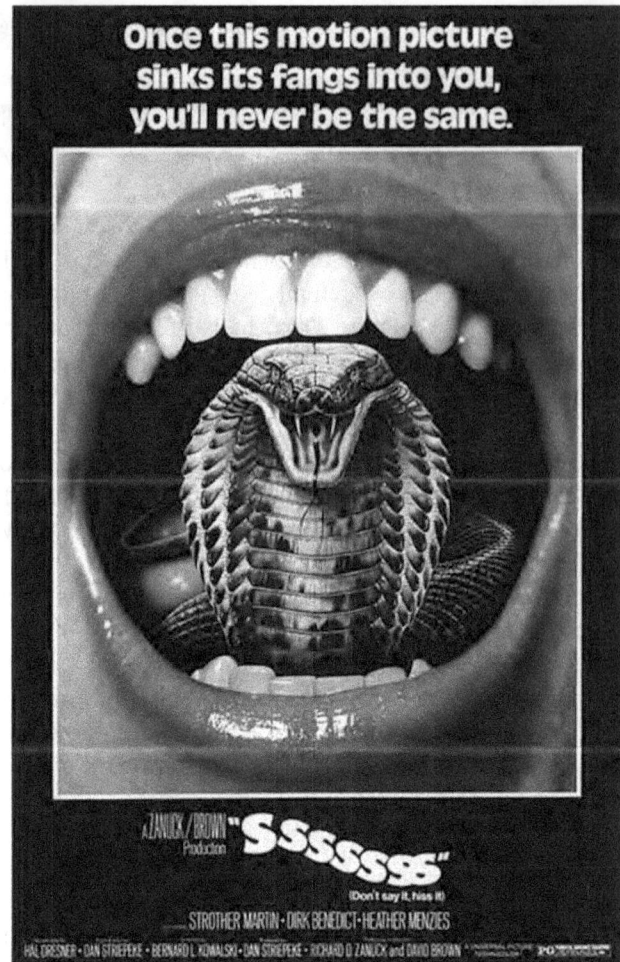

GREAT GRINDHOUSE DOUBLE FEATURES:
Sssss & The Boy Who Cried Werewolf

I was working the job of a lifetime, or so I thought, managing the Livingston Drive-in. It was the summer of '73, I was on break for college. I was soon to be on permanent break 'cause of the gas shortage of '74, but that's another story.

I thought this would be a great job, silly me. It was a split shift. You came in at 10am, did paperwork, cleaned up the field, painted, repaired speakers, and other hump work until 2pm. Then you had to be back at 5pm until whenever. I thought I would get to see some great movies. Unfortunately I wasn't privy to how these films were booked.

Union Drive-in got all the Blaxploitation stuff and Spaghetti Westerns. Morris Plains, Troy Hills & Totowa got all the horror, exploitation, and Euro Action films. We got Disney, Egg Head Films, and big mainstream shitty movies.

I could go on my day off to any of the other Drive-Ins for free. That I did. Then I finally got a horror double bill, ***Sssss*** and ***The Boy Who Cried Werewolf***. I was excited until I saw the PG rating. "Gonna suck!" I thought. I had to screen the prints when we opened Wednesday night just to make sure you could see them. ***Sssss*** was no problem, but ***Werewolf*** was dark. I complained, but the company didn't want to replace the film as it was a "package deal" from Universal. Actually, it was one of Universal's last double features. So now I had to leave a recorded message of the start times. How do you say *Sssss*? I just hissed it and hoped for the best. *Sssss* was arguably the better of the two films. Starring Strother Martin, Dirk Benedict, and Heather Menzies, and supported by '70s stalwarts Jack Ging and a young Reb Brown, *Sssss* used real snakes, a King Cobra, Black Mamba, and a Python, instead of the fake rubber ones. In fact none of the snakes were defanged for this film. Five King Cobras were brought in from Thailand and the python was from Singapore.

Directed by Bernard Kolwalski (*Attack of the Giant Leeches*) and the make up is credited to a John Chambers. Before the credits, Dr. Stoner (Martin) is selling something in a crate to a guy who runs a freak show. It seems the demented Doc has been trying to turn his lab assistants into cobras to survive the coming nuclear holocaust. The thing is the crate is one of his failures.

A new assistant is recommended by a rival doctor. David is his new assistant, who Stoner wastes no time giving him "immunization" injections. David has some hallucinatory dreams on this shit.

Stoner has a King Cobra that he calls "The King." He runs a venom show to get the cash he needs to keep his experiments going. Things go wrong when his pet boa, Harry, is killed by a drunken jock (Brown). Stoner releases a black mamba while the jock is taking a shower. David now is starting to shed his skin. He visits the carnival and comes face to face with his predecessor, now an exhibit, in the freak show.

The professor, who recommended David for the job, tells Stoner his grant has been refused. Stoner knocks him out and throws him in a cellar with a hungry python. Stoner's daughter, Kristina, is worried about David. She goes to the carnival and realizes that the snake man is Tim, Stoner's last assistant. She then knows that David is going to wind up the same way.

David now morphs into a King Cobra. Stoner, for some reason, decides to have it out with "The King." Things are deteriorating rapidly. A mongoose gets out of its cage and attacks snake Dave. Stoner is bitten a couple of times by The King. Kristina arrives to find Dr. Stoner dead and " The King" in attack mode. The sheriff takes the King's head off with a shotgun blast. Snake David is being chewed on by the mongoose as the film freezes on Kristina's screaming face.

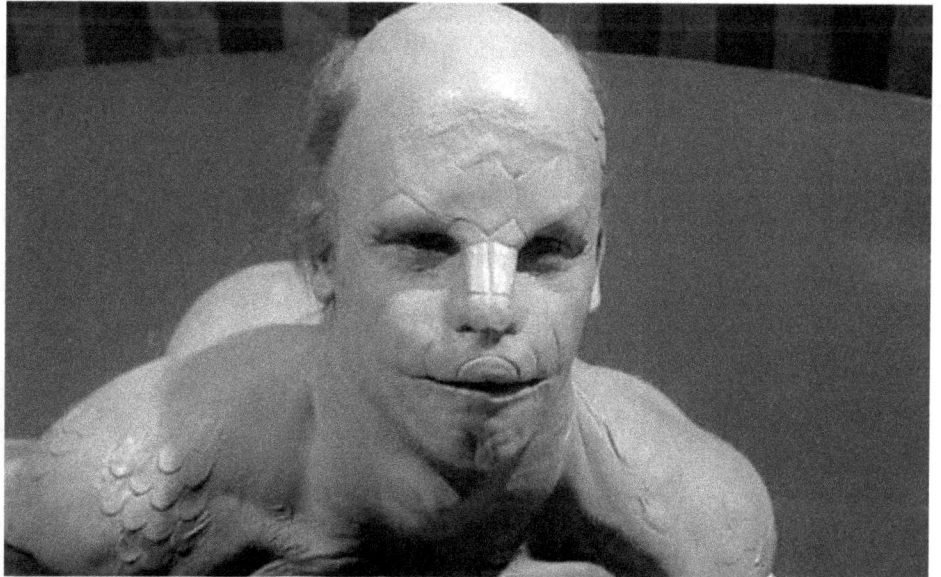

This was pretty good. The presence of the great character actor, Strother Martin, gave the project credibility. Martin's earnest performance of the deranged Dr. Stoner saves the film from being your typical 'mad scientist creates monster' roots. You actually feel sorry for David as he painfully turns into a snake.

Martin, who achieved fame in films like *Cool Hand Luke*, *The Wild Bunch* and others, did a few more genre films, westerns and TV shows before his death in 1980. Dirk Benedict found fame on the TV shows, *Battlestar Galactica* and *The A-Team*. Heather Menzies did a couple of more genre films, *Piranha* and *Endangered Species*, plus a lot of TV shows. Director Kolwalski directed a ton of TV Shows like *Magnum PI, Nightrider, Air Wolf, Jake and the Fat Man* and many others before his death in 2007. Look for *Addams Family* star Felix Silla as "The Seal Boy" in the freak show.

As good as *Sssss* is, *The Boy Who Cried Werewolf* sucked. I had more problems with rowdy patrons during that film. Where *Sssss* held their interest, *Werewolf* seemed to piss them off. First mistake was showing a fully transformed werewolf before the credits. Second was having this whinny bitch of a kid, Scott Sealey, in a pivotal role. The main star, Kerwin Mathews, was in a bunch of regular people meet big monster period pieces like *7th Voyage of Sinbad*, *Jack the Giant Killer*, *Three Worlds of Gulliver* & others. The director, Nathan Juran, was no strangers to giants either as he directed ***Attack of the 50 Foot Woman***. Both directors directed "Attack of the Something" films.

Let's see, we have an annoying kid, a werewolf that causes traffic accidents, pushes a camper off a cliff, and rips an arm off (off camera), Jesus freaks, a tough sheriff (veteran western actor Robert J. Wilke), some blood, and a lot of boredom. Like 'the boy who cried wolf' story, no one pays attention to this kid. Considering that he did this film and one episode of ***Emergency!*** no one was really paying attention to his career either.

The werewolf make-up was an early creation of Tom Burman. However a werewolf wearing a turtleneck sweater just doesn't cut it for me. I kept thinking about the Warren Zevon song "Werewolves of London", the line where "his hair was perfect." Even the cheap dissolve transformation scene bites more than this werewolf.

I never saw this film even though I had it running for a week. I was breaking up drunken fights and escorting the rowdies off the lot. ***Sssss*** ran twice a night, ***Werewolf*** ran only once as the co-feature. We started running films around 8:30 pm as the sun was setting. Intermission was at 10pm, then the second film at 10:20. Snack Bar closed at 11:30 pm. Last showing was around 12:30. I only recently caught up with this on a "convention" DVD. R. So I waited over 30 years to see this clunker and, trust me on this, it wasn't worth the wait.

Star Kerwin Mathews also did a lot of Euro films, ***Octaman*** with Pier Angeli and Jeff Morrow, ***Barquero*** with Lee Van Cleef & Warren Oates, and some TV appearances. He died in 2007. Director Nathan Juran also moved on to direct TV shows like ***Lost in Space, Time Tunnel***, and ***Voyage to the Bottom of the Sea***. He had won an Oscar for art direction in 1941 for ***How Green was my Valley***. He died in October of 2002. Looks like a lot of former B Movie directors found a home directing TV shows.

The Last Gasp of My Favorite Grindhouse:
THE EMBASSY THEATER

It was toward the end of the '70s when I last stepped into the Embassy Theater. It was a double bill with a film called *Shanghai Joe* on top and a shitty Kung Fu film on the bottom. I only wanted to see *Shanghai Joe* because Klaus Kinski was in it. And the Embassy was the only place it was playing.

The Embassy was my home away from home, starting in the early '60s. There was a thing called the Kiddee Matinee every Saturday. The program consisted of three Warner Brothers Cartoons, a Three Stooges short and two feature films. Parents would drop their kids off around noon with $1.50 cents to get in, the rest for soda and popcorn. For whatever reason, they never seemed to look at what the two movies were, assuming they were films "just for kids." They weren't.

Oh, you would get the occasional Jerry Lewis crappy comedy, but what parents didn't know was a lot of horror films were shown. No shit, my first matinee was *Curse of Frankenstein* and *Horror of Dracula*. I told my big mouthed little brother to shut the fuck up about these films or we would never be allowed to go again. Catholic parents + Catholic school = no fun of any kind like this. So thankfully he didn't blab.

The amount of double feature horror films was amazing. Here a partial list that my damaged brain remembers: *Dinosaurus* and *4D Man, Earth vs. The Spider* and *The Deadly Mantis, Horror of Party Beach* and *The Blob, Creature from the Black Lagoon* and *Revenge of the Creature, I Was a Teenage Frankenstein* and *Terror from the Year 5000, Killer Shrews* and *The Giant Gila Monster, Frankenstein vs. The Space Monster* and *Curse of the Living Corpse, Brides of Dracula* and *The Mole People* and a lot more.

I always said God bless those irresponsible bastards who booked the Kiddee Matinees. But in the mid. '70s, their booking of black and white horror films backfired as someone put *Night of the Living Dead* into the mix. Children were traumatized and the bookings stopped shortly after that. By the late '60s I was already haunting the Grindhouses on 42nd Street. I would revisit the Embassy on occasion, and *Shanghai Joe* was the last time.

The Embassy used to be pretty opulent and clean. Now it was anything but. I hadn't been there in a few years and deterioration had set in. The once. enticing Candy Counter was so foul that you wished you had snuck something in to munch on. The seats were broken and springy, with stuffing hanging out of them. There was a foul smell of burning PCP, the cheap drug of choice back then that would induce psychotic behavior. Ad that stench to the smell of cigarettes, pot, spilled wine and malt liquors, and body odor and you had Aroma De La Grindhouse.

The three balconies were closed off and the once. clean rest room now had broken urinals and piss-soaked

floors. Even the screen had stains on it like someone used it for a target for tossing half. full cans of beer at it. Alkies were still crashed out in the back rows. A couple of dust heads sat muttering to themselves. I picked a seat far away from the other patrons. I was getting some dirty looks from the all. black crowd, but I didn't care, I was here to see a movie, not socialize.

Any of the 'brothers' expecting another Shaw Brothers period piece were sorely disappointed. It stars Klaus Kinski for maybe five whole minutes, and Chen Lee, no relation to Bruce or Chris, as "Shanghai Joe." He is never called Joe though, during this 94. minute ordeal. He is usually called a 'chink' or 'dirty, yellow bastard' as one grizzled character remarks, "We just got rid of the Indians, now we got a bunch of chinks."

Joe has come to the old Eurowest to become a cowboy. After a few trials and tribulations, he's hired by some gunmen to herd cattle. The 'cattle' are Mexican peons used for slave labor. When the border patrol arrives, the gunmen start shooting the peons. Joe objects to this and Kung Fus the nasty gunmen. The culprit behind the slavers is a wealthy land baron who is fond of shooting peons for the amusement of his cohorts. See what you're forced to do for entertainment when you have no cable?

Joe is righteously pissed off and beats the shit out of everyone. The land baron decides that Joe is a threat to everything he holds dear, slave labor, bad acting etc. So he puts a $5,000 bounty on "that dirty chink" and hires four killers to take him out.

The first killer is Pedro the Cannibal, (Robert Hundar, *Sabata, The Cut Throats Nine*), who wonders how Chinamen taste. He's either living up to his nickname or he's real lonely out on the prairie. Joe kills him with a pot of boiling rice. Killer #2, Burying Sam (Gordon Mitchell, *Beyond the Law, Coffin Full of Dollars*) is a bit more creative. He digs a pit full of stakes and lures Joe into it. The crafty Joe is not impaled and tricks Mitchell, throwing him into the pit. Killer #3, Tricky the Gambler (Giacomo Rossi). Stuart, *Last Man on Earth, Kill, Baby, Kill*), lures Joe into an ambush. The ambushers kill each other when Joe turns the tables on them. Tricky survives and tries to lull Joe into a false sense of security. But when he pulls his hideout gun, Joe plucks his eyes out, a la *Queen Boxer*, where this stunt appeared first for all you Kung. Fu purists out there.

Killer #4 is Jack the Scalper, Klaus Kinski, looking weirder and acting more demented than usual. Jack shoots Joe in both legs, then knocks him out. When Joe comes to, he finds Jack trying to scalp a girl who had befriended him earlier. Jack keeps eight knives in his jacket, four on each side. Joe gets free and hits him with chops on both sides, driving eight knives into his chest. With all the local killers dead, the land baron ups the ante and brings in a martial arts expert to dispatch Joe for good.

A lively battle between the two martial artists ensues with swordplay, lots of jumping around, and the traditional—I guess—palm strike that rips Joe's opponents' hearts out. Joe has triumphed over evil. His new girlfriend wants him to settle down. But Joe has found his calling, to seek out injustice, right all wrongs and all that sentimental horseshit we have come to cherish. *Shanghai Joe* was a fun film with bloodshed, violence and over the top sadism.

I didn't stay for the next feature, as a few people seemed to be sizing me up for a rip off. I never returned to The Embassy; it was too dangerous an area by then. It lasted about another year before being boarded up. The once. proud marquee over shadowing the sidewalk was removed. The place was gutted later on and turned into offices. The place that I practically grew up in was no move, but the flickering images projected on to that majestic screen were etched into my brain. Now only the memories of a better time remain.

He Was Hardcore Before Hardcore Was Cool:

MAD DOG BUZZ SAWYER

By 42nd Street Pete and Cinemawasteland.com Ken

When wrestling fans talk hardcore, they speak of Mick Foley, The Sandman, Axl Rotten, Sabu, Terry funk and others. But back in the early '80s, one guy made Georgia Championship Wrestling must see TV for two hours every Saturday night. That guy was Terry "Buzz" Sawyer.

Born Bruce Woyan in 1959, he was known for his bizarre behavior early on in high school. According to a former classmate, Buzz picked the biggest black guy in the school and told him to "hit me in the head as hard as you can." He did and the blood flowed. Buzz just stood there and smiled. Between classes, Buzz would ram his head into steel posts in the hallways. According to former classmates, even at 15 years old, he was one scary motherfucker. For whatever reason, Buzz used to bait black athletes in PE that were six inches taller than him and outweighed him. Sometimes he'd win the fight, other times he'd lose. Little did anyone know that these actions would come to define Buzz Sawyer, Pro Wrestler.

I first noticed Buzz back in the days before cable TV. On the old UHF stations, I got a Spanish channel that had Lucha Libre from The Olympic Auditorium in Los Angeles. I saw Roddy Piper, Gorgeous Keith Franks (Adrian Adonis), Professor Tanaka, Tank Patton, Moondog Lonnie Mayne, and a young baby faced Terry Sawyer. Terry had a full head of hair and was a good guy. He got beat up a lot by the heels. That was the mid '70s.

Fast forward to the '80s and cable TV. Georgia Championship Wrestling, soon to become WCW, had a two. hour time slot starting at 6:05 pm on the Superstation TBS. Having been weaned on the WWWF in my area, as that was all we had, this wrestling was more realistic, more violent, and occasionally the blood flowed. Now I was seeing in action guys I had only read about in wrestling magazines, like Ole Anderson, The Masked Superstar, Tommy Rich, Abdulla the Butcher, Bob Armstrong and many others. But nothing could have prepared me for the antics of Buzz Sawyer.

Buzz might have been a baby face before I started watching GCW. He was a full. blown killer heel when I saw him and engaged in what would be almost a two. year bloody feud with "Wildfire" Tommy Rich. That feud may have almost ended Rich's career as he went back to working for regional promotions after it was over. Although he did return to GCW on occasion, he never was the same.

These two had such a hot feud going that it sometimes spilled out of the buildings and into the streets and parking lots. The two would brawl even if they weren't pitted against each other on the card. That led to speculation that this feud may be legit. They even took it on the road to Southwest Championship Wresting in San Antonio Texas and other promotions that GCW was swapping talent with. Their last encounter was a locked steel cage match billed the Last Battle of Atlanta at the Omni in 1983. Rich emerged victorious, but was never the wrestler he had been after the feud ended.

Buzz made GCW must see TV because no one could figure out what he was going to do next, even booker /part owner Ole Anderson. Buzz teamed with legend Ivan Koloff, who named him "Mad Dog." Buzz and Koloff attacked Tommy rich's cousin, Johnny Rich and shaved his head. Buzz fucked with everyone he could. He told black wrestler

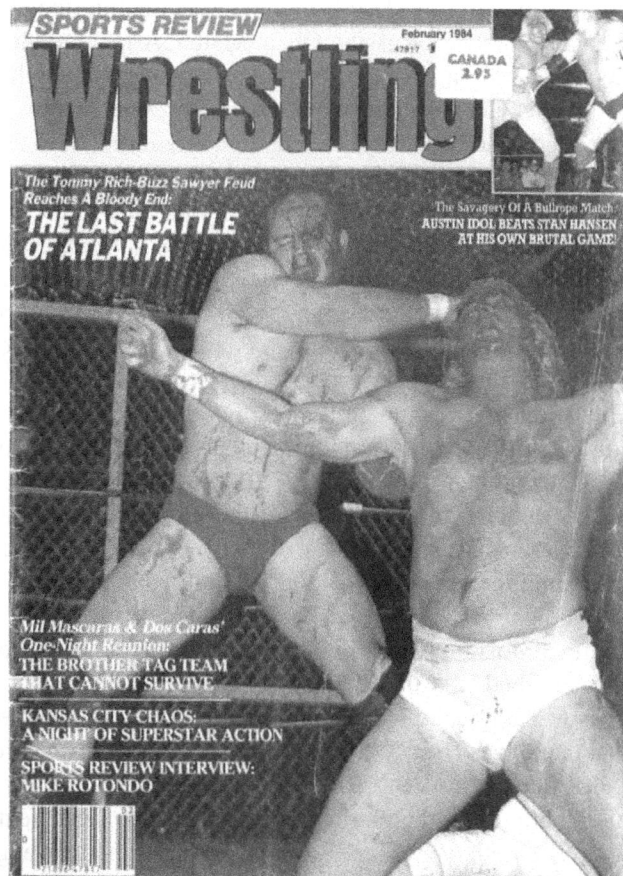

Butch Reed to "shine my shoes, boy." That comment got Buzz cold. conked by Reed on the air. When Ole Anderson said he had incriminating footage of Buzz and it went missing, Buzz showed up on camera chewing the incriminating tape. During a feud with Dick Murdock he made remarks about Dick's mother, prompting Murdock to attack him on the air. A Buzz promo consisted Buzz screaming, sweating, and his eyes bugging out. My wife at the time was a nurse and she said to me, "Look at that fucker, he's coked up out of his mind!"

Yeah, Buzz had "personal demons." Ivan Koloff remembered a night after a match when a group of wrestlers stopped at a store to buy beer and snacks before they went back to the hotel to unwind. Koloff has just wrestled his specialty match, a Russian Chain Match. A huge redneck called him out over wrestling being fake and asked Ivan to step outside. Ivan obliged but before anyone did anything, Buzz confronted the guy—who was over a foot taller and 150lbs heavier—and took him down. Buzz sat on him, rubbing his face into the gravel parking lot until the flesh was shredded. The cops were called, but Buzz didn't stop the beat down until the cops were forced to draw their guns.

Buzz became more unhinged. He would routinely beat the shit out of jobbers. Once he caught Tom Pritchard as he came off the ropes and threw him face first to the floor. Tom didn't get up for a while. Since no one on the roster could hang in there with him, guys like Roddy Piper, Ronnie Garvin, Abdulla, and other big names were brought in for a one. shot feud. In an interview, Ole Anderson claimed ignorance of Buzz's drug use. "I was booking four shows a night, how the hell was I supposed to know half my roster was on the shit?" Maybe he did, maybe he didn't, but in an interview with Matt Borne, a Pacific Northwest wrestler who teamed with Buzz early in their respective careers, Matt said that Roddy Piper took him to Georgia to work and after he signed his contract, road agent Wahoo McDaniels tossed him an 8- ball of coke. Borne was paired with Arn Anderson as a tag team, but was let go from the company after domestic violence charges were filed against him.

Buzz joined Precious Paul Ellering's stable, The Legion of Doom, which included The Road Warriors, Jake The Snake Roberts and King Kong Bundy. Bundy soon turned on the group when he overheard Ellering on TV saying they weren't keeping Bundy around because it cost too much to feed him. A new wrestler, Brett Wayne, had just come into the territory. A good. looking young guy, he was quickly targeted by the LOD. During a long, brutal match on TV against Jake the Snake, Ellering and Buzz were ringside. Buzz seemed really disturbed about something. Jake would almost pin Brett, then pull him up before the three count and beat on him some more. Buzz suddenly went bats shit, grabbed Ellering by the face and tossed him aside. He stormed the ring and fans feared he was going after Brett. Fans were shocked when Buzz beat the crap out of Jake and helped Brett to his feet. Then it came out, Brett Wayne's real name was Brett Wayne Sawyer, Buzz's younger brother.

Ellering, now out for revenge, brought in Abdulla the Butcher for the next Omni Show. Buzz and Abby had a bloodbath. Later that night the Road Warriors were beating the crap out of Brett. A bloody Buzz stormed the ring and took out both Hawk and Animal. Buzz remained a good guy, winning the tag team belts with his brother, and teaming with former enemies against the LOD. When Vince McMahon took over WCW's time slot and bought out the owners—everyone except Ole—Buzz left.

Buzz hooked up with the WWF who was grabbing any name talent they could. Buzz was renamed "Bulldog" Buzz Sawyer and was managed by Captain Lou Albano. He couldn't use the "Mad Dog" name because Mad Dog Vachon had also jumped from the AWA to the WWF. Buzz disappeared from the WWF. Ole managed to get airtime on TBS, but it was 7am Saturday morning. Ole still had a few guys that didn't jump to the WWF or guys that the WWF didn't want. Tommy Rich, Ronnie Garvin, Scott Irwin, Ox Baker, and a few others made up the roster. Buzz and Brett returned, but didn't stay long. Eventually Ted Turner and McMahon clashed over what Vince was doing. Turner wanted in studio wrestling, Vince just wanted to run tapes. Vince sold the time slot to Crocket Promotions for a million dollars. Vince figured Crocket wouldn't last.

Joke was on Vince because as he was marketing to kids, WCW was more into actual wrestling, brawling, and bloodletting. Buzz was brought back as part of Gary Hart's stable J. Tex Corporation with Kendo Nagasaki, Terry Funk, and The Great Muta. Around then, Buzz started to fly. By that I mean a coked out Buzz was jumping off the top turnbuckle on to the floor. During a cage match, Buzz found a wire sticking out and ran his face into it, ripping his forehead open. Then he fell off the cage, back into the ring, and landed on his head. He got right up. Then Ole Anderson realized what a liability Buzz was and fired him.

And yet it gets better. Before returning to WCW, Buzz opened a "wrestling" school. One of his first students was the almost 7. foot tall Mark Callaway, who would later find fame as the Undertaker. He paid Buzz $3,000 and the next day Buzz was long gone as he used the money to score drugs. Callaway was brought into WCW as Mean

Mark Callous. Seeing Buzz in the locker room, Mark sat right in front of him and said, "Remember me?" Buzz got weird, mumbling incoherently and promising to make good, then started laughing. Callaway wanted to pummel the cocky fuck, but knew he was one of "Ole's boys" and didn't want to lose his job. Other would. be students were also ripped off by Buzz.

Buzz bounced from territory to territory, usually lasting a month or so before his unpredictable behavior got him fired. Then in February, 1992, Buzz was found dead on his front lawn in Sacramento, California, of a massive cocaine overdose. In an interview with wrestler Billy Jack Haynes, Haynes claimed that both he and Sawyer were running drugs for Pablo Escobar and Buzz was the victim of a hit squad. Bear in mind that Haynes also accused Vince McMahon of having someone "stab him in the eye " while he was homeless and sleeping in a car to shut him up.

Had Buzz lasted a few more years, he would have wound up in ECW. Buzz was tailor. made for a promotion that flipped off mainstream wrestling and focused on bloody brawls, weapons, and actual edge of your seat wrestling. Can you imagine Buzz feuding with Sabu, Taz, The Rottens, Sandman, Raven, Balls, and the Dudleys? Sadly, we will never know, as Buzz was hardcore way before the phrase was coined.

How out of control was Buzz? I'll end this with a story told by Ken Kish, now owner and promoter of Cinema Wasteland. While working security in a Cleveland hotel, WWF ran one of its tour though the area and Buzz was on it. Here's Ken story of how things went down:

In the early 1980s, I was working as a security guard for the hotels around Cleveland Hopkins Airport. The WWF was slowly decimating regional promotions and there was a ton of great wrestlers coming through town every month. At just over 6'2" and weighing in at around 230 pounds, I was in the best shape of my life at the time. The WWF guys all stayed at the hotel on airport grounds. I believe it was a Sheraton at the time, and because I was a big guy, personable managers like Bobby "The Brain" Heenan used to pull me into the action whenever the wrestlers came in after a show beat down, tired, and in need of a few drinks and a meal but were met by groups of kids or fans, which was a pretty regular occurrence. It became my usual duties to wave off the crowds and get the guys to the elevators, front desk, or their rooms as they arrived and I had a blast doing my small part for the guys.

One night after a WWF show, I received a page from the front desk that there was somebody causing trouble in the bar. The bar was on the top floor of the hotel and it was after Midnight when I got the call. By the time I got up there, the place was quiet. I walked past a guy sitting at the end of the bar who had to be eight feet tall and 500+ pounds. He was drinking wine out of a big beer glass and had a couple of full bottles in front of him. You may know the guy. He went by the name of Andre The Giant. I went over to talk to Tony, the head bartender, and told him that if Andre was the guy causing trouble, I'm out of there as fast as my legs could carry me as there was no way I was going to tell a guy that big shit. Tony tells me that a big sweaty guy was indeed pacing around the bar shouting at nobody in particular and giving a couple of women—actually the regular hotel hookers who hung out most every night—a scare. But he left a few minutes before I got there after he scared the women away. Shit like this happened all the time so I didn't think anything of it and went out to fire up half a fattie in my pocket since the outside fire exit doors were right off the bar entrance.

Five minutes later, I get another page from the front desk. Then another a few seconds later. I head back into the bar and call the front desk from the bar phone just a couple of feet from where Andre The Giant is still gulping down wine. He must have polished off two bottles in the five or six minutes I was gone. When I call down to see what's up, I'm told that there is a big guy pacing the fifth or sixth floor hallway ranting, raving, ramming his head into the elevator doors, and generally making people fear for their lives. I'm not one to shy away from confrontation with a drunk, so I head out of the bar and go down the stairs instead of taking the elevator thinking maybe I can sneak up on the guy. Once I get to whatever floor it was, I open the stairway door and I can hear the guy ranting and raving down the hall from around the corner. I turn, and... Holy fuck, I know that guy! It's Buzz Sawyer! And yes, he was indeed sweating, pacing, ranting, and running his head into the walls and elevator doors! I not only turned and walked away at that point, I went straight up the stairs and back to the bar where I called the front desk. "That's Buzz Sawyer! There is no fucking way I'm telling that coked out monster anything!" I tell the front desk. "He's obviously on something and I don't get paid enough to have my ass kicked by a guy I know can kick it up and down the hallway twice! You don't even let me carry handcuffs, so call the cops and have them take care of him," I'm telling the front desk.

Now, I'm saying all this just a couple of feet from Andre The Giant with bartender Tony laughing his ass off behind the bar. I hang up the phone and I'm about to tell Tony to go and take care of the guy if he thinks it's so damn funny when Andre looks at me and tells me to show him where Buzz is. I tell him to follow me and we head off to the elevators and down to the fifth or sixth floor. When the doors open, there's Buzz. Still ranting and raving away. Andre grabs his entire face with one hand. His whole fucking head with his face in his palm, and tells Buzz something along the line of, "What room you in?", in a booming voice. Buzz mumbles and pulls out a card key from his pocket. I'm just standing there sort of dumb fucked. Andre the Giant has Buzz Sawyer by the face and starts to drag him down the hallway by his head until they get to a room. He gives me the keycard and I open the door. Andre shoves Buzz into the room where he must sail about eight or ten feet before he stumbles backward on his ass. Andre looks at him and tells him, "Stay there… Go to bed!" and turns to walk away as the door closes. He's heading back to the elevator without saying a word to me. I tell him, "Thanks, Andre," and he mumbles something along the lines of, "He won't be trouble no more," and heads back up the elevator. I head down to tell the front desk that hopefully things will chill out but just in case, what room is Andre The Giant in?

Things are quiet for about 45 minutes or so when I get another call from the front desk that there is some trouble in the bar AGAIN. Fuck me. I haven't had a night like this in all the time I've worked this hotel and it's going on 2:00am now. I usually head up to the bar and walk the last bartender down to deposit the night's receipts anyway, so I was just about to head up there to shoot the shit as they closed the place when that page came in. When I arrive, I'm relieved to see it's just Tony and Andre The Giant, still seated at the bar gulping wine. Tony leaves the bar and meets me ten feet behind Andre and whispers to me that "He doesn't want to leave and it's time to close up." I don't want to piss off the guy who may or may not have saved my life an hour earlier, but I know that you need to get everyone out of the bar by a certain time. I head over to Andre and try to tell him that he just can't stay in the bar after a certain time or the bar could get shut down. He's not really listening to either of us, but we do manage to get through to him that he could buy some more wine here at last call, sit at the bar with us until we close it down for the night, and take whatever he doesn't drink by closing back to his room if he wants. This seems to help and all is good. The bar closes down, Andre grabs a couple of bottles of wine for the road, and we lock the gate and head down to deposit the night's receipts.

The only thing I regret about the night was not asking Andre for an autograph. Sadly, on this night, he looked like he didn't want to be bothered, and since he reluctantly helped me out already once during my long twelve. hour shift, I wasn't going to bother him for anything. My shift ended at 7:00am and thankfully, I didn't hear a peep about Buzz Sawyer the rest of the night.

One of the Best Horror Novelists You Never heard of:

WILLIAM W. JOHNSTONE

Growing up in the '60s, we horror fans didn't have very much reading material, except for the works of Poe, HP Lovecraft, Ambrose Bierce, Robert Bloch, and Richard Matheson. Matheson's I Am Legend was a groundbreaker that may have been the inspiration for Romero's Night of the Living Dead. Then an avalanche of horror writers erupted in the late '70s, early '80s. A new breed of writer was on the horizon. Like the new breed of indie filmmakers, not much for them was taboo.

Jack Ketchum, Gary Brander, Richard Laymon, Graham Masterson, John Russo, Steven King and others put a new slant on horror. Depictions of murder, mayhem, and graphic violence were vividly illustrated by these talented artists. They took horror out of the musty tombs and graveyards. Now the real horror might just be living right next to you. Being a guy that reads a book a day during down time, I just ate all this stuff up. I loved prowling musty, used book store in NY/NJ for stuff I never heard of.

There was a huge, old bookstore in Passaic, NJ, The Passaic Book Center. You name it, they had it. From old comics and magazines to first edition books. Rooting through several boxes, I found two books by a guy I had never heard of, William W. Johnstone. The books were *The Devil's Kiss* and *Out of the Ashes*. Each was over 300 pages. Intrigued by the descriptions on the back of the books, I took a chance.

The Devil's Kiss was awesome; a brutal read involving how Satan tries, though his earthbound minions, to enslave an isolated mid. western town. The hero is former soldier turned preacher, Sam Balon. Balon rallies the few untouched by the Devil. But the Devil not only has his worshippers, he has the living dead, flesh eating beasts, and other horrors to throw at the faithful. In the end, Balon sacrifices himself to save the others. He battles a witch, Nydia, who needs to be impregnated by Balon to spawn a perfect demon child for the Devil. Johnstone ups the ante by throwing in rape, torture, mutilation, and religion into the mix. This book brought Johnstone national acclaim and he became a full time writer. Previously, he'd published two espionage books, *Eagle Down* and *Dagger*, under the name "William Mason."

The other book, *Out of the Ashes*, blew me away and pretty much made me a fan for life. This was the first of a series of close to 30 books. *Ashes* is the story of former special forces soldier and mercenary, now novelist, Ben Raines, who survives a worldwide nuclear, chemical, and germ warfare attack. Raines roams the devastated country, trying to document what happened. He encounters many people who convince him to help put the country back together. He takes the best of the best to an area in the west. The area is comprised of three states that didn't take that bad of a hit during the upheaval. The area was named "The Tri States." Raines and company got factories up and running, put people back to work, made military training mandatory for all residents, and had no crime.

The revamped United States of America, however, was not doing that well. In fact, it perceived the Tri States as a threat. Despite all of Raines's efforts to peacefully co. exist, war is declared on the Tri States. Americans vs. Americans and the descriptions are brutal. Most of the residents of the Tri States are massacred, characters you actually cared about. Raines and the survivors live to fight the corrupt government as the series continued. Raines' Rebels fought battle after battle. Biker gangs, Russian invaders, mutants, cannibals, Islamic terrorists, Neo. Nazis, drug lords, slavers, etc., were all soundly trounced by the Rebels. But after over 30 books in the series, it ended with

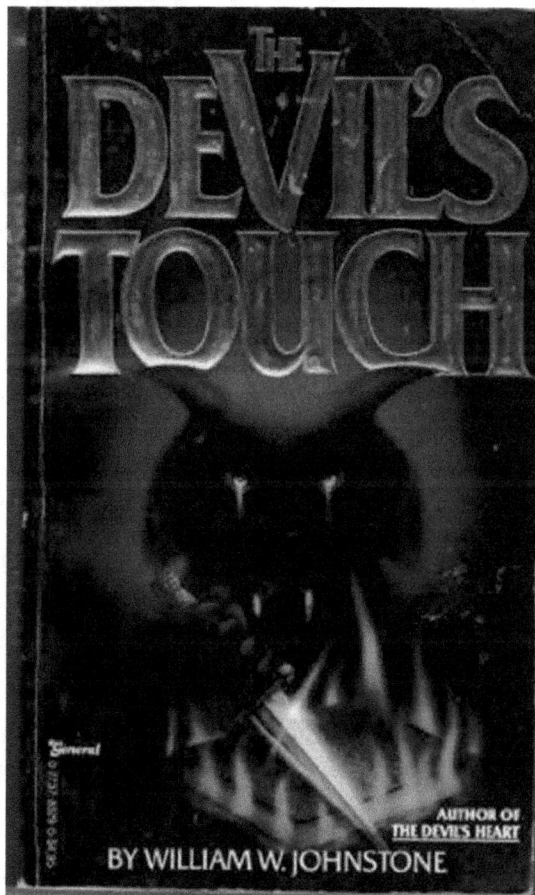

a whimper, not a bang. He tried, it seemed, to replace the series with **The Last Rebel** in 2004. But something was amiss, and that something wouldn't be revealed until almost three years later.

William Wallace Johnstone was born October 28th, 1938, in Missouri. He quit school at age 15 and joined The French Foreign Legion. He was kicked out when his real age was revealed. He went back and finished school in 1957. He worked as a Deputy Sheriff, did a hitch in the army, and started a 16. year career in radio broadcasting, where he honed his storytelling skills. After **The Devil's Kiss**, he wrote three more novels in the series, **The Devil's Heart, The Devil's Touch**, and **The Devil's Cat** with Sam Balon's son, another military man, picking up the battle where his father left off. More horror followed with **Wolfsbane**, witchcraft and werewolves in the bayous of Louisiana. **Baby Grand, The Rocking Horse,** and **Toy Cemetery**, were all about items possessed by evil. **Sandman** was about Voodoo rites. Them was about invaders from space. **Cats Cradle** and **Cat's Eye** were about evil Egyptian deities. Other books **Rockabilly Limbo** and **Rockabilly Hell**, dealt with ghostly roadhouses and their deadly inhabitants. **The Uninvited** had armies of killer cockroaches. Other books were **Night Mask, Carnival, The Nursery, Deathmaster, Watcher in the Woods** and **Bloodland**.

Darkly the Thunder is one of his best. A small town is under attack by something called the Fury, an ageless entity that feeds on human energy every 30 or so years. Usually it creates some kind of disaster to mask its intent, but not this time. There is no defense against the Fury as the town is sealed off. But help comes in the unlikely form of the ghosts of several '50s juvenile delinquents who were wrongfully murdered and want their names cleared. Blood soaked and vicious, but with a lot of humanity and characters you care about.

Johnstone was a keen observer of the political scene and didn't like what he saw. He wrote about it in not only "The Ashes" series, but book series like **Rig Warrior, Codename**, and books like **Ordeal, Breakdown** and others. This put him on a government watch list, something Bill never spoke about until later. But you sort of knew something was up as he sort of "toned down" his rhetoric for a bit. Bill stopped the horror novels and jumped into westerns. He devoted hours of research to find out as much as he could as to the weapons used in the eras he would write about. The westerns were just as brutal and violent as his other works. Again, he created characters that you grew to care about.

These westerns were epic in scope. The series were **The Eagles Legacy, the Last Mountain Man, The Last Gunfighter, Sidewinders**, and more. Gunfighters like Smoke Jensen, Frank Morgan, Preacher, and others took you places no other western novels had. But something went wrong in 2004. All of a sudden, Bill had a co. writer, Fred Austin. After a few books, Austin was gone and J. A Johnstone replaced him. Stranger still was the fact that while Bill never shied away from rape, torture, and violence in his books, things seemed to be toned down a bit. On the copyright page of 2006's **The Last Gunfighter: The Devil's Legion**, there was a statement that said following the death of William W. Johnstone, a carefully selected writer has been chosen to organize and complete Mr. Johnstone's outlines and unfinished manuscripts to create additional novels for all his series. Seems that Bill died in 2004, but his "estate" didn't confirm his death until 2006. He was 65, and that makes me suspect. He lived most of his later life in Shreveport, LA, but died in Knoxville, TN. I cannot fathom that a guy this tough just passes at that age. Call me suspicious but no details that I could find are available about his death. The carefully selected writer, J.A Johnstone is a "nephew." Since 2004, over 100 more novels have been published. An average of two to three a month are published. There must have been a shitload of unfinished work. But they honestly, with a couple of exceptions, have been good reads.

William W. Johnstone is an American original. All of his horror novels are out of print and go for big money. They are worth seeking out. I can honestly say I have never been disappointed by anything Bill has written. He not only was a great writer, but a visionary as he predicted The Gulf War, having a black president, and today's unstable political climate. He had his finger on the political pulse of this country and had the balls to write about it, bring heat on himself. I'm just sorry I never met the man and I'm even sorrier that he left us so early in life.

You can get a list of everything he ever did at williamjohnstone.net.

THE NORTHVILLE CEMETERY MASSACRE

Some films defy description and wind up actually better than they are advertised. Such is the case for *The Northville Cemetery Massacre*. Strolling around "The Deuce" I spied a one. sheet poster with a fat, redneck cop holding a shotgun with the tagline, "The Day Law and Order Went Berserk." My curiosity was aroused but this seemed to be just another biker flick and biker films could either be really good or really shitty. No middle of the road here. *Northville* was paired with a Spaghetti western, *The Ugly Ones*, so I figured it wouldn't be a total loss and, being it was around noon, admission was only $1.50.

So I picked up a pint of cheap hooch from Athena Liquors and stepped into the rank confines of The Empire Theater. Little did I know that this film was to become an International Motorcycle Cult Film. When you put the words 'Cemetery" and 'Massacre" in a title, you're going to draw a crowd. Thing was that most of this crowd expected a horror film. What they got was a kick. ass biker film that went against the grain.

In this film the bikers are good guys and the law are a bunch of sadistic pricks. A hitchhiker is on the road when he see some bikes heading toward him. He whips out a sign that says grass and one of the guys picks him up. Chris, the hitchhiker, is connected to someone in the club. He goes on a run with them, than sneaks off to an old barn with his girlfriend.

Cops arrive to break up the run. Two cops corner Chris and the girl. Lynn. Chris is knocked out and Lynn is raped by one of the cops. She is threatened by the cop if she talks. The cop has her taken to a hospital, then, to cover his ass, he goes to Lynn's father and tells him the gang raped her. The cop swears the father to secrecy and the two hatch a plan to get revenge on the bikers. They enlist a hunter, Armstrong, with a high. powered rifle. The cop recruits him with the story of the savage rape. Back at the clubhouse, two of the boys go out back to water the lilies. They are cut down in mid. piss by a high. powered rifle. Thinking a rival club is responsible, the leader calls for a sit down.

The two clubs meet at an abandoned Drive-in. As the two club leaders talk, the shooter guns down members of both clubs. They decide action must be taken, but the rogue cop has planted a seed with the other cops and the clubs are constantly hassled and searched at every opportunity. The rogue cop sadistically guns down a biker who has broken down in a ditch. The shootings are in the slo-mo Peckinpah style, lots of bloody squib bursts.

The clubs are not sure who's behind the killings but decided to even the odds a bit. They take a cruise out to see their local arms dealer. Lots of great shots of tricked out bikes on the highway. The arms dealer lives in an underground bunker that could withstand a "17,000 megaton blast at ground zero." The boys pick out a various assortment of shotguns, pistols, rifles etc. The dealer tells them that if they'd called in advance he could have gotten them some Claymore mines and a bazooka, but he thoughtfully throws in some hand grenades. Anyone have this guy's number?

Chris visits Lynn in the hospital and she tells him what really wet down. Chris and Lynn have to warn the club as the club is riding to the cemetery to bury their dead. The cops stop the club and search them for weapons, finding none. After the coffins are unloaded, the mayhem begins. A helicopter with the cop, Dad, and Armstrong attacks, but the club had loaded the coffins with weapons. The bikers fire on the 'copter, but are shot to pieces. Head shots, chests bursting, this was some heavy. duty violence then. These bikers had to be the worst shots in the history of western civilization.

The club fakes the shooters out by playing dead. The helicopter lands and the assholes get out to check their kills. Another gunfight starts and even the biker's women are killed. Finally someone tosses a grenade into the helicopter, blowing it and the pilot into a bloody mess. Chris is badly wounded and everyone is dead except the cop. The film ends with the two facing off. Typical '70s downbeat ending as the guy you wanted to die the most is alive at the end of the film.

The Empire crowd crapped all over this as the end didn't give you what you wanted: Rogue cop dead. An actual motorcycle club, The Scorpions from Detroit, played the club. *Northville Cemetery Massacre* did its "for one week only" run and vanished. In the early days of VHS, it was released by Paragon Video as part of its "horror" line with *Dr. Butcher M.D., Nightbeast*, and others. It has since been restored on DVD by VCI Entertainment.

THE CUT-THROATS NINE:

Remembering a Movie I Never Went to See

Strange times, the '70s, and even stranger behavior on my part. I never had any intention of seeing *The Cut Throats Nine*. I did, however, want to see the top billed film, a horror film, whatever it was. *Cut Throats* was the second feature. The sorry saga begins on a Saturday night at Club 44, my home away from home on 44th street. Right in the middle of Times Square, I had been drinking here since I was 15 and I had struck up a symbiotic friendship with two bar maids/call girls. They only worked high. end clients and I had met them at a bachelor party. We hit it off, partly because I was a complete stoner and always had or could get weed. Lisa was working this night and she didn't want to. She could be making more scratch on a call. Just my luck I stopped there before going to the movie, which was at The Liberty on "The Deuce." She was pissed and a lot of non. tipping out-of-towners were there. "This sucks," she tells me, "I was just working this afternoon and that cunt, Carol, just quit. Now I'm stuck."

"That does suck" I agreed. "I'm going to the movies."

"No, stay here and we can go later."

"Later," I said, "like 4am, when you get off?" No fuckin' way. It was close to 11pm, last show would be around 1am. "Besides," I said, "I ain't flush, so I can't stand here and nurse this beer all night, Nino will be pissed."

Nino was Nino Valdez, former boxer, now bouncer. Nino liked me, just as long as I was drinking. Lisa went on, "What if I feed you beer, free, will you stay then?" Now this was tempting and now I'll push my luck. "Throw in a couple of shots and let me crash at your place and we got a deal."

"Done, but put some $$ on the bar to make it look good."

So it went. I wasn't a pig, I paced myself. By 2:30 am, I was sloshed. I needed weed. I grabbed this drunk, Tony, and took him so I wouldn't get lost. Based on the theory that one of two drunks should be able to find their way back to the bar. We went down a couple of blocks to Chiba St., 40th something, but we called it Chiba Street because you could buy $20 bags of weed called Chiba, in honor of Sonny Chiba, *The Street Fighter*.

Twisting one up, we staggered back. That took an hour. It was close to 4am. "Let's get out of here, but give me one more," I said to Lisa. "No," she said, "we'll go upstairs by my place."

"Upstairs" was an afterhours joint in a warehouse loft. OK, we took the subway down to Avenue A then smoked all the rest of the stuff walking to 4th street. Two flights up and the door to the freak show opens. This was one of the more 'opulent' of the afterhours shitholes, and by that I mean they actually washed the glasses. I was really too trashed, but kept drinking anyway. Lisa was banging down shots of tequila. After trying to shoot some pool and almost impaling a transsexual hooker in the process, it was time to call it a night. Lisa wanted to go for breakfast—FYI, greasy bacon and eggs don't mix with tequila. I was too fucked up to eat, I didn't want coffee, I wanted sleep. I nursed a coke, she pigged out, then we left. By the time we got to her place, she was sweating and doubling over.

Oh, fuck—she drank all that on an empty stomach, then poured grease over it. She made it to the can and then

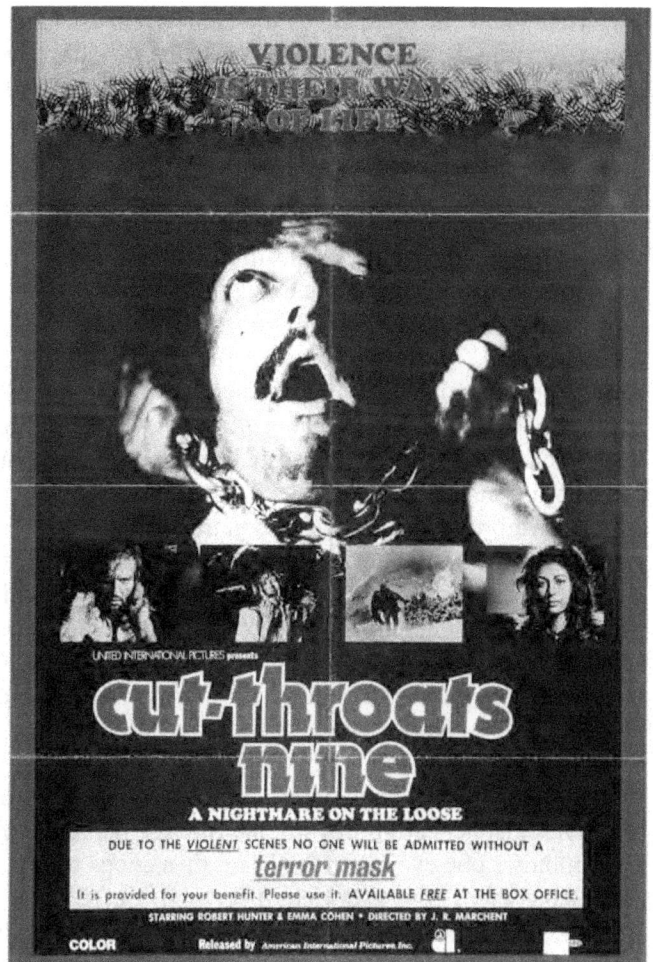

talked to god on the porcelain telephone. I brought her cold water; she puked for hours it seemed. Candy, her roommate, came home. She looked at me, looked at Lisa, and shook her head. "Better hit the road, chief, before it hits you." I was out of there. I took a bus, but had to change busses on Central Avenue, East Orange. I was waiting for the other bus, it was fuckin' cold, it was winter, grey, cloudy, and shitty.

Then I saw the marquee on the Hollywood Theater, the movie I'd wanted to see was playing there. Fuck the bus, now I can finally see this, a gift from the Grindhouse Gods. I paid $3.50 to get in. The Hollywood was an old cavernous place that didn't retain heat. I found a seat, sat down and passed out.

I woke up with a start, **where the hell am I?** It's snowing—wait it's a movie. What happened to me? Then I remembered. I tried, with no luck, to stand up. Credits appeared on the grainy print, **The Cut Throats Nine**. I figured that I might as well just watch it.

The film opened with a wagon leaving a mining camp, guarded by three soldiers. In the wagon are seven convicts, chained together. Also in the wagon is Sgt. Brown and his daughter. Brown is played by the only name actor I recognized, Robert Hundar, a hawk-faced actor who did a lot of Euro westerns, most noticeably **Sabata**.

Brown's wife was brutally murdered by one of the convicts. We are treated to flashbacks showing her being disemboweled. The wagon is stopped by some slimy looking bandits who are after gold. When no gold is found, the bandits become understandably upset. One shows his displeasure by caving in a soldier's head with a rifle butt. Lots of spurting blood and grey matter. Another soldier's throat is slashed from ear to ear. The wagon is sent stampeding until it crashes in a scene that makes you feel bad for the horses. Brown and his daughter jump to safety. One prisoner has his leg broken in the crash.

Brown orders the prisoners to march and has them carry the injured man. It seems to be snowing all the time; the scenery is bleak, desolate and cold. So was I as it was fuckin' freezing in this place. The prisoners amuse themselves by singing cute songs about how they are going to kill Sgt. Brown. After marching for a while, the prisoners are getting pissed about carrying the guy with the broken leg. After Brown tucks them in for the night, they draw lots to see who gets to kill the guy. Dawn breaks, and there is one less prisoner for morning brunch. "You can still carry him," snarls Brown. After a day of toting the stiff around, the boys set the corpse on fire. Brown isn't happy with the unauthorized cookout. They chop off the burnt leg to unchain the body. They then discover the chains are made of the gold the bandits were after. A big argument breaks out in monotone. If you haven't ever heard an argument in monotone, you don't know what you are missing. The dubbing in this film is really horrible.

The prisoners are in revolt, one refuses to go on. "You'll have to shoot me," he screams at Brown. No problem. Brown blows one eye out of his head, then chops off his arm from the chains. The boys now know that killing Brown will make them free and rich. The tired. out Brown is jumped when the group takes shelter in an abandoned farmhouse. Brown is brutally beaten and forced to watch the prisoners rape his daughter. He is left hanging from the rafters. The prisoners set the place on fire and Brown is burned alive in a scene that's hard to watch.

The prisoners march to freedom with Brown's daughter in tow. The guy who instigated the rape is hung by his chains by the one prisoner who was against the rape. The remaining members are perturbed, but not that much when they figure the pie now can be cut four ways instead of five. One prisoner, an alcoholic degenerate, decides to take off on his own. In a booze. induced hallucination, he imagines Brown coming back to life and chasing him. He runs into the group of bandits and is killed in a shoot. out. The surviving three arrive at a trading post run by a man named Caldwell.

Caldwell has a history with one of the guys. He is hung up on a hook and disemboweled. At that moment a wino, who had been passed out a couple of rows behind me, woke up and muttered loudly, "Lookit dem guts all hangin' out!", then passed back out again. The sympathetic prisoner is killed and it's revealed that he was the one who murdered Brown's wife. As the remaining two prisoners discuss their next move, Brown's daughter finds and lights a stick of dynamite, blowing the place to bits and ending her and my torment.

I now managed to stand up and stagger out of the Hollywood. It was snowing as I waited for the bus, adding to the weirdness of the last 24 hours. I got home and slept for two days.

Almost 40 years later, I still can't remember the name of that first movie I'd wanted to catch.

DOUBLE FEATURE REVIEW:
OCTAMAN (1971) & SPAWN OF THE SLITHIS (1978)

By Bill Adcock

I'll be honest with you: I'm too young for the true Grindhouse experience. I was born after the Grindhouse was dead, but grew up in the video era, watching tape after tape of the classics – Universal, Hammer, the 1950s Atomic Scare, Flying Saucer flicks…that's my movie. geek background, and eventually I grew up and my tastes evolved and I began hunting down more obscure films, weird horror flicks… I just really want to see something new and strange that I haven't seen before. Every so often, I'll catch a whiff of some cinematic oddity, read a two. sentence review, whatever, and I'll get it into my head: "I need to see this film."

Cue searching through eBay, trawling the gray. market vendors at conventions, etc., until at last I have my grubby paws on a copy.

Is it worth it? Sometimes the movie ends up being good, more often it's junk but at least I've had the satisfaction of hunting it down and seeing something that I wouldn't have seen otherwise. I don't get the opportunity to inflict screenings of strange horror flicks for friends as much as I'd like these days, but I'm a big fan of putting together double. feature screenings of movies that I think work well together. In this issue, I've got two films that were never shown together in the days of 42nd Street (*Spawn of the Slithis* screened with *Laserblast*), but they've both got rubber suit monsters created by the dumping of toxic waste, and they're both movies I put way too much effort into tracking down, only for them to basically fall into my lap.

Octaman was written and directed by Harry Essex, best known for writing and directing 1953's adaptation of Mickey Spillane's *I, The Jury*, writing the Universal sci. fi classic *It Came From Outer Space*, and most importantly for *Octaman*, writing the screenplay for *The Creature From The Black Lagoon*. Starring Kerwin Matthews (of *The 7th Voyage of Sinbad* fame) and Pier Angeli (in her final film appearance before being found dead of a barbiturate overdose), with Jeff Morrow (*This Island Earth, The Giant Claw*) in a supporting role, *Octaman* is basically a lower. budgeted rehash of the script of *Creature*, with an octopus. man (early work by Rick Baker) replacing the gill. man, and the action moved from the Amazon to the Everglades. Funnily enough, nothing I ever read about the movie in my search for a copy of *Octaman* ever mentioned, "hey, this is basically the exact same movie as *Creature from the Black Lagoon*." Though on the other hand, I'm kind of glad for that because if I'd heard that, I probably never would have bothered tracking this down, and it was kind of a cool thing to see.

Kerwin Matthews is playing a scientist who's been running tests on the people living in fishing villages along the Gulf of Mexico, and he's discovered that these people have been consuming about 100 times the amount of radiation that they should be—something about the ocean currents carrying radioactive fallout from nuclear testing into the Gulf, and he and his assistant (Pier Angeli's character) decide to look for mutant animals to prove that so much radiation is going into the Gulf.

Well, they find an octopus with human eyes that cries like a baby, and take it with them to try and score more funding for their research. This pisses off the octopus' mother (father?), the Octaman of the title, which looks a lot like the Creature from the Black Lagoon except instead of two finny arms it has four tentacles, two of which are pretty plainly connected to the other two by fishing line, so when the guy in the suit moves his arms, it wiggles the second set of tentacles too. It's got a big pulpy head with a saggy, open sphincter of a mouth and two bulging green. orange eyes which are actually pretty creepy looking. The eyes are effective, even if the rest of the suit is so-so.

So the Octaman starts killing people until it catches sight of Pier Angeli, and then all it wants to do is carry her off and empty his ink sac into her. Kerwin Matthews saves her, the Octaman is killed, we get the sense that she's going to be a lot more than just his research assistant, the end…or is it?

This is a film that would have really benefitted from keeping the monster in shadow. It's a good design, and it's probably the best Octaman feasible, but the creature is constantly shuffling around in broad daylight, which really doesn't hide the flaws in the suit any. And if that wasn't enough, the opening credits of the movie are shown over a long shot of the Octaman in a medium close. up, waddling, wiggling, shuffling and flailing, with nothing else in the shot. The Creature from the Black Lagoon was hidden from view for a big chunk of the film, with just a hand or a foot shown to increase suspense and let the audiences' imaginations do the work of keeping the creature scary. With Octaman, it's more like, "Tada! Look what we made!"

The other thing is, with *Creature* they made the effort to convince us that what we were seeing was an amphibian creature, especially with the long scenes of the "water ballet" between Ricou Browning in the Creature suit and Julie Adams. Octaman never looks like anything but a suffering stuntman waddling around in a foam rubber suit that's soaking up water like crazy, and you'll notice he never wades out into the water deeper than his waist. Swimming scenes were out of the question, given the budget and the limitations of the suit.

I looked forever for a copy of this in a format I could watch, I checked every bootleg and gray. market vendor I could find, and most of them had never even heard of *Octaman*, let alone carried it. Naturally, as soon as I stopped actively looking for it, the movie popped up on Netflix Instant, and in 2012 a 40th Anniversary DVD release happened, packaged with Harry Essex's next feature, *The Cremators* (which I haven't checked out yet) as a bonus feature.

While *Octaman* feels familiar, *Spawn of the Slithis* (1978) feels like a lot of things familiar. A lot of elements here are recognizable from appearing in many, many horror and sci. fi films preceding *Slithis*, making this movie something of a cinematic chop suey. And you know what? That works just fine for me.

This is one of only two films written and directed by Steven Traxler, who seems to have gone on to a much more productive career as a producer and production manager for such films as *Waterworld, Legally Blonde 2* and *Invasion U.S.A. Slithis* stars Alan Blanchard, Judy Motulsky and J.C. Claire, none of whom ever acted again in film and television. Better off was character actor Hy Pyke in a supporting role, who'd previously appeared in *Dolemite* and *Lemora: A Child's Tale of the Supernatural* and later went on to appear in *Blade Runner* of all things.

The story starts off with something killing pets in the area around Venice, California, and news anchors speculating that a Manson Family-esque group or maybe a bunch of Satanists are to blame, but local high school journalism teacher Wayne (Blanchard) isn't convinced. That's right, we've got the hoary old cliché of the investigative journalist ferreting out the truth the eludes the police, only this time the guy's not even an actual newshound – just a washed. up wannabe who ended up teaching high school. He decides he's going to investigate the case of the mangled pets himself, much to the worry of his girlfriend Jeff (Motulsky; very clearly a woman despite the name) and exasperation of balding, obese, pop. eyed chief of police (Hy Pyke, whose body language would have looked excessive even in the silent film era).

Pretty soon, the killer moves up from cats and dogs to drunks and homeless people, and at the scene of the latest attack Wayne finds weird muddy footprints all over the place. Taking a sample, he brings it to his friend and coworker, Dr. John (Claire) the biology teacher. His analysis figures out that the mud is alive – specifically, it's identical to mud taken from a lake contaminated with radioactive waste, identified years earlier in the scientific journals as "Slithis." Jeff asks why they named it that, and Dr. John replies, "for the same reason your parents named you Jeff." Oh, so the scientists were stoned off their asses.

Eventually Wayne figures out that this "Slithis" was created by a reactor leak at the nuclear plant up the coast, and unlike the original Slithis which stayed mud, this batch has evolved into a man. eating monster. Since the police won't believe him, he decides it's his duty to go out and kill it.

So we've got a couple guys in a boat hunting a monster in a seaside town where the cops won't close the beaches. There's your *Jaws* connection. The Slithis looks like the Creature from the Black Lagoon and one of the monsters from *The Slime People* had a kid, and that kid started abusing steroids. And the radioactive mud making it up could have come straight from *X The Unknown/The Quatermass Xperiment*. Like I said, it's a hodge-podge of a lot of different things brought together and somehow it all boils down smooth and works.

I'm not going to lie, it's not that great a film overall. The pacing is very slow, with the emphasis really being on Wayne's investigations. We see a lot of him wandering around looking at things and asking questions, and there's no real monster action on display until the end of the film. For those who aren't prepared for it, the film can be a real endurance test.

The monster suit really is worth the wait though, and after all the movies I've seen where a lousy suit is on display, it's almost heart. breaking to watch *Spawn of the Slithis* and see this fantastic suit kept mostly in shadow and saved for the last ten minutes of the movie. This is a suit that really should have been on full display.

Code Red released *Spawn of the Slithis* on DVD in 2010, but it came and went pretty fast, and now copies are selling for $75+ and quite honestly, I'm not in a place in my life, financially or whatever, where I can justify spending that much money on a DVD of a low. budget monster movie. I saw *Slithis* for the first time when someone uploaded a pretty decent print of it on YouTube. Hopefully Synapse or someone will get the rights and give it a release that doesn't go out of print a week later.

MIDWEST GRINDHOUSE: NOTHING BUT THE BLOOD

By Douglas Waltz

Growing up in Kalamazoo in the 70s and 80s made it a sure thing that I would never see the inside of a New York Grindhouse. Sure, we had two Drive-Ins; The Douglas and The Portage, but while they did show those kinds of movies, it wasn't the same thing. Safely tucked into your car, experiencing films like **Switchblade Sisters** and **The Devil's Nightmare** with just whoever might be in the car with you.

My Grindhouse experience came more from the VHS boom when there was a Mom and Pop store on every corner filled with those big boxes that had exploitative artwork screaming at you that was, for the most part, better than the film encased within.

I was lucky in that I worked with a lady who owned her own video store. Miller Rd. Video. Sue Mattimore worked as a banquet server at The Brown Derby where I tended bar. She jumped on the video boom bandwagon, smart enough to get a stack of VCPs (Video Cassette Players) that you could rent for a weekend if you didn't own your own VCR. She also knew that I read a lot about horror movies, primarily *Fangoria* back when it was good. She would listen to me and get whatever I said would be a big hit. She stocked anything horror. I still remember when she got **Tombs of the Blind Dead** in. Every time I went into her store I was like a kid at Christmas.

One of the bigger renters was anything with the word 'blood' in the title. It was like a buzzword that meant the movie was going to be different. Anyone who denies this would just have to be pointed to the film **Blood Freak**. Any movie where the hero becomes a drugged addled monster with a giant turkey head and craves blood is a sure winner, regardless of how bad it might be. **Blood Freak** definitely falls into the 'so bad it's good' genre.

Another prime example might be **Invasion of the Blood Farmers**. When a group of hillbilly Satanists captures people and harvests their blood to revive their long dead queen you know you're in the land of quality cinema.

And while I could go on and on with this particular theme, I think it might be better to focus on three lesser known 'blood' films.

WAS IT
THE NYMPHOMANIAC...
THE HUNCHBACK...
THE GANGLAND LEADER...
OR A MILLION DOLLARS
WORTH OF HEROIN...
THAT LED THEM DOWN
THE BLOODY PATH TO—

THE KILL

EASTMANCOLOR®

BLOOD HUNGER (1968)

Originally known as **The Kill** and lensed by Orson Welles' cinematographer, Gary Graver, **The Kill** never really experienced a life of its own. Rereleased in the '80s with a lurid cover that looked like the cover of a Blondie album with a little blood for good measure, **Blood Hunger** is not a horror movie.

Even Steven Productions took the original film and redubbed it. The dubbing is cartoonish and there are cartoon sound effects added to the proceedings to make it even, well, worse. But, in the movie there is this kernel of … something. Like a car wreck you can't turn your head from. **Blood Hunger** is unique in its execution.

The basic plot is a girl in trouble who goes to a private detective for protection. These murderous henchmen are after her. The films starts with a shot of a sun bleached city street, probably California. On the street is a dead cat. An actual dead cat and it doesn't look fresh. We are then introduced to our leading lady who gets captured by the bad guys and ending with them dragging her to this sleazy room and raping her. It's the classic completely naked girl while the guy keeps his suit on scenario. I did find it odd that the room was filled with old film cans. At this point I just assumed that Graver shot this in his basement or garage. Anyway, she escapes the clutches of the bad guys and runs to the detective who gets right on the case. The girl, meanwhile, gets on the blind hunchbacked janitor.

The only actor worth mentioning in the film is the lead girl, Antoinette Maynard. A staple in sexploitation films of the '60s and '70s, Antoinette is a long, lean, sexually charged creature that always looks like she is having a great time. *Blood Hunger* is responsible for my current Antoinette Maynard infatuation. I have managed to track down about half of her filmography and am on a constant search for more. If anyone knows of her current whereabouts please contact me via this esteemed publication.

Back to the film.

The movie is filled with tons of soft. core action and a little blood. For a film called *Blood Hunger*, this is pretty restrained in the blood. letting department. Unless you count the squashed kitty.

Towards the end of the film one of the bad guys approaches this woman in the woods. The woman is none other than Ushci Digard. Uschi was a fixture in many films of this type, but this is unique in that she manages to lose her top as she is wont to do and, realizing she is in danger, takes off running through the woods. With her particular 'attributes' this is an amazing sight to behold. One of the other reasons to sit through this butchered abomination. I am pretty sure that it was originally a porno. Either that or there was a girl giving a guy a blowjob who didn't know how to fake that. They hide it, but not all that well.

The movie got a third life when it was released again under the title *Reservoir Cats*. (See what they did there? Ain't that clever?) That print is even more cut up than the *Blood Hunger* version. I hope that someday, someone releases this under its original title with the original sound. It would be kind of cool to know what the actual story was supposed to be about before Even Steven Productions got a hold of it.

BLOOD SONG (1982)

Released during the slasher era, I remember renting one of those VCPs and going to a girl's house to watch a couple of flicks. This was the one I remember. I can tell you what the girl looked like, what the room her TV was in looked like. The movie froze that particular time for me for some reason. During a recent rewatch, I'm not too sure why.

The basic premise is there's a psychopath on the loose, Paul Foley, and because he gave Marion a blood transfusion—after her father Frank (Richard Jaeckel) crashed a car because he was drunk—she can see when Paul kills people. This in addition to her having to wear a leg brace all the time and her father constantly accusing her of being a slut with a local boy, Joey (William Kirby Cullen).

The visions come whenever she dozes off, which is all the time in this movie. They come faster and more intense as he gets closer and closer to her. Paul also plays a wooden flute that his father gave him just before he found his wife screwing some other guy. The father shoots them both before putting the gun in his mouth and that's all that Paul needed to make him a crazy for life. Notice how I didn't give away the actor who played the killer? There's a reason for that. It's a game changer for this movie.

This is two years before Donna Wilkes starred in the infamous *Angel* movie. (You know...Honor Student by Day, Prostitute by Night. Such a great sleazy flick.) Before that, you might remember that she was in McLean Stevenson's ill-fated TV series, *Hello Larry*. You know, the one he quit *M*A*S*H* for? Yeah, that one.

I noticed that a lot of the dialogue is looped...badly. Wilkes gives a fine performance, as does most of the cast. The movie plays a lot like the game of I recognize the actors face, but what was his name? The director, Alan J. Levi, is a veteran TV director who probably cast people he knew from his decades in television. He makes a fine, serviceable film, but it's not really a slasher movie. It's a movie about a broken family where a bizarre element is introduced which leads to a confrontation between a young girl and a homicidal maniac. The best part is that she gives better than she gets. Every time Paul gets close enough she is stabbing him, punching him, impaling him. It is much different than most final girls in slasher flicks where they run and whimper a lot. Marion is not putting up with

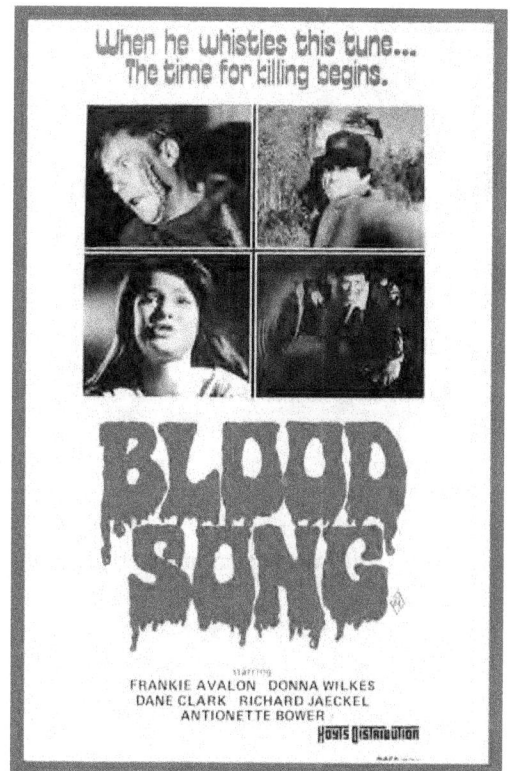

any of Paul's crap.

Now, for the game changer. If you already knew this it won't be a shock. For the rest of you…

The killer is Frankie Avalon.

That's right, king of the beach movies, Frankie Avalon. He plays Paul with this bizarre intensity. He isn't even aware that Marion knows what he has been doing. His plan is to escape and make his way to San Francisco. Coincidence drops him on her doorstep and once he sees her he becomes fascinated. Avalon plays him as this wiry, twitchy maniac that loves to kill people. You can see it in his eyes. There is a scene in a motel where he strangles a girl he just had sex with and it is bloodless yet brutal. Some of the best work I have ever seen.

The concept is unique in that the sharing of blood gives Marion an insight into the inner workings of a madman. I don't think I've seen anything quite like this. **Blood Song** is a different take on the slasher genre and the addition of Frankie Avalon as the killer makes it even more so.

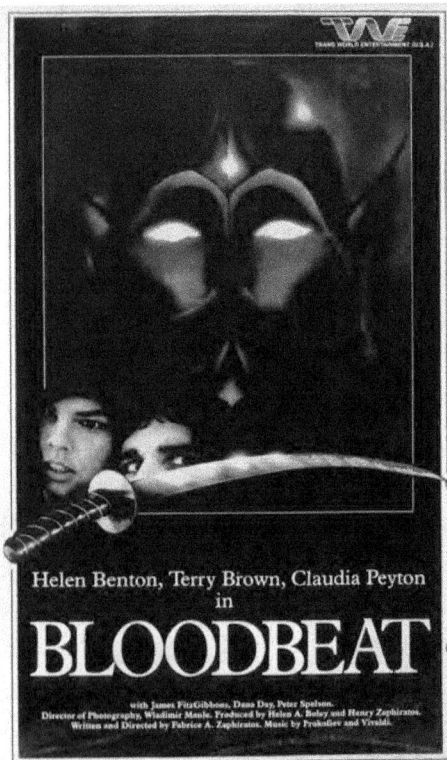

BLOOD BEAT (1983)

And we finish with what might be one of the oddest movies to ever come from the 80s slasher boom. *Blood Beat*. Set in the wilds of Wisconsin during Christmas, it has a rural family coming together for the holidays. One of the kids, Ted (James Fitzgibbons) brings his big city girlfriend, Sarah (Claudia Peyton) along for the fun. Unfortunately Ted's mom, Cathy (Helen Benton), is one card short of a full deck and gets a weird, creepy vibe from Sarah.

When Sarah finds a samurai sword in her room, things proceed from weird to bizarre. It seems that her presence has rousted the spirit of an ancient Samurai warrior (???). Now, whenever she has sex her orgasms send the spirit into a killing frenzy. This is actually a good thing as we get a lot of soft. core sex from the film. Hurray for nudity! The gore is standard '80s fare and there are some long stretches of dull that are obvious padding.

So, I know what you're asking. 'Why in the Hell would I watch this thing?'

You tell me when you would get another opportunity to watch a Christmas slasher movie with a samurai ghost doing the killing whenever a woman has an orgasm? That's right, you can't. Add that the mom has these weird psychic powers to fight the ghost and you're treading in the land of the bizarre and unusual. The final nail in the coffin of this being a must watch is this is one of those movies where no one in it did another movie. Sure, one of the minor characters (Terry Brown) ended up with a bit part in the film **The Princess Diaries**, but that's it. The writer, director, actors. Nothing else.

You will never find another movie like **Blood Beat**. Some might say that's a good thing. I wouldn't be one of them. So, there you have it. Three movies from the days of VHS during its heyday. All of them are available to watch. Well, **Blood Hunger** can only be seen in its **Reservoir Cats** VHS format, but the other two are on DVD. Not quite the same as haunting cramped aisles stacked with lurid, big box VHS, but you can just use your imagination and pretend.

FORGOTTEN BLOODY HORRORS

Horror history will tell us that HG Lewis created the gore film with *Blood Feast* in 1963. But right after *Blood Feast*, a couple of minor gems surfaced. Whether they were inspired by *Blood Feast* could be subject for discussion, but the fact is these films could have been in production at the same time *Blood Feast* was. *The Flesh Eaters* and *Horror of Party Beach* were released in 1964, a scant year after *Feast*. *Feast* was in color, the others black and white.

Both *Blood Feast* and *The Flesh Eaters* were offered to TV. Stations would have nothing to do with *Blood Feast*, but took the black and white *Flesh Eaters*. They cut out virtually all the payoff scenes. There was really never an intact print of the film releases until Sinister Cinema came up with a print that actually had the red tinted ending. Prior to that, Monterey Video released the TV Version. *Horror of Party Beach* was also picked up for TV with its co. feature, *Curse of the Living Corpse*. *Beach* was heavily cut, but *Curse of the Living Corpse* wasn't.

To understand the TV situation: it was the late '60s, early '70s. You got all the gore and violence you needed on the evening news with the Vietnam War. I did notice that during the Nixon era that films shown on television, films that I had already seen theatrically, had almost all of the violence edited out. Especially horror films and westerns. To add to the overall stupidity, horror films were booked at Kiddee Matinees, and no one ever checked their content. After *Night of the Living Dead* was shown, with disastrous results, the Kiddee Matinee ended.

One film that did slip through the cracks, both TV and screenings, was 1959's *Caltiki, the Immortal Monster*. 1958's *The Blob* was a huge hit; enter Italian Copycat Cinema with their version. Directed by Riccardo Frieda, and cinematography by Mario Bava under the name John Foam, it was a superior film, darker and eerie. It opens with a guy staggering though some Mayan ruins. He is part of a group of explorers picking over the ruins. He is scared to death after he and a buddy, Elmer, were attacked by something.

A group goes back to look for Elmer. There is a lake and they think Elmer fell into it. They go back to get some diving gear. As they leave, the camera pans in over some skeletal remains. They return with diving gear, Bob is the diver. He comes up with a lot of gold jewelry he finds mixed with human bones at the bottom of the lake. No Elmer however, but Bob wants to dive one more time. The rope goes taunt as something has happened. Bob is pulled back up and, in a gruesome scene, his face is reduced to a living skull.

A huge mass bubbles to the surface. It oozes toward the group. Max, one of the scientists, tries to grab the bag of gold. He stumbles into to the creature that engulfs his arm. John uses an axe to chop Max loose. John is in charge of the expedition. The creature is expanding and is almost out of the cave. John drives a gasoline truck into the mouth of the cave. It crashes into the mass and burns it.

Max is taken to a hospital. The blob like thing is peeled off his arm and that arm is eaten down to the bone. Max has a skeletal arm and hand from the elbow down. As gory as this scene is, it was never cut out for TV. The scientists discover that this mass is some sort of Mayan god. There is a comet that is going to pass close to the earth. This same comet passed years ago and the Mayan civilization vanished. Coincidence?

Max has now lost his mind and thinks John has the gold and Max wants his wife even though he has a girlfriend, Linda. Max uses his skeletal hand to murder a nurse and escape. Linda hides him out. Caltiki had been cut in two pieces; one piece is at a lab, the other at John's home. A burst of radiation cause the creature in the lab to grow and devour a watchman before being burned up. The comet is now passing the earth and the creature starts growing. Max has really gone around the bend. He corners John's wife and daughter. Linda tries to stop him, but Max kills her. Max hears a noise and thinks it's John. Calling him out with the intent to kill him, Max screams at what he thinks is John.

The door busts open and Caltiki engulfs Max. Blood spews from his mouth as he is crushed and his flesh stripped skull is spit out. Wife and daughter climb out on the roof to escape the army of Caltiki blobs. The army arrives with tanks and flamethrowers to save the two women and the world.

Reportedly director Freda turned over the director's chair to Mario Bava as he felt Bava had what it took to direct and just needed the opportunity. *Caltiki the Immortal Monster* is a lost classic that begs to be rediscovered.

Horror of Party Beach/Curse of the Living Corpse was a 1964 double bill directed by Del Tenney. From the opening sequence, obviously shot in a fish tank, it's good, bloody, cheesy fun. Drums of radioactive waste are dumped over a sunken ship full of human remains. The waste brings these remains back to life as scaly sea monsters with a taste for fresh blood.

A drunken bad girl incites a fight between her boyfriend and a gang of bikers. After the fight, no one wants anything to do with her, so she goes off on an outcropping to pout. She is attacked and ripped to bloody shreds by a creature with a mouth full of cucumbers. She is washed up on shore covered with blood. The creatures stalk the night, attacking various random women, truck drivers, and stranded motorists. They even slaughter a pajama party.

The gore effects are basically chocolate syrup used for blood and is liberally poured or smeared on the victims. Primitive, but effective back then. The monsters are dragging their victims to an abandoned quarry. A weapon is accidently found when a beaker of sodium is spilled over one of the creature's severed arm. The creatures are finally dispatched by having bottles of the chemical tossed on them, causing them to burn up.

Horror of Party Beach had all of the gore removed for TV. Prism Video released the TV version, but Admit One Video out of Canada released an uncut VHS tape. The film has since been restored and released on TV by Dark Sky entertainment.

The Flesh Eaters is another classic. Written and produced by Arnold Drake, who got the idea from an incident in the '50s where millions of dead fish were washed up on the coastline from Florida to South Carolina by some bacteria which turned the tides red. An ambitious film that may have taken three years to complete as, according to Variety, principal photography was completed in 1961. While filming on location on Montauk, Long Island, a hurricane destroyed all sets and equipment and the film was set back a year.

The story goes that a down and out charter pilot tries to fly an alcoholic actress and her assistant to an undisclosed location. They fly into a storm and are forced to land on a "deserted " island. The island is home to scientist Peter Bartel, played to the hilt by veteran character actor, Martin Kosleck. Bartel is doing 'research" on the island. After tucking in his visitors, Laura, the actress, decides she needs a nightcap. Bartel finds her passed out on the beach. He unties the plane and puts the rope in her hand.

The pilot, Grant, finds Laura, but the plane has drifted out to sea. Meanwhile Bartel finds hundreds of glowing fish skeletons on the beach. He does not seem surprised by this discovery. Obviously Bartel is up to something and doesn't want the others to leave. Laura needs another drink and spies her suitcase full of booze in the surf. She tries to retrieve it, but thousands of tiny, glowing creatures have her trapped on an outcropping of rocks. Grant moves in to save her, but water splashes on his leg and the creatures start eating through his clothes to get to his flesh. Cool effect here as we see the things eating his leg until Bartel cuts them away. They are now trapped on the island.

They hear music and see some weird guy on a raft headed right toward the creatures. They try to wave him off, but he thinks they are waving him in. Now the island has another prisoner, Omar, a beatnik. A supply boat is coming in, a couple of days early because of the storm. Bartel see the boat approaching and tries to shoot the sailor. Before he can pull the trigger, a wave washes over the boat and the creatures reduce the guy to a pile of bones. Now why would Bartel try to kill a guy who was coming to help them?

Bartel puts several flesh eaters in a glass bowl. He gets the group together and runs electricity though the bowl. The creatures sink lifelessly to the bottom. Electricity kills them and Bartel has a huge solar battery. The group runs cables to the beach to clear a path to safety. Bartel remains behind. He watches as he times the creatures coming back to life. They were only stunned. Bartel joins Omar and suggests they break for a drink. Bartel puts a couple of the creatures in Omar's drink. Omar screams "there's something inside me eating its way out." Bartel tape-records Omar's dying screams as blood bursts out of his stomach. This scene is so intense that it was not only trimmed for TV, the sound of Omar screaming was muted too.

Bartel ties Omar to his raft with the tape recorder playing screams. He tells the others Omar just took off. We see the dead Omar, tied to the raft with a huge hole in his abdomen that you see the ocean waves through. Now you know where they got the idea for John Morhgan's death scene in *Cannibal Apocalypse*. Laura senses Bartel is not all he seems to be. She seduces him only to get stabbed and buried in a shallow grave. Bartel walks away but Laura's bloody hand emerges from the sand. Now only Grant and Jan, the secretary, are left. Bartel holds them at gunpoint and comes clean.

Bartel was a scientist working for the allies during WWII. He was interpreting documents from German scientists when he found out that a U. Boat containing the canisters of flesh eaters had sunk off the Carolina coast. He destroyed the documents and waited. When he saw reports of fish skeletons washed up on southern coastlines, he tracked them to this island. He intends to capture them and sell them to whatever superpower gives him the best price. While Bartel is explaining this, footage of a Nazi laboratory is run with women being dunked by their hair into a pool of flesh eaters. This footage is not part of the original film. This footage was shot by exploitation czar, Mike Ripps, to make the film more "marketable" to southern Drive-in audiences. This footage was removed for the Dark Sky DVD release and used as an extra.

Bartel's plan is to shock the creatures, then put them in containers. Bartel sends Jan back to his tent to get containers. But when she gets there she find that the flesh eaters Bartel had zapped have morphed into a huge, tenticled beast. She tries to warn Bartel not to go through with his plan. But it's too late. The beast goes after the trio, but a bloody Laura appears and tries to stab Bartel. Bartel empties his gun into her and rolls her corpse toward the creature. The knife she hold in her death grip punctures the creature and her blood flows into the wound. The creature is destroyed. "Hemoglobin sensitivity" shouts Bartel. They now realize that a creature a hundred times the size of the first one is forming beneath the waves. They create a huge syringe that they fill with their own blood. Bartel, however, is not about to stand trial for two murders. He fights with Grant and is tossed into the waves. He is covered with the creatures that start eating him down to the bones in an incredibly gory scene. A huge creature emerges from the surf. It picks Grant up, but Grant managers to inject the blood into its eye. In a cool effect the entire screen turns blood red. The creature explodes and the seas are once again safe until Jaws.

This is a must see film that benefits from a tight script, decent acting, a great score and editing by Radley Metzger. The two female leads are hot in that '60s pinup girl mode. *The Flesh Eaters* got the full cover treatment from *Famous Monsters of Filmland Magazine*. This really irked rival publication, Castle of Frankenstein, a more "cerebral" horror mag. Castle felt that this film and *Blood Feast* was grade Z junk. Funny how "junk" is really classic exploitation stuff. Every film mentioned here deserves to be scene. It could be argued that *Horror of Party Beach* may have been the template for *Humanoids from the Deep* as it, too, had sea monster carrying off women— Same with *Piranha*, as it too deals with a bio weapon. Check these out; I doubt you'll be disappointed.

THE BLOOD ISLAND TRILOGY
GIMMICKS, GORE, and MORE

With the advent of Drive-Ins, films were needed to attract the younger patrons. American International Pictures were the first to make films for the Drive-in crowd. Horror films would draw huge audiences and after 1963's **Blood Feast**, the floodgates of gore opened. One company that would supply the gruesome goods was Hemisphere Pictures based in the Philippines.

In 1959 the team of Kane V. Lynn and Edgar (Eddie) Romero produced a film called **Terror is a Man.** Directed by Gerry DeLeon, it was a remake of **The Island of Lost Souls** with just one creature, a panther man. **Terror** starred Francis Lederer, Greta Thyssen, and Richard Derr. In the opening of the film, there is a map displayed and on this map is a place called **Isle De Sangre** which translated is "Blood Island." **Terror** did so-so business, but did better when it was rereleased as **Blood Creature** in 1965. But the stage had been set for what would become known as **The Blood Island Trilogy**, three gimmick-laden films that would make exploitation history.

Brides of Blood, 1968, was the first up and gave out plastic wedding rings to female patrons. Starring former **Beach Party** star John Ashley as Jim Farrell, Kent Taylor as Doctor Henderson, and Beverly Hills as Henderson's wife. **Brides** was co-directed by Gerry DeLeon and Eddie Romero. The team is here to study the effects of radioactive fallout on the flora and fauna of the island. As the trio arrives on the island, a funeral is taking place. A stretcher is dropped and severed body parts fall out on the beach. An ill omen at best.

The Chief and his daughter are the only English-speaking residents of the island. They inform our heroes that they have gone back to "the old ways." It seems some horrible entity known as "The Evil One" demands a sacrifice now and then. The natives have a lethal lottery and the unlucky winners are tied to stakes and left for the creature to satisfy its sex and blood lust. As night falls, the island gets downright creepy. Trees become tentacled monsters with a taste for human flesh. Butterflies become fanged, bloodsucking horrors and somebody morphs into a horrible monster that looks like a cross between Ron Jeremy, the Tasmanian Devil, and The Michelin Tire Man. The creature fill the night with ear splitting grunts as it stalks its prey.

Farrell stands idly by until a native girl who caught his eye becomes an unlucky winner of the lottery. Farrell tries, with no luck, to rally the locals against the monster. They respond to his efforts by tying him up and locking him in a shack. He gets loose and scares off the rubbery fiend with a flare gun. Now the locals are understandably upset at Farrell for ruining the evil one's night out. Farrell and company go to the estate of Don Estaban Powers. Backtracking here, Powers is an American who lives in a walled fortress with a hulking bodyguard and midget servants. Earlier, Don Estaban had invited the three to stay with him. Farrell declined, as he wanted to work with the natives. The Doc and his wife, however, accepted the invitation. By the way, Beverly is a very unfaithful wife and is quite enamored with Don Estaban.

When her seduction attempt of Don Estaban fails, she sulks off into the jungle to pout. Don Estaban morphs into the Evil One and takes her up on her offer, tearing her to pieces in the process. He throws what's left to the flesh eating trees. The Doc, while searching for his wife, has a run in with Estaban's bodyguard, who shows his sympathetic side by loping off the good Doctor's head. Farrell has now convinced the natives they can kill The Evil One. They trap it in a shack and set it on fire, ending The Evil One's reign of terror. ***Brides*** was rereleased in 1979 under the misleading title of ***Grave Desires***.

Returning to Blood Island a year later on the other side of the island, free from radiation, man-eating trees, etc., it's time to make an appointment with Doctor Lorca, ***The Mad Doctor of Blood Island***. But before we start, we must take the dreaded Oath of Green Blood:

"I, a living, breathing creature of the cosmic entity, am now ready to enter the realm of those chosen allowed to drink of the mystic emerald fluids herein offered. I join the order of green blood with an open mind and through this liquid's powers, I am now prepared to view the unnatural green ones without fear of contamination."

You were given a packed of green blood and told to drink it after reciting the oath. It was green food dye in sugar water. I would say this was Sam Sherman's idea as he had ties with Hemisphere and was the guy bringing these films into the states.

Mad Doctor of Blood Island again starred John Ashley, Angelique Pettyjohn, and Ronald Remy as Doctor Lorca. Directed by Gerry DeLeon and Eddie Romero.

A ship is heading for Blood Island. The passengers include doctor Bill Foster, Sheila Farrow, and Carlos Lopez. Each has their own agenda. Foster is there to do research. Sheila is trying to find her father. Carlos is there to persuade his mother to leave the island. Before the ship makes landfall, a girl taking a swim is attacked and dismembered by a horrible monster oozing green slime. The ship's captain tells Foster that they had rescued a man at sea only to have him attack and kill one of the crew. "I shot him a few times," says the captain. "Before he dove overboard, he bled all over the deck. His blood was green." An ill omen at best for our travelers.

Arriving on the island, Sheila finds her formerly respectable father is now a drunken bum. He gets tanked and wanders off into the dangerous jungle for days at a time. Carlos finds his mother unwilling to leave the island. Carlos's father, Don Ramon died seven years ago and mom just doesn't want to leave. She has taken in a couple of borders, Doctor Lorca and his assistant, Razack, a bald-headed thug with a penchant for machetes. Another woman is also living in the house. Marla is a voluptuous native woman who Carlos remembers as a childhood friend. Carlos astutely puts two and two together and figures out that there is bizarre love triangle going on here involving his late father, Marla, Mom, and Dr. Lorca. Ok, I know four sides isn't a triangle but it's the best I can do so cut me some fuckin' slack, ok? [***Ed.—Love quadrangle? Love trapezoid?***]

Sheila decides to follow her father into the dangerous jungle. She loses him, but is attacked by a green monster. One of the locals tries to intervene and is ripped open from neck to crotch by the monster's claws. Something scares the creature off and Sheila is rescued by Foster. Carlos is now starting to wonder if Daddy is really dead. Before he can act on that thought, and injured man with a dark green hue is brought into the clinic. Dr. Lorca is called in for a consultation. He tells all concerned that the man is suffering from chlorophyll poisoning. He says not to worry; he knows how to approach this. He sends Razack back after dark to decapitate the green guy and disembowel the man guarding him.

While this is happening, Foster and Carlos decide to exhume Don Ramon's body only to find a cobra and an empty coffin. Marla is extremely upset over this development. Back in the jungle, the green monster finds a young couple screwing and proceeds to tear them to pieces in an orgy of severed limbs and scattered entrails. Marla tracks down the creature that, amazingly, doesn't attack her and grovels at her feet. "I knew you weren't dead," Marla says, confirming that the rampaging creature is indeed the late Don Ramon. She orders Ramon to get up because "we have a lot more to do." One might wonder what kind of twisted relationship these two had before Don Ramon became what he is now. It is obvious that Marla has unsettled issues with Ramon's wife and Doctor Lorca. Marla lets Don Ramon into the house where, in a really grisly scene, tears his unfaithful wife to shreds. Carlos inadvertently walks in on this and is knocked out by his father. Luckily for Carlos, Dad recognizes him and doesn't fillet him like he did Mom.

Lorca comes in after the carnage and locks Carlos in a basement cell. Foster and Sheila are also captured. Lorca comes clean telling his captive audience that yes, the rampaging creature is indeed Don Ramon. Ramon was dying of leukemia. Lorca replaced his tainted blood with chlorophyll. That put the disease in remission for a while until the side effects turned Don Ramon into what he is now. Ramon escaped from the demented Lorca, hiding out in the jungle and killing anyone who he presumed was there to ferret him out. Lorca is determined to continue his experiments, so he orders Razack to dispose of his unwanted guests.

Marla, whose mind has snapped, sets the house on fire. Foster knocks Razack out and frees Sheila, Carlos, and some of Lorca's green colored victims. Lorca tries to flee the inferno, but is caught and mauled by Don Ramon. The lab blows up as Lorca, Marla, and Don Ramon are trapped inside. Foster and company leave the island and all is well. Before we fade to black, a dripping green hand reaches out from under some canvas assuring us that this is far from over.

As a ship departs from Blood Island, Dr. Foster looks back on the shrinking island and muses that he really never got to see the island or got to know the people. "Don't worry," the ship's Captain tells him. "The island will still be there when you retire." A sickening thud interrupts any further conversation. A member of the crew hit's the deck with his head split open by an axe swinging Don Ramon. Other crewmembers try to stop the rampaging creature and are sliced and diced all over the ship. The ship catches fire and explodes. Foster is the only survivor, but the crafty Don Ramon escaped the explosion and has washed up on shore. As he staggers into the jungle, the opening credits roll. It's the finally chapter in the trilogy, **Beast of Blood**.

It's seems the "troubles" have started again on Blood Island, prompting Dr. Foster to make a return trip to sort things out. Joining him on the tramp steamer this time is reporter Myra Russell of The Honolulu Clarion looking for some dirt. Also the ships Captain, a poor man's Alan Hale (Bev Miller) who's acting talents make Conrad Brooks look like Richard Burton. Foster's return is received with a less than enthusiastic response by the locals. It seems the green men have returned.

An island girl informs Dr. Foster that it was she and her father who found Foster after the ship sank. Now her father has been taken by The Evil One. This lady is not only hot, but swings a mean machete as she uses it to off at least a dozen bad guys during the course of the film. Foster decides to visit the abandoned Lopez mansion, the former stomping grounds of the late demented Dr. Lorca. The mansion is far from empty, it's loaded with booby

traps and corpses crawling with maggots. Foster decides to go back at night with the island girl as his guide. This time they find a freshly severed head and Razack, who obviously survived the last film. Chasing him though the mansion, they find a passageway leading into the jungle.

Going back for reinforcements, they find out that Myra has been kidnapped. After a few bloody shootouts and a rather nasty impalement in a pit of spikes, Foster finds out that Lorca is still alive. He is minus half his face from his previous altercation with Don Ramon. Lorca has also started up his experiments again. Lorca had managed to capture Don Ramon and decided the best course of action was to remove his head and put it in a big glass jar. Lorca keeps trying to transplant heads on Don Ramon's body with no success. Lorca, in some of the most hilarious dialogue ever committed to film, tries to talk to the head and is understandably pissed at the lack of response. Lorca mutters how the day may come when Lorca will no longer have any use for Don Ramon. After Lorca leaves, the head makes several snide comments about how "That day will come sooner than you think, Lorca." Ramon's head is slowly gaining telepathic control of the body.

Foster allows himself to be captured and hints that he and Lorca should join forces. Lorca has told Myra that they should have a child together, a sort of insurance for the future. Lorca sort of admits that he has gone around the bend. He tells Foster that his first impression is correct, "I'm as crazy as ever." Foster's "lets team up" idea was a ploy. Foster's buddies are outside Lorca's compound waiting to attack. And attack they do in a Sam Peckinpah. inspired shootout with blood squibs exploding everywhere. Lorca orders Razack to kill Foster first. No such luck as Foster blows two large holes in Razack's barrel chest. Lorca, realizing his forces are losing, gathers up his records and tries to escape. Don Ramon's headless body breaks its restraints and pummels Lorca with the head insanely cackles, "We can talk now, Lorca." Lorca is beaten to a bloody pulp and then Ramon crushes his head with piece of machinery. The lab catches fire as Ramon's head looks on helplessly. The island girl finds her father, Foster rescues Myra and the group leaves the decimated compound. As the sun sets, we bid Blood Island a final adieu.

Beast of Blood was the most heavily promoted of the three films. Being this was around the time of the first actual organ transplants, a major radio campaign hyped up that angle. If you had a radio on at that time, the ads relentlessly played up the head transplants. Fake, folded $10 bills were dropped all over certain cities with Don Ramon's face on them and the catch line "Ten Dollars Worth of Thrills, See ***Beast of Blood***." All three films played the Drive-in and Grindhouse circuit up until the late '70s. The films were packaged as ***The Blood O Rama Shock Show,*** which consisted of four films with blood in the titles. The show promised "More Blood Than You've Ever Seen." The films could be any of these Hemisphere releases: ***Brides of Blood, Blood Creature, Mad Doctor of Blood Island, Blood Drinkers, Blood Demon, Beast of Blood***, and/or ***Blood Fiend***. Another shock show, ***The Chiller Carnival of Blood***, used the same films.

The butchery and carnage in ***The Blood Island Trilogy*** could not compare to the butchery these films suffered at the hands of syndicated TV and Home Video. Packaged for late night television, all three films had their titles changed and all the gore and violence taken out. ***Brides of Blood*** became ***Island of Living Horror***. ***Mad Doctor of Blood Island*** became ***Tomb of the Living Dead***. ***Beast of Blood*** became ***Beast of the Dead***. Schlock video company, Regal Video released ***Brides of Blood*** as ***Brides of the Beast***. Their box synopsis for ***Return of Doctor X*** was ***The Mad Doctor of Blood Island***, but the film was some Japanese movie about killer plants. ***Beast of Blood*** had a limited video release on some obscure company that was listed in the Video Shack Catalog. ***Mad Doctor of Blood Island*** was release on Magnum Video, but without the main title/green blood intro. Here are some of the title changes these films went though:

Brides of Blood, 1968
TV Release as ***Island of Living Horror***
Regal Video Release as ***Brides of the Beast***

Mad Doctor of Blood Island, 1969
TV Release as ***Tomb of the Living Dead***
Regal Video Release as ***Return of Doctor X*** with the wrong movie
Magnum Video Release ***Mad Doctor of Blood Island*** missing opening credits

Beast of Blood, 1972

TV Release : ***Beast of the Dead***
Working Title: ***Horrors of Blood Island;*** Alternate Title: ***Blood Devils***

The ***Blood Island*** films set something in motion. Star, John Ashley realized how cheap it was to shoot in the Philippines. He formed a production company with Eddie Romero, then contacted Roger Corman, who had started a company called New World Pictures. The out-pouring of films included ***Beast of the Yellow Night, Women In Cages, Beyond Atlantis, Twilight People, Big Doll House, Big Bird Cage, Savage Sisters*** and more. Director Jack Hill was brought in, as were Sid Haig, Pam Grier, Margret Markov, Vic Diaz, Gloria Hendry, Cheri Caffaro, and others. These films were hugely successful and had a huge fan base.

Looking back, ***Mad Doctor of Blood Island*** could have been a homage to HG Lewis's ***Blood Feast,*** with its plethora of severed limbs and scattered entrails. ***Beast of Blood*** looked like it was influenced by Peckinpah's ***Wild Bunch,*** more action. oriented than the other films and was peppered by shootouts using exploding blood squibs. All films were considered "grade Z horror dreck" by some of the genre publications of the time. They were especially lambasted by ***Castle of Frankenstein*** magazine. They were a lot more than dreck as most fans will agree.

Sadly, most of the major player in these films are no longer with us. John Ashley suffered a major heart attack at age 62 in NYC in 1997. Angelique Pettyjohn succumbed to cancer in 1992 at age 48. Eddie Romero passed away at age 88 this year. The two actors who played Doctor Lorca, Ronald Remy and Eddie Garcia are still with us, as is ***Beast of Blood*** star Celeste Yarnell.

Celeste Yarnell

Here is a little interview I did with Celeste back in 2000 when these films finally got the uncut DVD release that they deserved. Celeste was also in *The Velvet Vampire, Star Trek* and was a Reingold Beer Girl at age 19.

42P: One of my all-time favorite Grindhouse movies was *Beast of Blood*. How did you get involved with this film?

CY: I've been trying to think of that all day because knew that's what you were going to ask me. It started as a phone call to my agent from John Ashley's people. I was selected by John himself for the movie. I believe he had seen *Eve* [aka *The Face of Eve,* 1968] or something I had done that he was excited about. They sent me a rough draft of the script and I said yes.

42P: What was it like filming in the Philippines?

CY: Remember I told you during the ride from the airport that right after I accepted the job I found out I was pregnant. I had signed a contract and made a commitment. It was a huge decision. When I got there, the conditions were horrendous. I had my own apartment at the Tropicana in Manila. It was nice, but outside of that, the conditions were beyond human belief. We traveled on a boat that didn't have any bathrooms, they had buckets. We went to islands that didn't have electricity or running water. We were eaten alive by insects. I had my own stuntman/bodyguard as we were under martial law.

42P: I remember that. That was when all that stuff was going on with Marcos, right?

CY: Exactly. Here I was, this tall blonde among these small, delicate people. I felt like an Amazon! This bodyguard was with me all the time. In the middle of a shot he would jump up and grab a pit viper that was inches away from biting me. The only way you know the difference between a Pit Viper and a Mock Pit Viper is if it's a Pit Viper you die within five minutes of being bitten.

42P: That sounds like a snake known as "karate" or Three-Stepper, because after it bites you, you took about three steps before you died. If my memory severs me right, it's in the Cobra Family.

CY: He saved my life! He was incredible. We would be four hours from the nearest road, which was four hours from the nearest paved road. He would shimmy up a coconut tree and hack one open so I would have something to drink. I ended up really falling in love with the Filipino people. There were two lunch services, a Filipino one and an American one. I would e sitting on the ground with the crew, eating off a big banana leaf. The Filipino food is really good, lots of fish and vegetables.

42P: You told me on the way back from the airport that you had a cave as a dressing room.

CY: Oh my God, my cave (laughing) the big cave was my dressing room, but the men used it for a urinal.

42P: Oh, great!

CY: Yeah, remember I was pregnant and had morning sickness. It was just monstrous.

42P: I can just imagine what it must have been in that tropical heat.

CY: Remember the scene where I was in the quicksand? That was cork floating on water with a platform underneath. It was held by ropes that the crewmembers lowered down. While filming that scene, my bodyguard's rifle slipped off his shoulder and the site hit me in the face, splitting open my skin under my eye. They didn't use that shot, but when you see me coming out of the quicksand, I'm really injured. I was blinded and knocked out. We didn't have a first aid kit, so I butterfly taped my face back together, put some make up over it and went back to work. For the next few days, I had a shiner and they couldn't shoot me. I was a wreck, it was horrible. But I love the Philippines, I love John Ashley. There was always that loving camaraderie, that magic time when you're doing a movie. If it's good, it's real good and we had that there on the set.

42P: Actually that was my next question. How was it working with John Ashley?

CY: I adore John. Even though we had a passionate love scene, he was a perfect gentleman, a total professional at all times. I have very kind thoughts of John and I think he is greatly missed.

42P: I feel the same way, he was more than people thought and he left us too soon.

CY: He was wonderful to work with. He was a good businessman; he had that laidback Mid. Western attitude. I believe he was from Oklahoma. He was strong and I always felt safe around John.

42P: John was instrumental in opening the doors for American films shot in the Philippines, including *Apocalypse Now.*

CY: I really didn't know that.

42P: John got a lot of people in the door over there. But I think the whole thing with the *Apocalypse Now* people with their "We'll burn it, than pay for it later," attitude put a big crimp into what was going on. I know he worked over there for quite a few years. He did three more horror films that I can remember, ***Beyond Atlantis, Beast of the Yellow Night,*** and ***The Twilight People.*** Then he was doing a lot of action shoot 'em ups with Eddie Romero directing. He had his own stock players like Sid Haig, Vic Diaz, Eddie Garcia, Bruno Punzalan, and even Pam Grier for a while.

CY: Wow, he never used me again.

42P: I don't see why he didn't. How would you rate Eddie Romero as a director?

CY: Under the conditions and budget we had, he was amazing. He was a very nice man and he let you alone.

42P: So you could improvise a little?

CY: Right! I have a story for you—remember the snakes?

42P: You read my mind, I was just going to bring that up. When you fell though the trap door and into the pit at Lorca's old mansion.

CY: They were real cobras and they were not defanged. This might sound funny coming from someone in the Holistic Animal Care Business. They had lightly sutured the snake's mouth shut. Can you imagine if the sutures had broken?

42P: A disaster in the making.

CY: Right. Now this is really gross. While I was in the pit with them, one of the Cobras decided to go to the bathroom.

42P: That must have been lovely.

CY: You cannot imagine. That smell would not only clear a room, it would have cleared a small county. I'm pregnant, in a pit with two Cobras, then after it's done it's business, they want me to provoke it so that it will rear up so that their hood would flare up and they only do that when threatened.

42P: Yeah, it's a warning before they strike.

CY: Yes and I had to make that happen.

42P: And all the while trying to keep from gagging.

CY: That right and now you have an exclusive with this little story because I have never told this to anyone. I don't think I'd want to do that again.

42P: I can certainly understand that. Did they actually shoot the snake or did they just jerk it back with something to get the effect?

CY: Oh, no! They didn't kill it; they were very valuable snakes.

42P: The way it looked, I saw John go for the pistol shot. Reality wise, he would have had to be a crack shot to have hit it. When I saw the snake jerk back, I would think they used a thin fishing line or something similar.

CY: I really don't know, but the sound of that shot was deafening in that confined space.

42P: What did you think of the finished film?

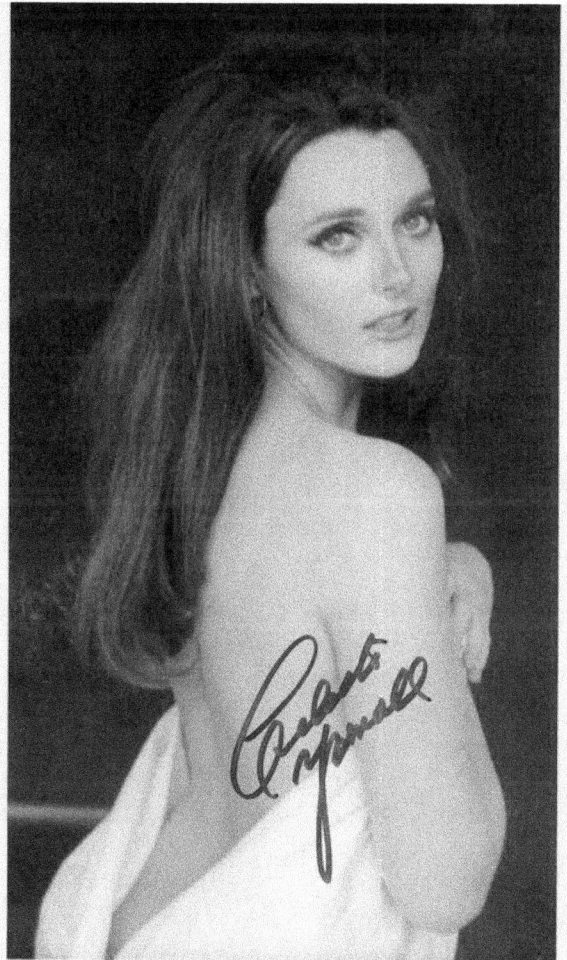

CY: (Laughing) I just saw it recently. It's a shame so many bits and pieces are missing. I don't remember doing that much nudity. I remember them telling me that they were going to use a body double for the version released in Japan. But how did I like the finished film? Well, it's not exactly *Gone with the Wind*, but now I'm becoming a fan of this stuff and I can appreciate it in a whole new light. It's fun to look back on this kind of thing. It had its moments. It's hard to believe it's been over 40 years. It's interesting to look at yourself back forty years ago; it's like you're another person, yet you're still the same person. I'm kinda tickled by it.

42P: To me it still holds up. I watched all three before this interview. I still pick up things I missed on the first go around.

CY: The gore effects are great and what an incredible monster. Eddie Garcia (Celeste imitates the monster's voice) Lorca was really great. Wasn't that cool. Remember he wanted to make love and have a child with me? What on earth would we have had, [laughing] a sequel? I would have given birth to a sequel, I would have been a mom.

42P: Was the film released under a different title over there? I had heard it might have been called *Blood Devils*.

CY: That I don't know. I know *Beast of Blood* and the TV title, *Beast of the Dead*. I was hired under the working title *The Horrors of Blood Island*.

42P: Any last comments for fans of the film?

CY: Check out the DVD that was finally released uncut. The whole trilogy begs to be rediscovered.

Dedicated to the Memories of
John Ashley 1934. 1997
Angelique Pettyjohn. 1942. 1992
Eddie Romero. 1924. 2013

EVERYBODY WAS KUNG FU FIGHTING

ENTER THE DRAGON, EXIT BRUCE LEE

It was 40 years ago that *Enter the Dragon*, the first "American" Kung Fu epic, exploded across Grindhouse screens. The film was low budget and ultraviolent for it's time. A Chinese Kung Fu film with American production values. It made its lead, Bruce Lee, a superstar right up there with Eastwood, Bronson, etc. Lee archived his dream of being the first Chinese superstar. Shame was he didn't live long enough to enjoy it.

So much has been written about how Lee was simply screwed over by a system that refused to cast him in pivotal roles because he was Chinese, that it would be redundant to cover all that. He was cast a Kato, sidekick to *The Green Hornet*. But that only lasted one season as it wasn't campy enough like *Batman*. Lee also got screwed out of the lead in the TV series *Kung Fu*. Lee was the black sheep of his family. He took up Kung Fu at age 13 to enhance his street fighting skills since he was a punk. He had been expelled from a private school and had a few brushes with the law for fighting. His well-to-do parents shipped him to Seattle to stay with a family friend.

Lee was a performer, but had no desire to be in a traditional Chinese role a la "Hop Sing" or a pig. tailed coolie. He started giving Kung Fu demonstrations at high schools and discovered, much to his chagrin, that Americans wanted to lean from him. He opened his own school in Seattle, teaching a fighting style he called Jeet Kun Do. He quickly found out that it wasn't enough to pay the bills. During this time he married blonde cheerleader, Linda

Emery, and had his first child, Brandon Lee, needed more income and at this time was cast as Kato. After that, he found he was in demand to teach Kung Fu to Hollywood's elite. Some of his students were James Coburn. Steve McQueen, Sterling Silliphant, Roman Polanski, and Warner Brothers chairman Ted Ashley. These people helped him get work, bit parts and fight choreography, but Lee inwardly seethed. He vowed to be as big a star as Steve McQueen. He was told that there was no way a Chinese man would ever play the lead in an American film.

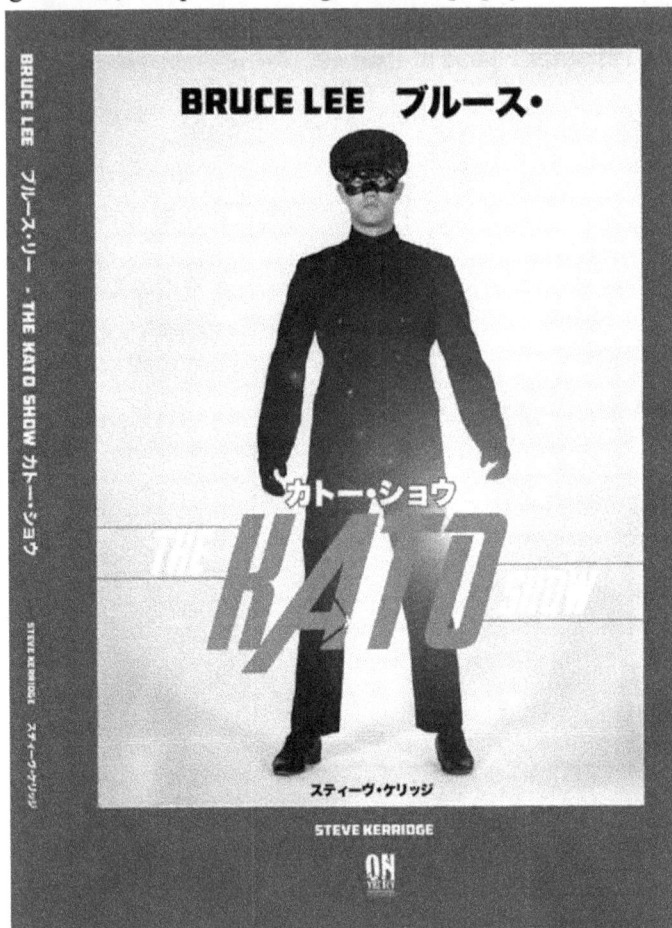

What Lee didn't know at the time was that *The Green Hornet* had been sold in syndication to Hong Kong. It was now *The Kato Show*. Lee went back to Hong Kong in 1970 and was stunned by the reception he got. He wasn't shit in Hollywood, but in Hong Kong he was the hometown kid that made good. Hong Kong movie producers made offers. Lee signed a two. picture deal with Raymond Chow and Golden Harvest Pictures. Chow had a nickname, "The Smiling Tiger", not a man to be trifled with in a business deal.

Lee's first film, *The Big Boss*, broke box office records in Hong Kong. His 2nd film, *Fists of Fury*, broke that record. Then he wrote, produced and directed The *Way of the Dragon*, which surpassed the first two films. Lee was now a huge star in not only in Hong Kong, but most of Asia. Lee's films hit the inner city grindhouses and outer borough Drive-Ins. His film were a huge hit with black audiences and opened the door to an avalanche of Kung Fu imports. One 42nd Street grindhouse showed three different Kung Fu films every week until it closed in the '80s.

Fred Weintraub, a producer at Warner Brothers, had seen *The Big Boss* and knew Lee was box office gold. Weintraub was certain that he could produce a film that he could pre-sell to Asian markets and would also be a huge hit in the States. Warner Brothers approved a budget of $250,000 to make *Enter the Dragon*. The story centered on three heroes that enter a martial arts tournament run by a criminal despot, Han. They intend to end his drug-dealing, slave trading ways. Lee was to star and choreograph all the action scenes. The one snag was dealing with Raymond Chow. Chow was afraid that Hollywood was going to steal his cash cow. At a dinner with Lee and Chow, Weintraub, frustrated with the elusive Chow, told Bruce he was leaving tomorrow because he couldn't make a deal. He told Bruce, right in front of Chow, "It's too bad that Raymond doesn't want you to become an international star." Lee turned to Chow and said, "Sign the contract." Chow was really pissed, but signed. Because of the animosity held by Chow, it was rumored that he might have had something to do with Lee's premature demise.

Everything was set in motion. Director Robert Clouse, who had made the violent film, *Darker Than Amber*, was hired because he worked cheap. Bob Wall, Lee's martial arts buddy, was hired to play O'Hara, the drug lord's bodyguard. Jim Kelly was a last minute replacement for Rockne Tarkington [*from the kids' adventure serial, Danger Island*], who pulled out over money issues. Weintraub needed a "name" actor. John Saxon was cast and told that he would be "the star" of the film. That illusion was shattered when Lee sparred with him and sent Saxon flying into a chair, which shattered beneath him. When Lee came over with a concerned look on his face, Saxon told him that he wasn't hurt. Lee replied that he wasn't worried about Saxon; he was upset that Saxon broke his favorite chair. Now the pecking order was established.

On the Chinese side of the casting, Angela Mao was cast as Lee's sister, Bolo Yeung, Shih Kien, and Wei Tung rounded out the cast. Lee, however, had an anxiety attack that lasted about two weeks. Clouse shot around him. When he finally did get in front of the camera, his first scene took 28 takes. While Lee fought with his nerves, the

Chinese and American crews fought with each other. Despite their differences, the two crews developed mutual respect for each other. Lee realized early on how valuable the stunt crew was and ate box lunches with them instead of eating in the hotel restaurant. One of the dozen stunt boys who worked on the film, someone who was insignificant to the film, would go on to superstardom himself. This boy was grabbed by the hair by Lee and flung around like a rag doll. He was accidently hit in the face by Lee's nun chucks. As soon as the cameras were off, Lee rushed over and picked him up, profusely apologizing. "He was very good to us and didn't care about impressing the bosses. He took care of us," the young actor said. That boy was a young Jackie Chan.

In any action film, you're going to have accidents. Bob Wall and Lee were rehearsing a scene where Lee would kick a broken bottle out of Wall's hand. Lee's kick missed and he hit the broken edge of the bottle with his fist. On the way to the hospital, Lee screamed that he would kill Wall. This, of course, was fed to the Hong Kong press that Wall intentionally injured Lee and that Lee intended to kill Wall. When Lee came back to the set, the stunt crew expected him to really kill Wall. Lee saved face by telling the crew that he can't kill Wall because the director needs him to finish the movie.

Chinese honor, however, requires some form of payback. A scene called for Lee to sidekick Wall hard enough to send him into the crowd of henchmen. Lee didn't hold back. Wall took off like a rocket when Lee kicked him. Lee insisted on 12 takes, one take was hard enough that Wall broke a stunt man's arm when he crashed into him. Not so subtle payback. Yeah, Bruce was pissed.

Another nightmare was the casting of the evil Han's harem. No Chinese actresses were willing to play prostitutes in an American film. So the producers went to Bangkok to get the real thing. It wasn't difficult finding them; the problem was convincing them to be in the film. They wanted to get paid more for being in the film than it would have actually cost to screw them. The stuntmen almost went on strike when they found out how much these 'ladies' were getting paid. Sexual antics abounded. Jim Kelly wound up in the hospital after screwing everything that walked in Hong Kong. Lee also was busy, sexually, with his mistress. He broke up with her after word hit the tabloids. She was hospitalized with a nervous breakdown.

Lee was often challenged by young upstarts, especially street gang members that were cast in the film. He tried to ignore them, realizing there was no upside in accepting a challenge. If he lost, it would be front-page news. If he won, it would still be front-page news that he bullied an extra. These guys were running their mouths and Lee finally had enough. He challenged one kid to "Come on down." The kid charged in hard and fast looking to do some real damage. Lee methodically took him apart. Lee turned the duel into a private lesson, at one point correcting the kid's stance. After the "lesson", the kid bowed to him.

Lee became thin and pallid during the shoot, seeming high at times, which he was. Lee was having migraines and self-medicating with hashish. Lee seemed to have a fondness for the drug that could be smoked or ingested. One form of hashish, Temple Balls, was produced in very unsanitary conditions. While smoking it might kill off some of the germs and bacteria, eating it wouldn't. Lee was rushed to the hospital and nearly died of acute cerebral edema, excessive fluid surrounding the brain. Deeply shaken, Lee returned to Los Angles for a complete physical. Doctors found nothing wrong. Lee was in a great mood, returning to Hong Kong for a meeting with several people about his next film, *Game of Death*. Lee also reunited with his mistress. At the meeting, Lee was munching on hashish and complaining of a headache. After the meeting, Lee went to his girlfriend's apartment to talk about the scrip and the major role he was giving her. Lee complained about the headache and she gave him Equagesic, a pain medication with aspirin and muscle relaxant.

Lee was supposed to meet Raymond Chow, George Lazenby, and others for dinner, so Bruce went to lie down for a while. He never woke up. An autopsy showed the cause of death to be acute cerebral edema, the same thing that almost killed him 10 weeks ago. Traces of cannabis and Equgesic were found in his stomach. At age 32, Bruce Lee was dead. Rumors flew, some said that Raymond Chow hired a triad hit man to take out Lee with a mythical "palm strike" that left no marks. Other said Lee was a raging hashish addict and that killed him. 40 years later, the debate still rages. Bruce Lee realized his dream; he broke though the Hollywood system. He was now as big as Eastwood, Bronson, Van Cleef, Reynolds, Connery, etc. Shame is he didn't live to see it. But he kicked open the door for other Asian stars, many who had small supporting roles in *Enter the Dragon*. Jackie Chan, Sammo Hung, Michele Yeoh, Chow Yun Fat, etc., all owe a debt of gratitude to Bruce Lee. In the words of producer, Fred Weintraub, it used to be that every American town has a church, a beauty parlor, and a corner bar. The change is that now every town has some kind of martial arts school with a framed picture of Bruce Lee somewhere in the office.

Dedicated to the Memory of
Bruce Lee 1940-1973
Robert Clouse 1928-1997
and our friend
Jim Kelly 1946-2013

HAND JOBS AND HAMBURGERS
THE WONDERFUL WORLD OF NYC MASSAGE PARLORS

In the late '60s, there was a huge explosion of streetwalkers in NYC. A change in certain laws made prostitution a lesser offence. So ladies now flocked to Manhattan to ply their trade. Picking up a streetwalker was a risky proposition as you could be robbed. It was not all that uncommon to have a girl take you to her room, then when your balls ass naked, a big black dude busts in screaming, "What are you doing with my wife?" Then you fork over you valuables.

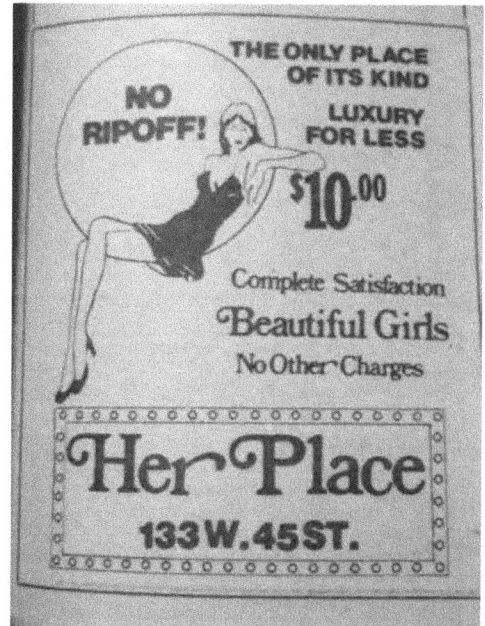

Some genius figured out that it doesn't take a lot of time to get a guy off. Why do you think the Internet killed porn? Because some guys can rub one out in under a minute. So the vice lords came up with a solution, a place that offered fast, assembly line sex, the massage parlor. Being that there were plenty of empty offices, storefronts and lofts, guys would get cheap rent. They would go in and make a small reception area, then build small cubicles that would house the women, a bed, or a massage table. Admission was cheap, $8 to $15. But that just got you in the door—anything else depended on how you wanted to "tip."

The girls cut of the deal was whatever they could hustle the mark for, be it a hand or blowjob. These "services" would range from $10 to $50. Guys who came in expecting an actual "massage" were usually chased out. Other early places that tried the same hook were Photo Studios and Nude Body Painting places. Most of these places, depending on who was being paid off, didn't last too long. Massage parlors were usually mob controlled. The Papa of the Peeps, Marty Hodas, turned a couple of Adult Book Stores into Parlors. The stores weren't doing that well, and Hodas, always on the cutting edge of new ways to bring in cash, decided this was the way to go. But with success come problems. When a couple of black pimps decided to open their own places, they got fire bombed and Hodas was arrested.

Hodas was beholden to the mob. He was the first guy to put the Peepshows in the Adult Bookstores. One day he got a call that the mob had dragged his machines out to the street and put theirs in the stores. Hodas had to make a deal and that actually opened doors for him in other cities. The mob really wanted nothing to do with street prostitution as the they felt the girls were too hard to control and pimps were too stupid to deal with. But when they horned in Hodas' massage joints, accidents happened. The parlors dotted the Time's Square area from the late '60s up until the mid '80s. These were quickie sex joints, nothing fancy, sometimes not even a bed. Some were OK, others were filthy. Operators would pay winos and bums to hand out fliers on the street to passing pedestrians advertising these places.

Here are some of the places I remember and what they offered:

Basheba's Hidaway on 17th street on the 11th floor. Two big rooms and $25 for a half hour session. Caesar's Retreat was an "upscale " place on East 46th Street with a sauna, baths and hot girls. Membership required. Club Utopia was on W 16th Street and was sparse and uncomfortable, but if your budget was under $10, that was the place to go. Middle Earth Studio was on 3rd Ave at 51st street, 2nd floor, $18 a session. Photo and Art Studio on East 19th Street,5th floor, had two room that were private, but uncomfortable. Body painting and photography available, so bring a camera. Secret Life Studio on 26th street, 3rd floor with 4 rooms and camera rental available. Swinging Fun City on West 46th Street, 2nd floor, was anything but fun. Unfriendly hoes, shitty atmosphere and $17 a session. The Body Shop on 49th street, 2nd floor, had a nasty looking, mugger's entrance, but comfortable inside. The girls ranged from pretty to nightmarish. Relaxation Plus on 36th street was great if you like paying $20 for a shower and a bad back rub. The Cathouse on 49th Street, 2nd floor had polite and attractive girls for $20 a session.

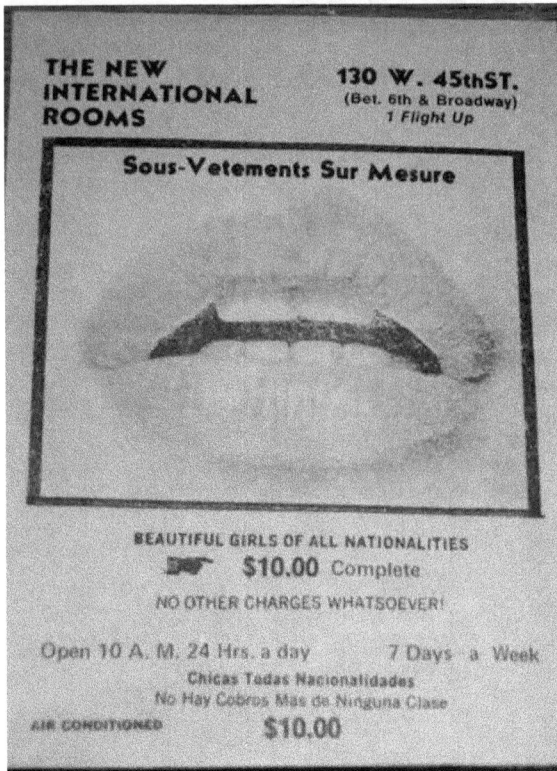

Other places were The Galaxy 1 on east 47th street that had girls that could turn you gay. The Conference Rooms claim to have girls of all nationalities, one visit I discovered Ethiopia. The Studio on E 51st was dingy with thin cubicles. Four unattractive women are available who would let you get undressed in front of them for $12. Anything else was extra. Favela on w 56th Street was a dingy shithole with low rent girls. $10 to get in, then a $7.50 room charge. Sign said no tips, but the girl would ask for more money anyway. The Delicate Touch on w 42nd Street offered half-hour shoeshines in cubicles with a girl and a shoeshine stand for $10, anything else is extra starting at $25. Cupid's retreat offered six pitched pup tents in a scummy loft, just perfect for the 42nd Street outdoorsman. $15 got you in, moderate tipped would get you off. The Red Ruby has girls wearing nurse's uniforms offering manicures and pedicures for men. $15 got you in the door and a ten spot would get you a blowjob. Holiday Hostesses boasted four or five girls of questionable health, dressed in shabby lingerie in a shabby waiting area. The Luxor Hotel had girls stationed at the bank of elevators. You picked a girl and rode the elevator to a shabby room.

So now you're asking, "Pete, did you ever go to a massage parlor?" Well *duhhh*. How do you think a 287 lb., big hairy guy get laid back in the day? Well my first spot was called The Dating Room on 42nd Street, close to 8th Ave. It was an office suite on the 3rd floor. I took the elevator up and got frisked for weapons by a bouncer named Leon, who was a career bouncer making the rounds of massage parlors, bookstores etc. Admission was $13, plus $2 for a "membership." You got a card that got you a free visit after 10 visits. Fool that I was, I assumed that the $15 would cover everything. I was wrong as the big tittted, longhaired biker chick I picked asked me what I would tip. Here I was 18-years-old and didn't know the score. Sonny was her name and she took pity on me. She asked what I needed to get my car out of the lot. I told her and that left me with $8. She gave me a blowjob for that.

I felt bad about the miscue and promised I'd make it right by bringing her a couple of sweaters that I lifted from the warehouse I was working in. Two days later, I double. parked and delivered the sweaters. That made me an OK guy with her, Leon and the management. I never saw Sonny after that as these girls rotated around the city. But one Saturday night, the strangest thing happened. I was stoned and horny so I went to The Dating Room to release my buildup of toxic semen. I exchanged pleasantries with Leon and picked out a petite Hispanic blonde, Celia. After negotiating the tip, I settled in for a BJ. In the middle of it, Celia stopped and said, "I want you to fuck me." I sensed a ploy and told her I had no more money. She didn't care; she said she wanted to get off. She slipped rubber on me and climbed on top. We had some kind of chemistry as we both got off at the same time. She gave me her home number and said to get in touch next time I was around. Somehow during that evening, I lost the number. I went back and she wasn't there. I knew better than to ask management and still curse myself out to this day. That could have been "Mrs. 42P." The Dating Room got raided and shut down. It re-opened as "Tanfastic", a pseudo tanning salon. I went there once and it had all the comforts of a pay toilet.

Another place that had several name changes and was the bane of NYC was "Her Place" on West 45th Street in close proximity to one of the first tranny bars. The girls at Her Place would subject customers to a painful and unnecessary VD check. It was shut down then re. opened as "The Silver Slipper." That didn't last too long either and it re opened again as The Lucky Lady. That's when I had the misfortune to get roped into going there. I had been out all night drinking and smoking. I was at The Tick Tock Dinner on RT. 3 when my friend Richie came in and saw me staring into my cup of coffee. He wanted to go into the city to this great massage parlor he heard about, The Lucky Lady. Problem was that Richie wasn't a drinker or smoker, so he didn't know how fucked up I really was.

I agreed to go with him. If he said we were going to go fuck a dead alligator, I probably would have agreed to do that too. Halfway though the Lincoln Tunnel, I made my 2nd mistake, my first was agreeing to this. I lit up my last joint. Now I was flatlined; I had no motor functions and Richie had no clue how bad a shape I was in. He parked the car close to the place and we went in. Everything was in leopard print, adding to my fucked-upness. Richie grabbed an Asian girl and disappeared. I am now in the 'reception" area, holding my ticket. I walked up to a smoking hot brunette and shoved the ticket in her face. She was having coffee and was pissed, but I was too fucked up to pick up on that. We went to a room and she gave me a lackluster blowjob, then I was told I had two minutes to come. I argued the point, and a knife came out, about an inch from my eye. Fuck this, I got dressed and got out of there.

Now I'm outside, waiting for Richie. He likes to bullshit with these chicks, so he could be in there for a while. Now the 12 hours of booze and smoke is wearing off and a shitty hangover is creeping up on me, and it's fuckin' cold out here. I was sitting on the curb with my head in my hands when I found I had company. A huge, dirty guy, wearing three overcoats started yapping at me. I tried to make out his gibberish, then it dawned on me that this guy wanted to take me somewhere and fuck me. Now I'm up and moving. I'm circling the parked car and this big bastard is right behind me. I was tempted to try and run around the block, but if I did, I might not have a ride home. The big fucker was gaining on me so I turned around and shoulder blocked him with all I had, which wasn't that much. He went down, but his knee came up and hit me right in the nuts. I proceeded to puke up about 12 hours' worth of tequila and bar food all over him. Richie came out as I was puking and had a 'what the fuck happened?' look on his face. "Start the fuckin' car1" I yelled at him.

"What the hell was up with that?" he asked

"You really don't want to know" I replied. A couple of months later, The Lucky Lady and the tranny bar were padlocked.

The city cracked down on all of these places and by the mid-'80s the sole survivor was a place on 14th Street that, for all I know, may still be there. The spirit of the massage parlor lives on today with many "spas" offering "The Happy Ending."

CANNIBAL COOKOFF: LENZI vs. DEODATO

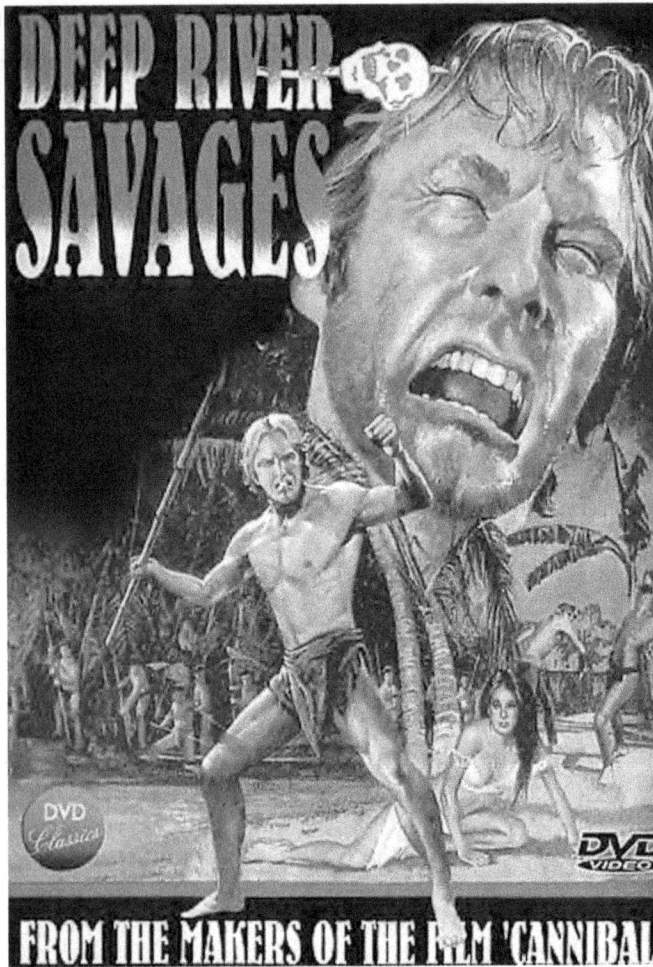

A twisted spinoff of Italian Zombie films was the creation of the dreaded cannibal subgenre. Two directors would be responsible for some of the most violent, depraved, and nauseating scenes ever committed to celluloid. There seemed to be genuine animosity between directors Umberto Lenzi and Ruggerio Deodato. They also seemed to be trying to top each other as to who could capture the most vile images to gross out the audience. Lenzi started directing in 1958 with sword & sandal epics, then westerns, crime films, and violent giallos. In 1972 he directed a film called *Deep River Savages*.

This was not the first film about cannibalism, but it was the first to actually show it. Previous films like 1939's *Five Came Back* had a plane crash in a cannibal infested jungle in South America. Directed by John Farrow, it starred Chester Morris, Lucille Ball, John Carradine and Kent Taylor. Long on suspense, only five people can fly out before the cannibals close in. Farrow actually remade the film in 1956 as *Back from Eternity.* Same plot, this time starring Robert Ryan, Anita Ekberg, Rod Steiger, and Jesse White.

The Sky Above, The Mud Below (1961) was a documentary about six Europeans on a 450 – mile trek across New Guinea. The trek took seven months and three people died during the expedition. The crew encounters headhunters, cannibals, and witnessed weird tribal rites. The film won an Oscar in 1962 for best documentary. The public was fascinated by this film. Little did they know that ten years down the road they would get an "in your face" look at cannibals.

Deep River Savages was picked up for American Distribution by Joseph Brenner Associates. Brooklyn – born Brenner worked in a movie theater as an usher, then theater manager. He was booking films for others when he decided to start his own company Joseph Brenner Associates He had said that if all my movies were as good as my trailers, I'd be in great shape. Brenner, like fellow distributor, Terry Levine of Aquarius Releasing, would get European horror, action, and crime films, retitle them, and have a crazy ad campaign and a lurid poster. Brenner released *Deep River Savages* as *Man from Deep River*, then changed it to *Sacrifice* and put it on a double bill with *Autopsy* in 1975. I caught this double bill at The Castle Theater in decrepit Irvington, NJ. I was with my buddy, Big Al, and we had just smoked a Thai stick. We decided to take in the matinee.

The film opens with a photographer John Bradley (Ivan Rassinov) in Thailand having a fight with his girlfriend. Drowning his sorrows in a local dive bar, he has a few choice words with a local low life and ends up in a bar fight, knifing a guy in the guts. Escaping the authorities, he has a guide take him up river into uncharted territory. He puts on a wet suit and does some diving. When he surfaces, he finds his guide dead with an arrow in his throat. He is caught in a huge net by a Stone Age tribe who thinks he's a fish.

John is taken to the village and kept as a slave. There he witnesses all kinds of torture and degradation. Since the tribe decide he is a fish man, so he is put to work catching fish and turtles for the tribe. During an attempted escape, he kills a warrior in one on one combat. He is accepted into the tribe after undergoing a sadistic ritual. He is tied to a device that keeps him immobile as the tribe shoots darts into his back and chest. Surviving this, he wins the affections of the Chief's daughter (Me Me Lai, who would appear in three of these type of films). He wins her in a courtship ritual, but he incurs the wrath of the resident witch doctor. The witch doctor secretly poisons her and she is slowly dying.

Up until now the violence quota was a tongue cut out, a hand hacked off and the usual animal cruelty that abounds in this type of film. Now it gets taken to a whole new level. A native couple are pursued by a raggedy – looking bunch of savages. The man is mortally wounded trying to protect his woman. She is stripped, raped, and killed. The man makes it back to the tribe to get help. John leads the group to rescue the girl, but the rescuers are greeted with the horrific sight of cannibals eating her dismembered limbs while one of the filthy bastards slices off a breast and eats it. This scene stunned the usually rowdy patrons into shocked silence. My stoned – out partner, now lucid, mumbled something about "this is really fucked up" and left the theater. I stayed to the bitter end. The cannibals are dispatched by the angry tribe.

Another tribe attacks the village, burning it and killing the witch doctor in the process. As the chief's daughter gives birth, she asks John to stay and help her people. She dies and John decides to stay, ending the film on an almost upbeat note. I didn't stay for **Autopsy** as I had seen enough and Big Al was understandably perturbed, his afternoon ruined. And he was not the type of guy you wanted to leave to his own devices. I suggested we go to a titty bar or something to calm his frayed nerves. He agreed, so off we went. Little did I know that about two years later I would be sitting in the same theater watching the film that would set the bar for cannibal films to come.

Ruggero Deodato's first film was **Hercules, Prisoner of Evil**, in 1964. He replaced Antonio Marghereti after he quit the production. He was second unit director on the classic Spaghetti western, **Django**, in 1966. He worked in television from 1971 to 1974. In 1977 he directed a film called **Last Cannibal World**. The film was originally supposed to be a sequel to **Deep River Savages** with Ivan Rassinov and Me Me Lai to star. This, however, fell though when Lenzi held out for more money. Filming in remote areas of Malaysia and Mindanao in the Philippines, Deodato did the impossible: he made a film that hammered jaded grind house patrons into stunned silence.

Originally released in 1977 by import specialists United Producers Releasing Organization, which also released stuff like **They Call Her One Eye, House of Whipcord,** and import soft-core porn. It was re-released by AIP in 1978, who changed the title to **Carnivorous** and paired it with **Raw Meat**. The double bill was called **Gorerama: For Those With a Thirst for Blood**. Then it was released under a different title, The Last Survivor. It was a sweltering summer night and I was walking past The Castle Theater and saw the one sheet. Thinking it was just another jungle action adventure, I downed my pint of chilled cheap hootch, bought a ticket and got comfortable, but not for long.

I was not prepared for what I was about to see. Deodato was about to take this emerging genre to a whole new level. He created a film full of disturbing and convincing images. Some of them, convincing enough to be taken and used by **Faces of Death** rip-off, **Dying: The Last Seconds of Life**. The film opened with the, "This is a true story," bullshit. The story is about Robert Harper, a corporate oilman takes a charter plane with his friend, Rolf, a female assistant, Swan, to visit a camp in New Guinea that is doing oil exploration. They radio the camp, but get no answer. Landing, the plane loses a wheel. The pilot inspects the damage as John and Rolf inspect the camp. They find the camp deserted. Checking out the nearby jungle, they find human remains that appeared to be gnawed on.

Darkness falls; the pilot says it is too dangerous to take off, so the foursome spends the night in the plane. Swan has to answer nature's call, so she leaves the plane. She is grabbed and carried off screaming into the jungle. The pilot wants to go after her, but the others want to wait until daybreak. The three head into the jungle to find Swan. The pilot notices a piece of clothing Swan was wearing. When he picks it up, he sets off a trap. A huge, swinging ball of spikes impales him, leaving him a blood spurting mess. Harper and Rolf are now lost. They smell smoke and go to investigate. To their horror, they find a group of savages have killed and cooked Swan. The camera dwells slowly over this barbecue from hell.

The two men are now desperate to avoid a similar fate. They construct a raft to take them back to the area the plane is. They hit some rapids and the raft breaks apart. Rolf is swept away and Harper is captured by the cannibals. He is put though all kinds of torture and humiliation. Because of the plane, the savages think Harper can fly. They strip him naked and put him in a primitive harness. He is tied to it and then flung around the huge cavern the tribe calls home. Then things take a grimmer turn. He is put in a cage with two large birds. Wondering why he hasn't been killed yet, Harper watches the tribe interact. A fellow who obviously has fallen out of favor has his arm tied over a nest of fire ants that eat it down to the bone. Native children taunt Harper by pissing on him.

Harper discovers that his cellmates, the birds, are bait for larger prey. The first is eaten by a large python that is dragged into the cave. The snake's skull is crushed by rock wielding savages in a hard-to-watch scene. The other bird is set out to catch a crocodile. The living croc is sliced open and the bird is pulled out of its stomach. Several patrons left the theater after this scene. Harper realizes he is next. He needs to escape. He had been sort of befriended by a native girl, who gave him a hand job though the bars of his cage. He plays dead and caves in a tribesman's skull with a rock. He finds the girl who befriended him being raped. He kills her attacker and takes her with him.

More shocks follow. Harper and his reluctant companion hear a moaning and find a native girl giving birth. Upon seeing the baby is a female, mom throws it to the crocodiles. The native girl tries to escape, but is run down by Harper who rapes her. She becomes subservient to him, bringing him food and things. Taking refuge in a cave, they find Rolf who survived the river. Rolf has a badly injured knee, infected so bad that he can hardly walk. They know the plane is their only hope of surviving. As they get closer to the plane, the tribe attacks. Rolf is wounded and the girl is taken. Her skull is caved in, she is decapitated, gutted, and split open from chin to crotch, filled with hot coals and eaten. You see it all, this scene hits you like a baseball bat to the balls. The usually rowdy crowd was stunned. Aside from some gasps and gagging, there was an almost eerie silence. A few people headed for the exits, but it wasn't over.

Harper battles with one of the tribe. He kills him, then in full view of the tribe, rips out his liver and eats it. This stops the attackers cold. Harper and Rolf make it to the plane, but Rolf dies. The credits roll and the producers assure us that this really happened and Robert Harper is alive and now living in Mexico. Every title the film was released under got an "R" rating, which was probably just slapped on the posters and ad mattes by distributors. Just the sheer level of violence and depravity wouldn't have let this slip by the MPAA to get that rating. Video City changed the title to *Jungle Holocaust* obviously to cash in on the director's more notorious *Cannibal Holocaust*. Being that this would be the 2nd film in the Cannibal cycle, it topped *Deep River Savages* in the brutality department. It may have also fired up the rivalry between Lenzi and Deodato.

Eaten Alive, 1980, was Lenzi's return to the genre. He also brought back Ivan Rassinov and Me Me Lai. Shown on "the Deuce" as *Doomed to Die*, it was also known as *Eaten Alive by Cannibals*. This was a true cannibal film, in the sense that Lenzi cannibalized footage from three other films to make it. Lenzi lifted atrocity scenes from his own film, *Deep River Savages* as well as *Mountain of the Cannibal God*, and *Last Cannibal World*. Me Me Lai's death scene from *Last Cannibal World* was taken and used in its entirety in *Eaten Alive*. In an interview, Lenzi claims he had the producer's permission to use those scenes—yeah, sure you did—and he referred to Deodato as "that other director" contemptuously.

Eaten Alive had Ivan Rassinov as "Jonas", a Jim Jones type living in a compound in the jungle with his followers. Sheila Morris (Janet Agren) is looking for her sister, who vanished with the family's money. She is a disciple of Jonas. She hires a mercenary, Mark, to help her find her sister, Diana. Mark is played by NYC porn regular, R. Bolla under his real name, Robert Kerman. Kerman would be a regular in these films. Diana was played by Paola Senatore, who also did a lot of Italian porn. Shiela and Mark make their way though the jungle to Jonas's compound. They are captured and told they can never leave. The jungle surrounding the compound is infested with cannibal footage. Sheila finds Diana drugged by Jonas. She has turned the money over to him. Sheila is drugged by

Jonas and, in a twisted scene that was way over the "R" rating, she is raped with a dildo dipped in cobra venom.

Sheila and Mark grab Diana to make a run for freedom. They are helped by cult member Me Me Lai. Jonas's henchmen waylay the group and one rapes Diana in the dirt. The cannibals attack the group, decapitating one guy, and grabbing Diana and Me Me. In a cheap but grisly effect, Diana is cut up and eaten alive. This scene is very unsettling because she is moving and moaning as the savages cut off her arms and feet and eat them. The effect was achieved by burying her arms and legs in sand and then pouring blood on them. Me Me has a chunk of meat torn off her back, then her death scene from *Last Cannibal World* is inserted. With the authorities closing in, Jonas has his cult do the Kool Aid treatment. Sheila and Mark escape the jungle only to learn that Jonas has also escaped and has the missing money.

Pretty much a cop-out for Lenzi. *Eaten Alive* bounced around "The Deuce" under different titles for a few years. Continental Video released it as *The Emerald Jungle* to try and cash in on John Boorman's *The Emerald Forest*. Bet that one gave a lot of renters a WTF moment. Deodato would make a similar film, *Cut and Run,* in 1985 as perhaps a final *fuck you* to Lenzi. Both directors would make one more cannibal film. And these two films would become two of the most notorious and reviled exploitation films ever made.

In the mid. '70s rumors persisted of an 8mm porn film in which people were killed and dismembered. Pseudo—snuff loops started appearing in various porn emporiums in Times Square. Whether these were real or fake is still debated today. The exploitation team of Michael and Roberta Findley made an incoherent film called *Slaughter in South America*. It was sold to distributor, Robert Shackleton, who titled it *Snuff* and added fake footage to it. Phony as it was, it was a huge hit. Now you had people wondering if there were real snuff type films. *Cannibal Holocaust* was the film that had people wondering if it was real. "Eat or Be Eaten!" screamed the trailer. "The Men Who Filmed This Were Killed And Eaten By Cannibals!" the print ads informed us. For almost 30 years this film was shrouded in mystery and controversy. Legally unavailable until Grindhouse Releasing put it out a few years ago, grainy bootlegs of the cropped Japanese Laser disc made the rounds of the horror convention circuit. The film was released in Japan as the same time as *E.T.* and out-grossed *E.T.,* in terms of money that is.

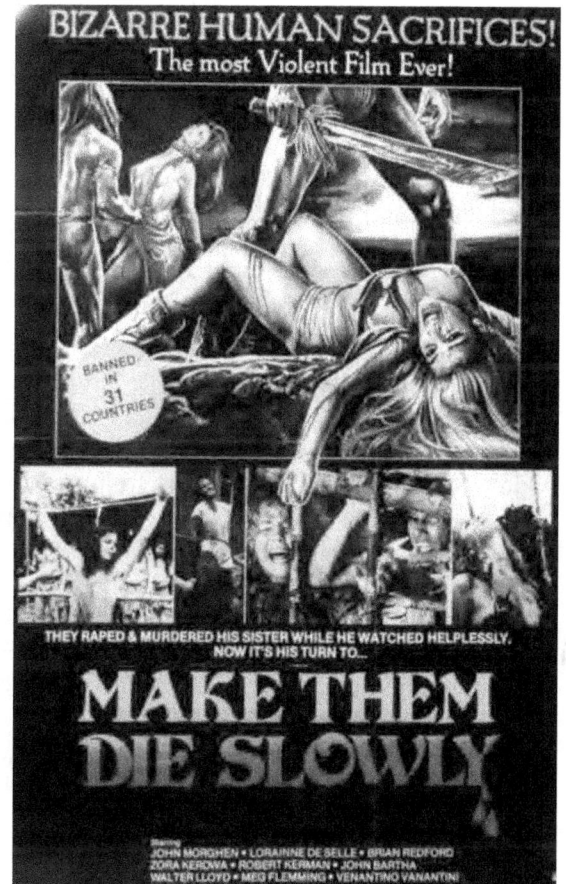

Horror fans were well aware of *Cannibal Holocaust* as it was praised by Rick Sullivan's *Gore Gazette* and Chas Balun's *Deep Red.* If my memory serves me, both guys got in trouble for selling it. The film was playing at skuzzy grind house in Montclair, The Wellmont Theater. It was pulled out after three days due to complaints about the animal cruelty. I caught it at The Liberty on 42nd Street on a Friday night with an SRO crowd. The usual unruly crowd of drunks, stoners, dust heads, working girls, thugs, etc., was pummeled into stunned silence by what they saw. The smell of vomit permeated the place. Some people headed for the exits. A couple of the drugged out working girls were openly crying. The film vanished quickly. Unlike *Man From Deep River, Eaten Alive, Mountain of the Cannibal God,* etc., it didn't bounce from theater to theater as the others did. This actually encouraged people to seek it out.

Some people saw beyond the geek show theatrics. The film was actually a political statement about the news media. When there is no story, create a story and consequences be damned. One of the main characters, Alan (Carl Gabriel York), is an egomaniacal douche who is not above murder to get his "story." His smarmy attitude is what predicates the violence to come. In a art – imitates – life moment, the makers of *Africa Addido*, released hereby Jerry Gross as *Africa: Blood and Guts*, were accused of delaying an execution so they could get a good camera shot of it. They were initially charged with murder. (Deodato would also face murder charges, more on that later.)

The premise of the film is that four reporters go into the Amazon and vanish. A search party, led by Robert Kerman tries to find them. During the search, they find evidence that something has gone terribly wrong. Encountering a Stone Age tribe, they find what has to be the remains of the four, now part of a bizarre shrine. The native won't allow the remains to be buried. They trade some canisters of film for some trinkets. The film has the answers. The four documented their journey. They didn't find a story, so Alan committed some atrocities and filmed it. They heard a bunch of natives into a hut, set it on fire and film it. They rape a native girl, then find that girl impaled on a pole that is shoved up her ass and out her mouth. The natives stalk the four, picking them off one at a time. It is gruesome and hard to watch. After the footage is screened, the station orders it burned. The film was offensive on so many levels. People were outraged when the turtle was cut up alive. Another scene with a muskrat impaled squirming on a knife also infuriated people.

Deodato was arrested shortly after the film's premiere in Italy and charged with first – degree murder. It seems that the authorities believed that several local actors from Columbia were killed on camera. He was exonerated when the actors were brought into court. It seems the actors had a clause in their contracts that ordered them to lay low for a year to hype up the film. *Cannibal Holocaust* was outright banned in Italy and prints were confiscated and destroyed. Even though Deodato was found not guilty, he was banned from making films for a few years. Almost 35 years later, *Cannibal Holocaust* still has the power to demolish the viewer.

I was lucky enough to have 'Alan', Carl Gabriel York, on my radio show around the time Grindhouse Releasing put out the film. He gave me a great interview and then I met him at Cinema Wasteland. I also met Ruggerio Deodato when they had a reunion of sorts at Wasteland. For guy who put some of the most violent, depraved, and vile images on film, he was a sweetheart of a guy. He was great to the fans and to me in particular. Robert Kerman was supposed to be there too, but backed out at the last minute. Kerman has strongly denounced these films, especially *Holocaust*. In one interview he claims he prayed for the film to fail. While some directors had claimed that the producers put in the animal atrocity footage after the films were completed, Kerman has said that Deodato himself shot that footage. Oddly Kerman seems to have gone from one form of pornography to another, the pornography of violence.

It was a hot, sticky summer day in NYC. It was 1981 and the death knell had started for 42nd Street. Three things were happening. The AIDS epidemic had just started. At first it was just thought to be a "gay" disease as it hit the Gay Community first. The health officials started shutting down the gay bathhouses, then gay theaters. When it became apparent that this wasn't just a gay problem, the city had the excuse it always had wanted to shutdown any sex related business in NYC. Police would put undercover cops in both gay and straight theaters. They would document sex acts taking place, then the health department would close the theater.

The emergence of the drug, crack was also a factor. Crack was cheap and it really fucked people up. As dangerous as the area had been, crack made it worse. Cracked-out hookers became more aggressive. Robberies were more common and Port Authority was infested by crack heads and homeless people. Fun City wasn't fun anymore, it was dangerous. The emergence of home video also factored in. Why risk your ass in a shitty grindhouse when you could just take a tape home and watch it there? This just killed off most of the porn grinders and broke the Mob's hold on the sex trade. When the multi years leases that the Mob had taken out on formerly unrentable properties ran out, greedy realtors swooped them up. A place would be open one day, then boarded up the next.

So on that humid summer day, a title was slapped on the marquee of The Liberty Theater that was the most enduring title ever to grace a "Deuce" marquee. *Make Them Die Slowly* was sadly apropos as the area was slowly dying out. Originally called *Cannibal Ferox*, Aquarius releasing changed the title and had a completely misleading ad campaign. "They Raped and Murdered His Sister While He Watched Helplessly, Now It Was His Turn To… *Make Them Die Slowly*." Bullshit, it wasn't a rape/revenge movie, but that title and poster art brought in the crowds. The film was paired with a Mondo film, *Savage Man, Savage Beast*. The monitor in front of the Theater, which would run trailers for the films playing, was turned off. This added to the twisted ambiance that the film was too fucked up to even show scenes from.

I wanted to see it, but my friend was too scared to go in. "Look at those fuckin' people going in there. We might not get out alive." He was being a tad melodramatic, but he was driving that day so I was fucked. I managed to catch it at the mildew-infested RKO Twin a few days later, feeling no pain due to the amount of weed and liquor I ingested before entering. I settled down and watched as a disclaimer scrolled down the screen. A soft female voice read it for the benefit of the patrons who were too fucked up to read. "This film contains over two dozen acts of barbaric torture and cruelty," she tells us, and she ain't lying. This one lives up to its supposed "Banned in over 30 countries" disclaimer. Lenzi tries the same formula Deodato did in **Holocaust**: Four people go into the jungle, one guy starts trouble, etc. Lenzi's might have been trying to make a social statement, but the film is an unrepentant geek show. Four students go into the Amazon to prove or disprove the existence of cannibals. They run into two drug dealers who have ripped off the mob and are hiding out in the jungle. The main dealer, Mike, played with demented gusto by John Morghen, has gone insane from too much coke.

Prior to running into the students, Mike tortured and killed a native guide. Mike's partner, Joe, tell this story to the group. Mike lights up one of the women with coke and then shoots a native girl. The natives capture the group and the fun starts. Joe dies from some jungle fever and is gutted. One guy is chewed on by piranhas before being shot by a poison dart. The most infamous scene has one girl hung up with huge hooks through her tits. Mike gets the most abuse. Trying to escape, he has a hand chopped off. Then he is tied to a pole and castrated. For the finale, his head is put though a hole in a board and the top of it is lopped off and the tribe eats his brains. The last girl escapes with the help of a native. That poor bastard is killed when he sets off a spring trap. The girl returns to civilization and writes her paper stating cannibals are a myth.

Make Them Die Slowly was a huge hit on "The Deuce." Patrons could identify with Mike as people like him prowled "The Deuce" in demented, drugged-out hazes that could turn violent in a heartbeat. **Make Them Die Slowly** was a fitting finale in the cannibal cycle from the director who started it all. The cannibal cycle lasted roughly 10 years. While a lot were total shit and relied on lifted surgical and autopsy footage, the ones that really delivered the demented goods were **Man From Deep River, Last Cannibal World, Eaten Alive, Cannibal Holocaust, Make Them Die Slowly, Mountain of the Cannibal God, and Trap Them and Kill Them**.

Supposedly Ruggerio Deodato is working on a sequel to **Cannibal Holocaust**. In the last few years, a few "revisions" have come out: **Welcome to the Jungle** and **Uncharted**, direct-to-DVD turds that sink to the bottom of the DVD toilet. Supposedly Eli Roth, when not sucking Tarantino's dick, is making his own version, **Green Inferno**. What these people fail to realize is that these films worked back then because of the time period and because no one had ever done anything like them before. Back then, grindhouses were almost living, breathing entities and these films were their lifeblood. You can't recreate that kind of ambiance, so don't even try.

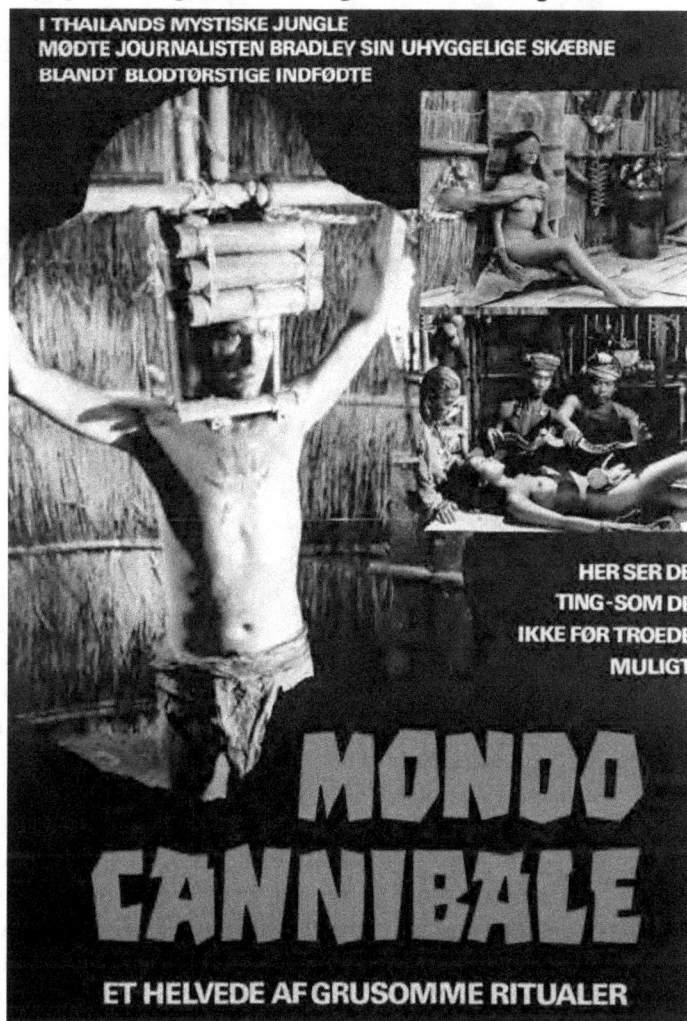

MY OWN VHS ODESSEY

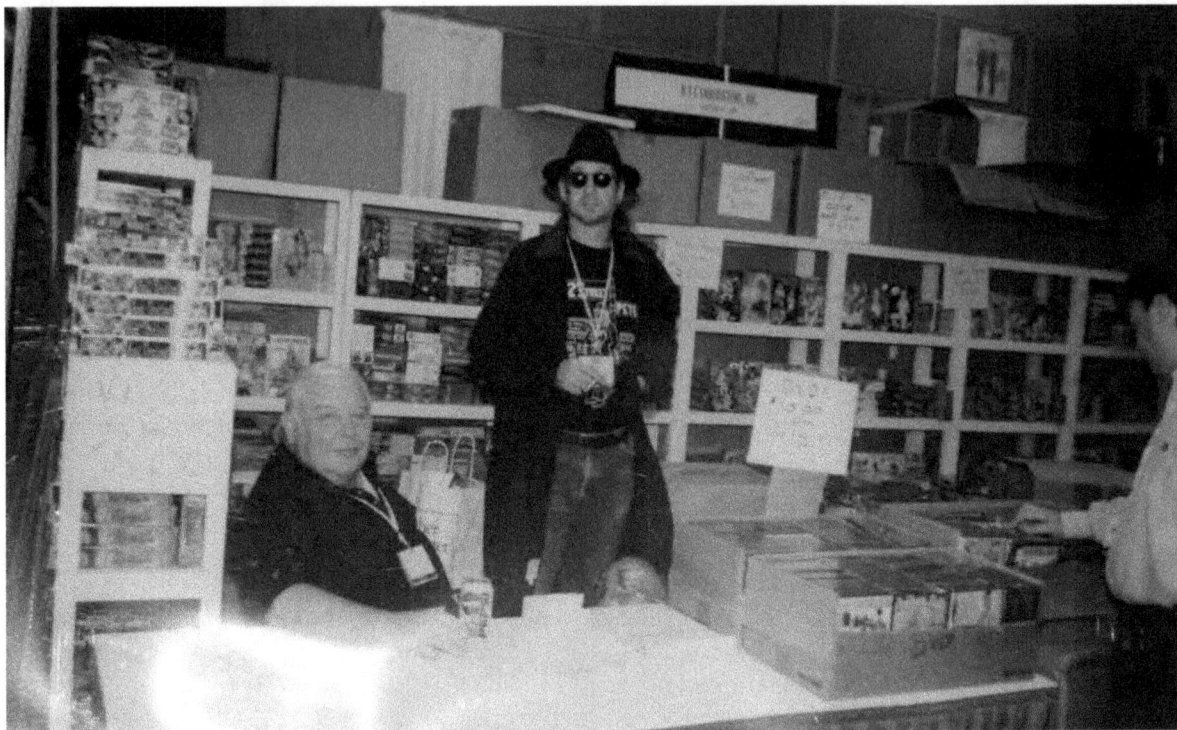

As a horror movie-obsessed kid, I often though how cool it would be to see my movies anytime I wanted to. But that was impossible in the era I grew up in. Closest thing to it was 8mm films. Certain companies put out 12-minute versions of horror and other films. Castle Films had all the Universal Monster Films. Ken Films had a lot of AIP films. I got an 8mm projector for Christmas and started collecting films.

Still, my fertile mind conceived that in the future there would be a way to watch an entire movie in your home. The years rolled by and Home Video was born. Like any new thing, Video Decks were expensive and so were the tapes. You could pay close to $1000 for a unit. Blank tapes were around $20 each, regular movies about $60 each and porn went $100 each.

There were two formats, VHS and Beta. JVC was VHS (Video Home System), Sony was Beta. JVC shared technology, Sony wouldn't. Beta was the better format, but Sony's position allowed VHS to steamroll over Beta, making it the more popular format. Sony would repeat this mistake throughout the years. I really wanted a VCR. I saved my money and bought a Magnovox VCR for $800. A blank tape cost me $22. I was hot to own movies. I drove to Video Shack in NYC around midnight. Video Shack was the first video store and the one in NYC was open until 2AM. My first two tapes were *Night of the Living Dead* and *Assault on Precinct 13* for $59.95 each.

This would be one pricey hobby. But I was a mechanic back then and making decent money. Being that I was the first one in my circle of friends to have a VCR, I should get a porn tape. But not for $100. I went into a store called Theater Vision to look around. There was a basket of tapes in generic white boxes. They were bootleg porn tapes for $30 each. Porn was a bootleggers paradise then because it was still a gray area, legally. Borderline illegal, who could you complain to without the off – chance of getting yourself busted? I picked one out, went home and called the gang.

We all got smoked up and I put in the tape. It was Japanese TV Commercials. I hit Fast Forward and got more of the same. Completely pissed, we all got in my van and drove to the store. The store was closing as we got there. The guy tried to blow us off, but I banged the tape on the window and yelled, "You fucked me!" Considering there were eight of us and we weren't leaving without a tape, he let us swap it around. In a funny twist, the store manager's name was actually John Holmes.

I was spending a lot of money on this stuff. *Hills Have Eyes, Texas Chainsaw Massacre, Zombie*, etc., all at

$59.95 a pop. Then I thought, why not open a video store? I had a guy who wanted to be my partner, so we started looking for locations. Problems arose when we would find a place then find out that town ordinances prohibited the sale of adult material. I had a relationship with Caballero Home Video, which distributed adult product and Wizard horror titles. Prices were $30 for an hour tape of Swedish Erotica and $50 for a complete feature. I wasn't going to order anything until I found a location that wouldn't give me a hassle. My "partner' had other ideas.

This jerk took $500 of our seed money and bought ten porn tapes. Seems, unbeknownst to me, he was a porn addict. Now I was pissed. We had a huge fight and I wasn't about to go into business with this guy. I wanted that $500 back. His answer was we each take five tapes each and call it a day. If that's what it was going to take to get rid of him, cool. But I'm still out $250. Then I had a thought. If I had another VCR I could copy these things, sell them for $25 each and get my money back. I got another VCR and found a place in NYC to get blank tapes for $10 each. It took a couple of months, but I got my money back. Then I had another idea, instead of buying movies for my collection, why not just rent and copy them?

So that's what I did. There was no anti-copy guard back then so my collection grew. An outfit called Goodtimes put out some bargain tapes, usually movies that fell into the public domain as their copyrights expired and not renewed. The movies were a lot of PRC and Monogram titles like ***The Apeman, Vampire Bat, Giant Gila Monster, Indestructible Man***, and others. Quality was so-so, but they were priced around $10, so they sold. People wanted to own movies, but not for $59.95. My mechanic days were coming to an end. I had supplemented my income by doing flea markets on weekends. I sold just about anything, but I noticed no one was selling videotapes. I formulated a plan and that plan was to sell videotapes.

First you have to realize what was happening back then. Video Shack was the first big chain store on the East Coast. It was owned by the same porn people who owned Video X Pix, Distropix, and others. Video Shack had a huge porn section and it wasn't in a back room, it was out in the open. I was actually amazed to see what they had. Bondage, Avon Titles, weird stuff and more. But in the '80s the government, under the senile Ronald Reagan, was going after porn. The Meese Commission was formed and they went after any adult stuff. They used Avon titles in particular to go after as they, in Ed Meese's own words, were 'the most vile and violent examples of Mob. produced pornography'.

Video Shack was sold to RKO, who sold off their freestanding theaters to buy it. RKO basically bought a turd. A new company called Blockbuster Video came in. Blockbuster had a lot of money behind it and would be more family friendly, as it would not carry porn. RKO Video was so messed up that you would find porn titles next to family titles. RKO Video only lasted a couple of years before liquidating their stores. Blockbuster would be the death knell for Mom & Pop stores. Where the small stores could only afford a couple copies of new releases, Blockbuster would stock 20 copies of each new release. Independent stores were closing, not being able to compete. That's when I made my move and never looked back.

I would go to these stores that were closing up. If the tapes were cheap, like $5. $7, I'd go shopping. If not, I'd approach the owner and ask him to call me when he was down to the end. Back then horror and exploitation was considered dreck and it would be left over as people took all the mainstream titles. I'd go in and buy what's left cheap. I got a shrink wrap machine from one store and I'd clean up the tapes and wrap them. I'd sell them $10 each, or 3 for $25. The stuff sold great, but the supply wasn't keeping up with the demand. Any used porn I got would fly off the table. That was where the real money was. But new porn, as I stated earlier, wasn't cheap. I needed a steady source of product and my seeking out these sources would introduce me to a real cast of characters and thieves.

There was no Internet back then. You had newspapers with offerings for sale and a weekly paper called the Want Ad Press that had stuff for sale. I found a place called Video Warehouse in Neptune, NJ. An old timer named Lou was the owner. He had a lot of PD titles, but he also had adult stuff. 30 minute highlight tapes were $7, 60 minutes were $10, and features were $15. I went with the $7 and $10 stuff. I could get $12 and $15 for them. I wasn't greedy. The flea markets I did let me sell them as long as I was low key about it. The stuff flew off the table. But I needed regular movies to offset the porn.

There was an ad in the Want Ad Press for new and used tapes. I called the number and talked to a guy named Mike. He gave me an address in Jersey City. The address turned out to be a bail bonds office. I went to a pay phone—yeah, no cell phones back then. I called this Mike guy and said, "Where the fuck are you?" He was operating out of the basement. I was buzzed in. A guy named Lou Renero owned the place. He rented Mike the basement. Lou hated Mike's customers, but liked me for some reason. Lou's real life persona would be the template for Robert De

Niro's character in **Midnight Run**. De Niro came to the office and spent a lot of time interviewing Lou to prepare for the role.

Mike was another story as he was an unorganized slob. His 'warehouse' was boxes stacked on top of boxes. You literally had to dig though tons of crap. Sometimes you would score some good stuff, other times you would waste a whole day. His price for porn features was $12. There were about 200 titles that were footballed around as no one seemed to own the rights to them. Guys would repackage these titles every couple of months as "new" releases, something that was still going on when I left the business in 2003. The price of these tapes would eventually bottom out.

Lou from Video Warehouse called me with a $10 price if I took 100 tapes. I took the deal as I could get $15 for them. Now a price war began. A wholesaler in NYC had the tapes for $9, then I found a place, Playtime Video, in Union, NJ, that had them for $8. I went to Playtime only to be rudely called out by the clerk in front. "How do I know you got any fuckin' money?" were his exact words. I had the money, but this asshole's attitude made me never go there again. His attitude got him killed years later. The front of this place was open to the public for retail. It wasn't the best of areas. This guy mouthed off to the wrong person and got shot. I wasn't surprised this happened.

RKO Video was getting crushed by Blockbuster. They started liquidating their inventories. Trouble was they had cut a lot of the big boxes to fit in plastic cases. I cherry picked as much as I could, but it wasn't enough. Then I saw another ad in the paper. They said they had titles like **Rambo, Raiders of the Lost Ark**, etc. I made an appointment and met John Zuchowski, who owned Prime Time Video. He was the guy who put tapes in supermarkets for rentals. He was a weird guy and when I got there, he was reluctant to sell me anything.

He had advertised a $5 price, but wanted $7 when I got there. I took some of the hotter titles. Every time I went back, the price was different, Zuch was a lunatic. The end for this came when I was browsing a room full of tapes and he locked me in there for three hours when he left for lunch. I was really pissed off, even more so when he upped the price. I just said fuck it and left. I was at a flea market and a guy had a truckload of tapes. I picked one up and saw a Prime Time Video sticker on it. I called the guy over as he was selling the same stuff for $4 that I was paying $7 for.

Seems he was one of Zuch's franchisees. Zuch was screwing him when he sold the tapes back and he was getting more money at the flea market. I cut a deal, I told him I'd take everything he had for $5 each. So every month I'd go down and clean him out. Between him and the stores I was cleaning out, I had a load of broken tapes and empty display boxes. I got snowed in one day and taught myself how to fix tapes. Unless the actual tape was damaged, I could fix it. I kept a list of the movies I had boxes for. This would come in very handy down the road.

The price wars kept up with the adult guys. Lou called me with a "special" deal. He had slow speed tapes for $6 each. What these cheap fucks did was record the tapes on the SLP speed. That way they could fit 90 minutes on a 30. minute blank tape. Lou sent me a box of 50 tapes. I tried one; it sucked. The image was blurry and grainy. Lou probably never cleaned his machines, which probably added to the problem. I couldn't sell these. I told Lou he was getting them back.

I wasn't the only guy who sent them back. Lou had a bunch of 20. minute cartoons. To recoup, he told his employees, a group of drunks and druggies, to copy the cartoons over the porn and let the tape run out to erase the last ten minutes. They just rewound them after the cartoon ran out. The tapes wound up in Toys R Us stores. Kids got ten minutes of porn after the cartoon. Lou had problems, but would bring more problems on himself.

He called me up and told me he had a great deal on Beatles tapes. I went and checked them out. He had them all right, but they weren't legal. He had other concert footage of Cream, The Stones, and others. I passed on the deal. Watching TV late one night, there was a commercial for these tapes. I thought he must be out of his mind. It even had the Video Warehouse address to mail your check to. Two weeks after I saw this ad, Video Warehouse was no more.

I had been selling at two flea markets. One was The Rockaway Market Place in Rockaway, NJ. I used to set up in the parking lot, but the town killed it. The owner let me set up in front of his store. It was on a highway and people stopped. I think they thought I was doing something illegal. Never the less they bought a lot of tapes. I developed a loyal clientele, but after a few years I was give a choice by new management: either take a spot inside or leave. I took a spot and created Past Midnight Video, a store that catered to grind house type films.

I made a separate area for the porn and my customers followed me inside. I still needed product. I was at one of my stops during the week. A bunch of hustlers like me would wind up at Placid Lakes Salvage. You never knew what these guys might have. A guy named Tony told me he could get new releases for $10 each. He showed me a list; I gave him an order. When I met him to get the tapes, they were all in clamshell cases, bootlegs. I told him forget it, no way could I sell this stuff. What I didn't know was they came from a place that I would frequent every week and eventually wind up working there.

For some reason, I walked into a local Blockbuster and checked out their sale bin. It was loaded with horror, exploitation, and cult titles, all for under $5 each. This was the stuff from all the places they had bought out, stuff they deemed "unrentable." That week I hit every Blockbuster within a 70. mile radius. At the end of the day I had a carload of great tapes. I kept running into this guy, Tony. He told me to go over to NYC and look for a place on 27th street called New York City Liquidators and ask for Norman.

I found the place, went in and asked for Norman. Norman was 5. foot nothing with a shock of white hair. I told him who sent me and that I needed regular movies and cheap porn. He sold me the porn for only $3 each. Liquidators was huge and had box after box of VHS and Beta tapes stacked four feet high. Norman had connections to the XXX industry. He was also a crook and made no bones about it. He used to have a huge store on Broadway called Norman's House of Deals. He lost that store when he got arrested for selling counterfeit Rolex watches.

Norm told me that a friend of his who owned Cinderella, an Adult Tape company, fronted him $10,000 worth of tapes to get him back on his feet after the bust. Norm also had "new "releases" behind the counter. These were bootlegs and they were good enough to pass as the real thing. Then I put two and two together: those clamshell bootlegs came from Norm. Bootlegging was huge back then, not only with camcordered taped of films still running in theaters, but new released VHS tapes.

Backtracking a bit, it was the greed of the video industry itself that enabled bootleggers to flourish. The big chains got in bed with the studios and raised the wholesale price of the tapes. They new this would kill off the smaller indie stores. What they didn't know was theses stores weren't going down without a fight. Where Blockbuster and others could stock 20 copies of a new release, small stores could only afford one copy. Some stores ran off extra copies in their back rooms. Others went to Norm.

Norm's stuff had boxes and labels that passed for real. He sold them for $15 each and customers were lined up three deep at the counter to get them. I didn't buy any, except for me to watch. I didn't need a problem, plus I was making enough with the used tapes and the porn. Norm's competitors would tell me I was crazy for going there because the place was being watched. They knew I was dropping a lot of cash at Liquidators and wanted my business. I didn't give a shit about being watched because I wasn't buying the bootlegs and nothing I was doing was illegal, so I had no worries.

I may have had no worries, but Norm did. I was working on of my many part times jobs when I got a phone call. "Turn on the news," I was told. Local camera crews were outside of Liquidators. Norm and the entire staff were taken out in cuffs. I was like, "Holy shit, they got him." Strangely though, I didn't see the three Mexican stock boys. Wonder how they got away. This was big news as it was the biggest bust of pirated taped ever. District attorney, Robert Morganthal, was pictured with a pile of the tapes. They claimed to have found everything from Disney films to animal porn. Supposedly it was selling Tinto Brass' *Caligula* that got him busted. I had never seen that tape in the store and I was there at least once a week.

Considering I did see *Fantasia* for sale I questioned the whole *Caligula* story. What really happened was an employee got stupid. I would get there early and wait until Norm opened. Some of the help used to get there early, so we'd hang out and get coffee. This one guy, Steve, was coked out and pissed off at all the $$$ that was coming in. He bragged he could get a $50k reward if he turned five people in for piracy. I didn't want to hear this shit. A week later, Norm overheard him on the phone, he was making a deal to make some stuff go out the back door. He got fired, a week later the bust went down, you do the math. Norm was on Riker's Island for about a week. I was up the block when I ran into Tony who told me Norm just got out and was reopening.

I went down to see him as I was sorry the crazy fuck went to jail. I told him anything I could do to help, just ask. He thanked me, then asked me to go outside and flag down a garbage truck. I got the driver and Norm gave him some cash. The truck pulled up to the door and Norm had the stock boys bring out all the tapes the feds missed and cases of empty bootleg boxes. It was a lot of stuff. I don't know what deal he made to get out of jail, but this was federal strike two. One more bust and it would be goodbye Norm. Norm stopped the bootlegging business, at least the regular movies. Any porn tape in a clamshell box or ameray hard box was fair game. Since it was still a gray area, there wasn't much they could do to stop it. Well, yeah, *legally* that is. But when the guy who was bringing in the nasty German tapes, a thug named Eddie Mishkin, found out Norm was copying them, he went to the store. He went into the XXX section, picked up a bootleg copy of his tape, then walked up to the counter. "Take off your glasses," he said to Norm. Mishkin bitch-slapped him and gave him a black eye.

That ended that.

One thing I did need was better product as those titles I spoke of were played out. Norm got better stuff from a great company, VCA. That company got a major fine from the government for shipping to states where the stuff was still illegal. To pay off the fine, they dumped their back catalogue stuff cheap. They also had Magnum Home Video titles like **Mad Doctor of Blood Island, Brain of Blood, Torture Chamber of Dr. Sadism**, and more for around $3 each if you bought a mixed case of 50 tapes.

I found another place, Video Wholesalers of America, in Newark, NJ. They had what was known as "catalogue" titles, tapes that were discounted because they were a year or two old. They ran between $3.50 and $5. I filled my back room with this stuff. I also picked stuff up for these guys from Norm, like those sick German scat, piss, and fisting tapes. This kept me in their good graces. I wound up just dealing with Norm, Mike, and these guys. Norm would call me when he bought out a store, so I would get first crack at the horror and exploitation stuff. Norm also had boxes and boxes of tapes without their display boxes. I would sit there for hours with my list of boxes, matching the tapes to the boxes on my list. Norm gave me those tapes for $1. With a box, I sold them for $10.

Norm was doing great until he cheaped out and started using cheap VHS tapes for his bootlegs. One out of two wouldn't work, so now he had a ton of returns lying around. He wasn't the only one who cheaped out. XXX companies would cut corners any way they could. First it was those slow. speed tapes, which sometimes they would forget to record on slow speed and the movie would run out in mid. stream. I was at a trade show and someone was selling off a load of tapes from a company called Video Treasures. Video Treasures was cranking out titles that fell into the public domain or that they had bought limited rights to release. They used 60. minute blank tapes on the LP speed for their releases. They would eventually become Anchor Bay.

I looked at the list of titles. 300,000 copies of **The Texas Chainsaw Massacre**, Cartoons, Shirley Temple movies, etc. Too much for me, but the deal stayed in my mind. Some cheap porn company bought them, then copied porn over them. Or at least they were supposed to. Liquidators got cases of this shit. They sold someone a porn tape and they came back bitching that TCM was on it. I had been staying away from the cheap stuff because it was bad for business. My business, however, was about to come to a screeching halt.

Someone wanted to buy The Rockaway Market Place and upgrade it. They expected us to move out, then come back in six months at three times the rent. We said if we are out for six months, we are out, period. I was fucked. I had nowhere to go with this. I started taking my inventory to the outdoor markets. Business dropped because others had gotten into the game. I had a great reputation and following, but even when I dropped the price to $5, they weren't selling. The run was over. I called Ken Kish from Cinema Wasteland and offered him the 1,000 horror, cult, Kung Fu, exploitation tapes I had. He took the deal. The rest of the stuff I tried to sell off. I ran Past Midnite Video for over 10 years. It sucked to close it up. Now I had no income. That would change in a weird twist of fate.

I was still going to Liquidators as I was still selling, but now out of my car. Norm asked me what I was going to do now. I told him I had no idea. He said, "Why don't you come down to Atlantic City with me for the East Coast Video Show? It won't cost you anything," he said, "it's all on me." Yeah, I thought and you don't do nothing for nothing, there had to be a catch to this. The guy who ran Norm's adult section was a lazy fuck. He couldn't sell heaters to Eskimos. We set up the NYC Liquidators booth.

This guy was supposed to be selling and taking orders. Instead he was roaming around, getting autographs from porn stars. I said to Norm, "Isn't he supposed to be selling this stuff?" Norm turned to me and said, "Why don't you show me what you can do? "Ok, I went into full tilt bozo mode, I started making a lot of noise about great deals and by the end of the first day I had sold half the stuff we brought. This pissed off Zito, the guy who was supposed to be selling. I kept it up for the next two days, pretty much blowing out everything. Then Norm offered me a job.

I wasn't thrilled about commuting into the city, nor was I thrilled about the distinct possibility of getting arrested while working there. However I had nothing else lined up. I told him that I'd take the job but Point #1, I wasn't going to jail if he decided to do something stupid. He laughed and said, "You'll have to keep me honest." That was a full time job in itself. Point #2, I didn't want to pay for anything I wanted. Done, I got that. So I was now working for one of the biggest crooks in NYC.

Of course Zito was less than happy with this. As far as selling, I blew his doors off. He never attempted to sell anything other than what someone ordered. I always took an order, but pitched other stuff to the customer. I was selling my ass off and in a couple of months I doubled his sales. Zito got pissed and started some shit with me. He eventually got into a screaming match with Norm over how he was the boss. Norm fired him then put me in total charge of the adult section, both buying and selling.

Norm had some kind of connection with a company called Intermedia in California. He was getting truckloads of VHS tapes from them. All was well until they stuck him with 50,000 Greenbay Packers highlight tapes. Norm refused to pay and the relationship went sour. I though we would never get rid of this shit, even at .25 cents a tape. Enter NYC mayor and rabid anti-porn guy, Rudi Giuliani. Rudi hated any form of adult product with the zeal of a religious fanatic. He got a law passed where any adult store had to have 60% of their inventory as non-adult product.

Now every porn store in the area was scrambling to get cheap non. porn tapes to stay open. Those Packers tapes went up to $1.50 each. These stores bought every VHS piece of crap we had lying around. Norm made peace with Intermedia and started getting more product, including the new format, DVD. I was reading one of the video trade magazines and they had an article about Intermedia. Intermedia was a company that was supposed to destroy any VHS tape or non. DVD that stores returned. I laughingly showed this article to Norm. He told me the company was run by "made" guys. I didn't need to know anything else.

When Bush got his second term, he made avow to the religious right to wipe out porn. This panicked a lot of the adult companies. They felt they should get rid of explicit boxes and anything else that might draw unwanted attention from the feds. Who would buy all this stuff? We would, that's who. We cut deals that got us the tapes for $1 each. Bush never made good on his promise because of the attack on 9/11. National security was more important than busting fuck films.

One really funny thing that happened was a huge Sexpo was planned to run in NYC. They rented the Jacob Javits Convention Center. This happened right under anti-porn mayor Rudy Giuliani's nose. He was livid, but there was no way he could shut this down. Norm took a booth there. He also took out an ad in The Village Voice that said we would be there with special guests Menage and 42nd Street Pete. This was a classy event, not a sleaze fest. They had seminars, workshops, and more. My old friend, writer Jack Ketchum, was there as well as Troma Films, Candida Royal, and another old friend, Al Goldstein. I was bullshitting with Al and he said, "Fuck Giuliani, this is a classy event, the only thing sleazy here is me, and you." Long story short, we sold $25K worth of tapes in three days.

With DVDs coming in, porn companies decided to liquidate all their VHS. VCA would sell us 10,000 tapes for a $1 each until they ran out of boxes. What these companies didn't realize that older masturbators were resistant to change. They still wanted VHS. Companies had to rethink things and still have VHS available. So the price went back up. Norm found another gold mine, this time out of Canada. Someone hooked Norm up with a guy in Toronto, Vito. Norm would wire $30K to Vito and three days later a truck would arrive loaded with VHS tapes and some DVDs. When this stuff came in, I'd go shopping. One load had a lot of DVDs. I was slow on my end that day, so I volunteered to count them. It also gave me a chance to pluck out what I wanted. The invoice said there were 3,000 DVDs. I counted over 5,000. When I told Norm, he said, "You never told me this."

Ok, cool, but how would Vito not miss over 2,000 DVDs? Every load we got had more product than on the invoice. When Norm was out, Vito called and I wound up talking to him for a bit. He mentioned he had other "items" that maybe Norm could use. I said I'd pass this on to Norm. Norm's bookkeeper asked me about the invoice and why Vito never billed us for the overage. Now my light bulb went on. Vito's company was a container company, aka a garbage collection company. This stuff was supposed to be disposed of. I would have to say that Vito was mobbed up, as Toronto was primarily Italian. Regardless, it was a great deal and we would get a truck every other week.

With that 60% law, any non. porn VHS would sell. Other states adopted that law. I sold 3,000 broken VHS tapes to a store in Florida. We shrink. wrapped them and they looked new. The guy slapped an $89.95 price on them so no one would mistakenly buy them. Norm's health went bad in 2001. By 2003, his kidneys were failing and he had a triple bypass. He died in 2003. I did have a handshake deal to keep the place going. His greedy stepsons overrode that. The place was liquidated for next to nothing. DVDs changed the entire landscape. Cheap, multi. hour porn DVDs flooded the market.

Most of the players I had dealt with were gone. Lou folded up after his bust. Fat Mike went from place to place, but then had to lay low after selling fake Viagra. Johnny Zuch was the guy supplying Wal-Mart with the bins of $5 DVDs. Even The East Coast Video Show stopped running in Atlantic City. I really thought VHS was dead. What I never thought of was, while I saw everything in Grindhouses, a generation of fans grew up watching stuff they rented from cool Mom & Pop Video Stores.

Certain VHS tapes are now going for $20 to over $100 each. Big box horror and exploitation from companies Like Wizard, Regal, Midnight, Magnum, World, Continental, and others command big bucks. Right now there are no more video stores. Blockbuster, who killed off the independent stores, has been in its death throes for the last few years. As of this writing, it's last few stores are closing. Blockbuster died a slow and painful death. A fitting end for accompany that changed the face of an industry, but stomped others out of existence in the process. My time in the business was very profitable and a lot of fun despite the over all chaos involved. I lived my dream of actually owning a video store that catered to the fans of all grindhouse genres. So that's my story.

My Attempt At A Non Confrontational Article

By Cory Udler

For some reason everyone likes lists. Top 10 this, best that, worst this. I know I'm a sucker for that shit. If Cracked has a Top 10 Movie Mistakes or Top 10 Painful Venereal Diseases you can bet your bottom dollar I'm clicking on it. I always find it interesting to read filmmaker's lists of films that inspired them or made them want to make movies. I can't point to any one film or collection of films that made me want to make movies. The only thing I ever say is that I loved "weird" movies and wanted to make "weird" movies. Vague, I know. While many no budget sleaze merchants like myself may have the dream to make that one "opus", I don't. I just want to continue to make weird shit that will be shunned by film festivals, overlooked by distributors and celebrated by oddballs like myself. So, with that, the following is not a list of my favorite movies of all time (I'll put those in bullet points at the end). What awaits you in this list are

The Top 5 Movies That Sculpted My View Of What "Weird" Movies Are And Can Be.

1. ***THE ASTRO-ZOMBIES***, 1968. Directed by Ted V. Mikels

I have said a million times before that it wasn't so much one movie or one director that really turned me on to the underworld of cinema. It was a TV show titled *The Incredibly Strange Film Show* hosted by Jonathan Ross. The episode with Ted V. Mikels stood out to me more than any others. Ted showed a true gusto, a sheer love towards making the movies he made. Upon seeing this episode I was only familiar with *The Corpse Grinders*, unaware of the man behind the madness or the rest of his body of work. *Astro-Zombies*, in my mind, has it all. With a Ted V. Mikels movie, you get everything including the kitchen sink. From the wind up robots in the opening credits to Tura's wardrobe, to an Astro-Zombie using a flashlight to recharge his solar panels in the middle of his forehead, THIS is a "weird" movie if there ever was one. I was fortunate enough to get to write *Astro-Zombies M3: Cloned* for Ted a few years back. As I said in a previous issue, if you would have told a 12 year old me that I would have written a sequel to the one movie I always cite as being a turning point in my quest for the fringe in the world of movies I would have said you were insane. The movie was a labor of love for Ted who, in turn, received none of the fruits of his labor. A bad distributor and some obvious shady shenanigans insured that Ted would not receive his due (monetarily) from *Astro-Zombies*. But, it is in this writer's opinion that *Astro-Zombies* is one of the main reasons that we all still celebrate Ted's body of work.

2. ***DERANGED***, 1974. Directed by Alan Ormsby and Jeff Gillen.

"Pretty Sally Mae died a very unnatural death. But the worst hasn't happened to her yet." So reads the tagline to what is the perfect oddball '70s Drive-in horror flick. Starring an obviously dedicated Roberts Blossom as "Ezra Cobb", *Deranged* is loosely based on the crimes of Wisconsin grave robber, Ed Gein. Having lived my entire life no more than a 90-minute drive from Plainfield, Wisconsin, I fancy myself a bit of a Gein enthusiast. Not much of a legacy for my daughter, I realize, but the story of Gein, coupled with the fact that Plainfield is located in what many in Wisconsin call the "Great Dead Heart" of the state was just way too fertile and enticing to a warped young mind like mine. Deranged not only has a very playful tone about it, much in the way that Ormsby's *Children Shouldn't Play With Dead Things* had, but it turns on a dime from moments that actually make you laugh out loud to moments that have you squirming in your chair. The landscape in which the film was shot (Canada) is a pretty close representation to what Plainfield was, and is, like. A

lean 82 minutes of gonzo performances, Technicolor blood flow and one of the most anarchic scripts you could ever hope to see brought to life, *Deranged* is a movie I will forever celebrate. Just because it's so strange, so fun, so wrong, and so perfect.

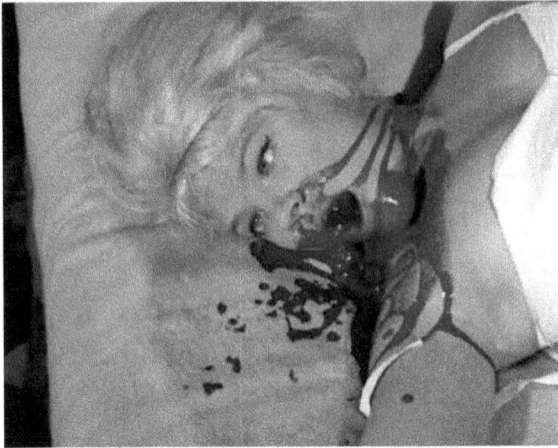

3. *BLOOD FEAST*, 1963. Directed by Herschel Gordon Lewis

Often credited with being the first "gore film", that isn't why this movie inspired me or made this list. It's because I have been watching this movie for the better part of 25 years and every single time I watch it I say the same thing. "It's almost as if aliens from another planet studied our Drive-Ins, made their own movie and birthed *Blood Feast* onto the unsuspecting public." It really feels like it was made either on another planet or by people from another planet. Lewis's entire body of work feels that way to me. H.G. Lewis not only made movies that the studios either "couldn't make or wouldn't make" he made movies that nobody on this planet could make. His sense of space, framing, pacing, music, dialogue, shot selection, lighting. It all goes into this boiling cauldron of fucked-upedness, comes to a simmer, reeks up the entire house, has the neighbors thinking you have liquefied human remains rotting in your crawlspace, and then finds it's way into your heart (somehow!) and once you get that first taste, you're hooked. Wooden acting, more blood than you will ever see in a movie and that music. Jesus H Christ, that music. *Blood Feast*. I'm still not convinced that it wasn't made by an alien race.

4. *LEGEND OF THE SEVEN GOLDEN VAMPIRES*, 1974. Directed by Roy Ward Baker and Chang Cheh.

This movie should have NEVER worked. If this were made today it would be done in a "faux grindhouse" style that would fall flat and be loaded with irony and in-jokes. Basically, it wouldn't work today. Give credit to Roy Ward, a Hammer staple, for his direction of the movie. In 1974 when Hammer Studios partnered with The Shaw Brothers something was obviously aligned in the outer reaches of our universe because *Legend of the Seven Golden Vampires* is a brilliant, sleazy, violent, classy, well. told movie that I'm surprised isn't celebrated by more weird movie fans today. Peter Cushing classes this thing up as he always had a tendency to do. But, don't let Cushing's class fool you. This is pure unadulterated sleaze hijinks. Plenty of naked women, lots of great kung fu, dusty faced vampires and, to be honest, a pretty damn interesting plot line make this one of those "late, late movie" staples that I remember seeing on KMSP out of the Twin Cities when I was a young kid. It never left me. Still a weird movie heavyweight.

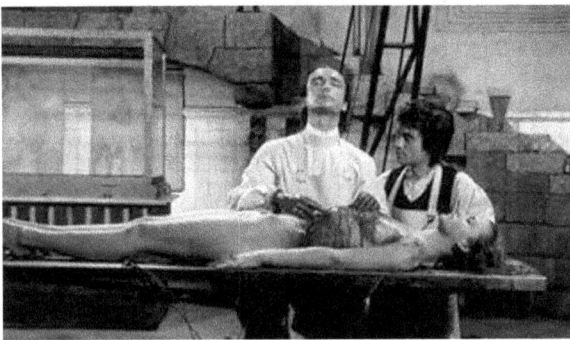

5. *ANDY WARHOL'S FRANKENSTEIN* aka *FLESH FOR FRANKENSTEIN*, 1973. Directed by Paul Morrissey.

I first watched a heavily edited broadcast of this movie on the USA network's *Night Flight* show in the late 80s. By that point I had already seen *Andy Warhol's Dracula* aka *Blood for Dracula* several times. I don't really know what I can say about this flick. I can tell you a friend of mine, who is no stranger to the outer reaches of cinema, watched it with me one night and subsequently got sick after the viewing. Could have been the Jagermeister, could have been the movie, could have been a combo. To this day I think Udo Kier is in search of a Serbian male with the perfect "nasum", but I have zero idea and I, quite frankly, don't care. If there were ever a movie made that said, "I don't give a fuck what anyone else is doing", this is it. It's a middle finger to every Frankenstein that came before it and after it. Udo Kier chews up every single frame of the film he's in, and for that alone this is a classic weird movie. And let's not forget him ripping open his "female zombie", fucking her insides and then proclaiming, "to know death, you have to fuck life in the gall bladder." Genius. A fucking gem of a movie. Originally shot in 3D, I had a chance to see the 3D print in a local weird movie theatre many years ago but had to pass it up. I can't remember why, I've blacked it out. It's one of the few regrettable things I have done in my life (keep in mind, I'm writing this a few months before the April 2014 Cinema Wasteland show, so there will probably be a half a dozen regrettable things added to the list after that). Oh, and from my understanding Andy Warhol had fuck. All to do with this movie. Just some of his hangers on were involved in some capacity. So, there they are in their wonderfully bizarre glory.

The American Western:
An Early Grindhouse Staple

Before cannibals, zombies, bikers, etc., took over the stained screens at the grind houses, one genre was a constant at these places, the western. Yeah, the 40s and '50s product was so dull that it was like watching paint dry. You had Randolph Scott, Joel McCrea, Rory Calhoun, and the "duke" himself, John Wayne. Aging WWI veterans and disenfranchised WWII Vets would go to these grind houses and get lost for a few hours watching the guys in the white hats take out the bad guys.

Slow moving and predictable, the films had simple plots of good vs. evil. Toward the mid-'50s, this was about to change. *Vera Cruz* (1954) was one of those westerns that took a new approach. Starring Burt Lancaster and Gary Cooper, the film center on a group of "adventurers" hired to escort a countess to Vera Cruz. Cooper wore the "white" hat in this one. Lancaster was the 'bad guy', complete with a gang of killers. The gang was made up of hungry actors, many fresh out of the service. Ernest Borgnine, Jack Elam, Charles Bronson, Jack Lambert and others were Lancaster's gang. A bit more violent than the usual western, Vera Cruz was a huge hit.

THE **MAGNIFICENT SEVEN**

They fought like seven hundred

STEVE McQUEEN   JAMES COBURN "BRITT"   HORST BUCHHOLZ "CHICO"   YUL BRYNNER "CHRIS ADAMS"   BRAD DEXTER "HARRY LUCK"   ROBERT VAUGHN "LEE"   CHARLES BRONSON "BERNARDO O'REILLY"

The Magnificent Seven (1960), was called the last great American western. It wasn't, but it had a huge impact. Based on the classic Kurosawa film, *The Seven Samurai*, a group of seven gunmen are hired to protect a Mexican village from bandits. Yul Brynner, Steve McQueen, Charles Bronson, James Coburn, Robert Vaughn, Brad Dexter and Horst Buchholtz were The Seven. It was a big hit and spawned three sequels and a TV series. It also upped the ante in the violence department as bandits were dispatched with knives, machetes and axes. *Rio Conchos,* 1964, opened with an unknown gunman shooting down members of an Indian burial party. Richard Boone is the vengeance crazed, booze soaked ex. Confederate Major Lassiter, whose family was massacred by Apaches. Stewart Whitman is a Union officer Captain Haven, who has a shipment of rifles stolen and Lassiter is caught with one of those rifles. Lassiter won't reveal where he got the rifle, so he's thrown in the stockade. Another prisoner is Rodriguez (Anthony Franciosa), who Lassiter has encountered in the past. Lassiter is offered a deal to find the rifles. He must team up with Haven and Sgt. Franklin (Jim Brown in his first film role). Lassiter got his rifle from a Cornel Pardee, who is still fighting the Civil War.

Pardee's plan is to arm the Apaches with the stolen rifles. Haven is given a wagon load of gun powder to lure Pardee out. Lassiter agrees to go, but wants Rodriguez to go also as he's knows the territory and gives him an edge against a double cross by Haven. After a violent shoot out with bandits and an even more violent battle with Apaches, they find Pardee's stronghold. Lassiter loses it when Apache Chief Bloodshirt (Rodolfo Acosta) arrives and attacks him after being taunted. The three are tortured and beaten until a sympathetic Indian squaw frees them. Lassiter and Franklin ride the wagon of gunpowder into the stash of rifles, blowing up the rifles, Bloodshirt and themselves. Look for wild man Timothy Carey in an uncredited role as a bartender. When the film was shown on TV, all the violence was edited out. I saw it as part of a Kiddee Matinee at my local grind house.

Young Fury (1965), was another film that hit the kiddee matinee. It was juvenile delinquents on horseback as JD films were popular in that era. It was also the template for Young Guns. A gang of young toughs take over a town because their leader's father is an ex gunfighter who supposedly sold out the Dawson Gang. That gang just got out of prison and Dawson (John Agar) is out for revenge. Tige McCoy baits his father, Clint (Rory Calhoun) that the Dawsons are coming for him. What he doesn't know is that saloon girl, Sara (Virgina Mayo), is his mother.

After several vicious brawls between members of the gang, most ride off, but Tige and a few stay to see how Clint will fare against the Dawsons. The gang arrives and the sheriff and Sara are killed prompting Tige and the others to take a side. A bloodbath ensues as the two sides battle it out. For a '60s film, there is a lot of blood and Dawson is shot in the face in a bloody close up. AC Lyles produced the film using his stock company of older stars. Lon Chaney is a bartender, William Bendix is a blacksmith and Richard Arlen is the sheriff. Lyles was a technical adviser for HBO's *Deadwood*.

The Professionals (1966), was a violent shoot 'em up about a millionaire that hires four mercenaries to rescue his wife from a notorious bandit. Burt Lancaster, Lee Marvin, Robert Ryan and Woody Strode are the mercenaries. Jack Palance is the Mexican bandit and Claudia Cardinale is the abducted wife, or was she really abducted? The film was a vehicle for Lancaster, but Burt was overshadowed by Marvin, who was reportedly drunk throughout the film. So drunk in one instance that assistant director, Tom Shaw had to intervene, as Lancaster wanted to throw Lee off the mountain. Burt also had to deal with a scenery chewing Jack Palance.

Marvin and Woody strode became good friends during filming. Marvin graciously gave Strode the rub, advising him to only wear his vest as Woody was pretty buff in those days. That gesture on Marvin's part opened the door for more roles for Woody. Being that *The Professionals* was an international hit, Strode was offered roles in Spaghetti Westerns and crime dramas.

Major Dundee (1965), was Sam Peckinpah's first epic western that went way over budget and kept Sam from working for a bit. Sam's battles with producers were legendary and Charlton Heston offered to return his entire salary if Peckinpah was allowed to keep going and reshoot several scenes. Much to Heston's chagrin, the studio kept his money. Heston also had problems with Sam. At one point Sam infuriated Heston to the point that Heston actually charged after Sam with his saber. Sam's cut of the film was 156 minutes. The studio cut it down to 123 minutes, rendering it a semi-incoherent mess.

Lee Marvin was the original choice for Indian scout, Mr. Potts. Marvin, however wanted too much money, so his agent suggested James Coburn, who got the role. Marvin also wrote a treatment for a western, which he gave to Sam and he intended to be the lead in it. Marvin's agent, however, didn't want Lee to appear in another violent western so soon after doing the Professionals. That "treatment" became *The Wild Bunch*. As incoherent as *Dundee* might have been, it featured a lot of actors who would become uniquely entwined with Peckinpah. Warren Oates, LQ Jones, John Davis Chandler, RG Armstrong, James Coburn, Ben Johnson and Slim Pickens worked for Sam in several films.

Nothing could have prepared the viewing public for 1969's ***The Wild Bunch***. Sam Peckinpah's classic was denounced as violent, stomach churning trash. Even the Eastwood/Leone westerns took a backseat to the violence in ***The Wild Bunch***. So much has been written about this film, that I would be hard pressed to add anything new. When I originally saw the film, I was mesmerized by it and stayed for a second showing. Ten years after it's release, I saw it at a revival house, The Park Theater in Caldwell NJ. It was on a double bill with ***Mean Streets***. During the opening credits, a tangible excitement went through the crowd. When William Holden uttered the line, "If they move, kill 'em," the crowd actually cheered. ***The Wild Bunch*** was the ultimate grind house western and changed the face of the genre. It is worth noting that based on the success of ***The Wild Bunch***, Columbia pictures offered Sam a chance to reshoot some of the scenes cut from ***Major Dundee***. Sam pretty much told them to fuck off.

The Wild Bunch-inspired films started to pop up. Some used the stars from that film. ***The Revengers*** (1972), reunited William Holden and Ernest Borgnine. This violent film has rancher Holden using a group of prisoners to track down the gang that killed his family. Lots of action, but an ending that really tanks the film. ***The Hunting Party,*** 1971, had a sadistic Gene Hackman tracking down a gang that had abducted his wife, Candice Bergen. The gang leader is Oliver Reed and one of the gang members was ***Wild Bunch*** co-star LQ Jones. Hackman and his friends use high-powered rifles to shoot Reed's gang to bloody pieces. Reed reportedly hated the film and, unlike his British counterparts, didn't relocate to America to beat the higher taxes in England.

Aging name stars were cast in some of these films. ***Four For Texas*** (1963), had fellow rat packers Frank Sinatra and Dean Martin as the leads. Their costars were Anita Ekberg and Ursula Andress. The supporting cast of Victor Buono, Richard Jaeckel, Mike Mazurki, Jack Elam, and Charles Bronson as the heavy covered the shortcoming of the two stars. A fun bit had the Three Stooges do a short cameo appearance. Martin, however, stayed in the genre with ***Rough Night in Jericho*** (1967), where he played against type as a former lawman gone bad. ***Something Big*** (1971), had Martin looking to steal a Gatling Gun to pull off a heist.

The story of a man who took the law into his own finger!

"SUPPORT YOUR LOCAL GUNFIGHTER"

JAMES GARNER / SUZANNE PLESHETTE
"SUPPORT YOUR LOCAL GUNFIGHTER"

Burt Lancaster was another fixture in the genre. In 1968's ***The Scalp Hunters***, he is a fur trapper who was forced to trade his furs to a group of Indians for an educated slave, Ossie Davis. Tracking the Indians, he finds them dead at the hands of a party of scalp hunters lead by Telly Savalas. Now the scalp hunters have his furs and the slave. The film focuses on the relationship between Davis and Lancaster. ***Lawman***, 1971, had Lancaster as a no. nonsense marshal who's town had an old man accidently shot by some cattlemen during a drunken celebration. He goes to their town to arrest all involved. The town is run by Lee J. Cobb, who offers restitution, but Lancaster wants all concerned to go back and stand trial. Robert Ryan is that town's sheriff who is owned by Cobb. Robert Duvall, Sheri North, and Albert Salmi co-star. The film ends in a bloodbath and a suicide, pretty much a first in westerns.

If the violence in ***Lawman*** was extreme, you'd be hard pressed to top the carnage in ***Ulzana's Raid***, 1972. A group of Indians jump the reservation and slaughter all in their path. Burt is a grizzled scout joining an inexperienced officer tracking the renegades. Highlights include scalpings, mutilations, hearts cut out, torture and horse killings. The film is outright brutal. Richard Jaeckel, Bruce Davison and Jorge Luke round out the cast. Burt was also the lead in 1971's ***Valdez is Coming*** were he is a Mexican American sheriff trying to get compensation from a powerful cattle baron after his men wrongly kill a black man in front of his pregnant Indian wife. Lot of underlying social commentary in Burt's films. After being brutalized, Valdez seeks bloody revenge.

People may think that ***Blazing Saddles*** was the first comedy western. It wasn't. ***Support Your Local Sheriff*** (1969), may not have been the first either [*it wasn't—ed.*], but it did set the bar. James Garner is a drifter on the way to Australia, but is made the sheriff of a boomtown. The biggest threat to the town are the Danbys, who demand 20% of all the gold. The Danby family is Walter Brennan, Bruce Dern, Gene Evans, and Dick Peabody. Director Burt Kennedy discovered that veteran character actor, Jack Elam, had a undiscovered comedic flair, and paired him up with Garner. Harry Morgan, Joan Hackett and Henry Jones co-starred. The film warranted a sequel, so Garner, Elam and Morgan returned for ***Support Your Local Gunfighter*** in 1970. Jack Elam was on a roll as he appeared in ***The Over the Hill Gang, Dirty Dingus McGee, The Cockeyed Cowboys of Calico County*** and ***Rio Lobo***, where he stole every scene he was in with the "Duke" himself, John Wayne.

John Wayne was no slouch either. Either he or someone in his camp realized that the "Duke" would have to up the ante in the violence department to stay viable, Wayne made a series of westerns from 1970 to 1973. ***Chisum, Rio Lobo, Big Jake, The Cowboys, The Train Robbers***, and ***Cahill: US Marshal. Big Jake*** may have been the most violent as a gang led by Richard Boone kidnap Big Jake's grandson after raiding his ranch and killing everyone in sight. This was the most violent film that Wayne ever did. In ***The Cowboys*** it is worth noting that Bruce Dern was the only guy who killed Wayne on screen (to this point). Wayne, obviously trying to cash in on Clint Eastwood's ***Dirty Harry*** success, did two "cop" films, ***McQ*** (1974) and ***Brannigan*** (1975). Both films failed as the public didn't buy an out of shape, toupee'd Wayne in a suit chasing crooks. Wayne returned to westerns in 1975 with ***Rooster Cogburn*** and ***The Shootist*** in 1976. Wayne passed away in 1979.

The Good Guys and The Bad Guys (1969), and ***Barquero*** (1970), were both filmed in parts of Colorado as veteran character actor, John Davis Chandler, appeared in both films. ***Good Guys and Bad Guys*** was directed by Burt Kennedy and costarred Robert Mitchum and George Kennedy as an aging lawman and outlaw. David Carradine is the outlaw leader and father, John Carradine also appears. ***Barquero*** costarred Lee Van Cleef, in between spaghetti westerns, and a manic Warren Oates. Co-starring Forrest Tucker as Mountain Phil, Oates's gang wipes out and loots a town and needs Van Cleef's barge to make their getaway. Van Cleef looked to be in great shape for a guy in his mid 40s. Oates as bad guy, Jake Remy, gives a completely over the top performance. Remy's gang is a who's who of character actors including John Davis Chandler, Kerwin Mathews, Armando Silvestri, Harry Lauter and Brad Weston. The film cashed in on Van Cleef's name as that was the last American western he appeared in before returning to Italy.

Welcome to Hard Times (1967), was a serious western directed by Burt Kennedy. The town of Hard Times is visited by The Man from Bodie, Aldo Ray in great performance as a psychotic outlaw. Ray kills a saloon girl, then half the cast, Lon Chaney, Elisha Cook, Fay Spain, before running off the sheriff (Henry Fonda), and burning down the town. Fonda urges the survivors to stay and rebuild. Keenan Wynn, Warren Oates, Royal Dano, John Anderson, Denver Pyle, Edgar Buchannan, and Janice Rule rebuild, but The Man is coming back and Fonda will have to face him or lose his town again. Great film loaded with good actors.

Clint Eastwood hung up his serape and returned to Hollywood in for ***Hang 'Em High*** in 1968. Clint is hung and left for dead by a posse who mistakenly thinks he murdered a rancher and stole his cattle. Clint survives and takes a job as a lawman so he can hunt down those responsible. The exceptional cast includes Ben Johnson, Pat Hingle, Inger Stevens, Bruce Dern, LQ Jones, Ed Bagley, Dennis Hopper, Alan Hale, Bob Steele and Charles McGraw. Eastwood continued with westerns: ***Coogan's Bluff, Two Mules for Sister Sara***, and ***Joe Kidd***. Then he directed and starred in ***High Plains Drifter, The Outlaw Josey Wales, Pale Rider*** and ***Unforgiven***. Eastwood became a 'macho' icon and one of the best American directors of all time.

By the early '80s westerns had sort of faded out and were replace by urban crime films. Similar plots prevailed as marauding Indians and bandits were replaced by street gangs and drug dealers. One film with Keifer Sutherland and Lou Diamond Phillips, ***Renegades***, was an urban remake of the Charles Bronson film, ***Red Sun***. Westerns would return with a vengeance with ***Young Guns, The Quick and the Dead, Unforgiven, Tombstone, Wyatt Earp, Open Range*** and others. The western will never die and has always found a home in the Grindhouse.

FROM FIVE STAR FILMS TO GRINDHOUSE ACTION:

Woody Strode

When you think of the first black action stars, I'm sure Jim Brown and Fred Williamson come to mind. But it wasn't them. Long before they ever graced a grindhouse screen, Woody Strode had already made an impact. Strode was born in 1914, he attended college at UCLA and starred on the UCLA Bruins football team with Jackie Robinson and Kenny Washington. Woody played for the LA Rams in 1946. He also played two seasons on the Calgary Stampeders of the Western Interprovincial Football Union in Canada where he was a member of Calgary's Grey Cup Championship Team before retiring in 1948 due to an injury.

In 1941, as a lot of former football players did, Strode tried his hand at professional wrestling. After the end of his football career, he wrestled part time until 1962, wrestling the likes of Gorgeous George and other big stars of that era, mainly in California. In 1952 he was wrestling every week, He was the Pacific Coast Heavyweight Wrestling Champion. He also teamed, at times, with Bobo Brazil and Bearcat Wright. He became close friends with Gorgeous George (George Wagner). Strode visited him in 1963, and was shocked at George's declining health. When more acting jobs came his way, Woody left wrestling for good.

In 1940 he married Luukialuana Kalaeloa, a descendant of the last Queen of Hawaii. Strode's film roles contrasted with the stereotypes of that era. He was nominated a Golden Globe award for his role in **Spartacus** opposite Kirk Douglas. He made his screen debut in **Sundown** in 1941. He was very active in the '50s as there were a bunch of "jungle" TV shows like **Ramar of the Jungle** and **Jungle Jim** with former Tarzan star, Johnny Weissmuller. He also was in the Monogram cheapie film series, **Bomba the Jungle Boy**. Other roles in the '50s were his dual role in the **Ten Commandments** where he played both an Ethiopian King and a slave. He was also the cowardly Private Franklin in **Porkchop Hill**. Other '50s films included **Bride of the Gorilla, The Lion Hunters, City Beneath the Sea, Jungle Gents, The Gambler from Natchez** and others.

Woody could "heel out "also as he played the villain in two **Tarzan** films. In 1958 he was opposite Gordon Scott in **Tarzan's Fight for Life**. In **Tarzan's Three Challenges** he played a dual role again as a dying leader of some small country and that leader's evil brother, opposite Jock Mahoney. He was also on the **Tarzan** TV series with Ron Ely in the '60s. Strode's stock rose dramatically when John Ford cast him in the lead role of **Sergeant Rutledge**, 1960. Rutledge was a cavalry sergeant accused of rape and murder. Strode and Ford became close friends. Strode appeared in minor roles in other Ford films: **The Man who Shot Liberty Valance, The Two Rode Together** and **Seven Women**. Ford preferred Strode's company over other actors. Strode became Ford's caretaker, sleeping on Ford's floor for a few months as Ford was dying from cancer. Strode stayed at his side until his death in 1973. Strode was considered for the role of Mr. Potts, the scout in **Major Dundee**. The director, Sam Peckinpah thought he looked too Indian and James Coburn got the part.

In 1966, Strode got the role that would establish him as a major star. And it was on that film he would meet a life-long friend who would graciously give him the rub that elevated Strode's stock as a major star. The film was *The Professionals*. Strode co-starred with Burt Lancaster, Robert Ryan, and Lee Marvin as four mercenaries hired to rescue a rich man's kidnapped wife. Marvin and Strode became fast friends and Marvin advised Strode not to wear a shirt, just a vest as Strode had a build that was impressive to say the least. When Strode was on screen, all eyes were on him and he stole the show from the established stars. Burt Lancaster, who was a very strong man, would challenge Woody to tests of strength, much to the amusement of Marvin. Lancaster lost every time and wasn't happy about it.

This role opened up more roles for Strode. In Sergio Leone's *Once Upon a Time in the West*, the original plan for the opening would have been extraordinary. Leone wanted *The Good, the Bad, and the Ugly* stars, Clint Eastwood, Lee Van Cleef, and Eli Wallach to be the gunmen waiting at the train station for Charles Bronson. Eastwood refused—in fact he was the only one of the three that refused, ending his shaky relationship with Leone. Leone changed the scene and it was Strode, legendary character actor, Jack Elam, and Al Mulock, who were waiting for Bronson.

Strode's brief role in that film opened the door to other Spaghetti Westerns and Italian crime films. In 1968 he did a film called *Sedvto Alla Sua Destra*, released here as *Black Jesus*. It was an unauthorized "biography" of African leader Patrice Lumumba. Strode got a lot of press on this film as the torture and interrogation is seen though his character's eyes. He appeared in 1969's *Che!* with Omar Sharif, Jack Palance, Frank Silvera, Sid Haig, and others. Then he was off to Europe.

Boot Hill was Strode's second Spaghetti Western with Terence Hill, Bud Spencer, Victor Buono, Lionel Stander and George Eastman. Strode was 2nd billed. *Boot Hill* was a huge hit at grind houses and Drive-Ins. Next was *The Unholy Four*, directed by Enzo Barboni, where again Strode was 2nd billed after Leonard Mann. *The Deserter*, 1971, was tailored for Bekim Fehmiu, who was being pushed as the next huge star. He wasn't. Co-directed by Niksa Fulgosi and Burt Kennedy, the film was a mess. To shore up their "star" Fehmiu, he was surrounded by a who's who of character actors. Strode, Richard Crenna, Chuck Connors, Slim Pickens, Ricardo Montelban, Albert Salmi and Ian Bannen were "The Bloodbath Brigade." Audiences couldn't buy Fehmiu as a star and the film tanked. A reviewer's quote on Fehmiu was that he had seem more vivid performances from driftwood.

The Last Rebel, 1971, was a spaghetti western designed to get former football player, Joe Namath over as a new star. It didn't. Even with veteran character actors, Strode, Jack Elam, and Ty Hardin holding Namath up, Joe didn't produce the box office magic his handlers hoped for. *The Revengers* (1972) tried to be a *Wild Bunch* clone with two of that film's stars, William Holden and Ernest Borgnine. Rancher Holden frees several convicts from a Mexican prison to help him track down the gang that murdered his family. Great action, but a shitty ending marred the film. Strode is one of the convicts that sides with Holden's character.

Fernando Deleo's *Italian Connection* teamed Strode with Henry Silva as two hit men dispatched from New York to kill a pimp who may have stolen some heroin. The two characters Strode and Silva played were the template for Tarantino's team of John Travolta and Samuel Jackson in *Pulp Fiction*. Strode returned to the states for *The Gatling Gun* (1972) with Robert Fuller, Guy Stockwell, and Barbra Luna. Fuller played against types as a bad guy who wanted to sell the gun to the Indians. Pat Butram, John Carradine, and Patrick Wayne rounded out the cast. Strode did a lot of TV movies and TV shows. *Key West*, a 1975 TV movie and the series *Manhunter*. He did another crime film for Deleo, *Colpo In Canna* (*Loaded Gun*) co-starring with Ursula Andress. *Winterhawk*, from director Charles Pierce was released in the westernless year of 1975, featured a Native American as the central figure in the film. It was a bold move for Pierce who had directed *Legend of Boggy Creek, The Town that Dreaded Sundown* and *The Evictors*. The film came and went quickly.

Strode had a small part in *Keoma*, 1976. More TV roles followed, then he appeared in Bud Cardos's classic horror film, *Kingdom of the Spiders*, with William Shatner. This was Strode's first foray into the horror/sci-fi genre. *The Ravagers*, 1979 was a post apocalyptic thriller with Richard Harris and Ernest Borgnine. *Jaguar Lives* 1979 was a kung fu film that had Strode as Sensei and co-starred Christopher Lee as the heavy. Strode roared into the '80s with roles both here and abroad. Cuba Crossing (1980) and *Scream* (1981) in the USA, Angkor Cambodian Express and Raiders of the Lost Gold 1982 abroad. Woody was never out of work and always in demand. Other than the occasional hit man, I can't remember Strode in any stereotypical roles like drug dealer or pimp. Woody was too good and too cool for roles like that.

Strode was featured in William Lustig's *Vigilante*, 1983, and *The Black Stallion Returns*. 1984 saw him return

to Italy for director Fernando DeLeo in *The Violent Breed,* in which again he co-starred with Henry Silva. *The Final Executioner* was another Euro lensed post apocalyptic thriller 1984's *Jungle Warriors* had Strode as drug lord Paul Smith's henchman. *Jungle Warriors* features a who's who of character actors including Marjoe Gortner, Alex Cord, Sybil Danning, and John Vernon. Next was *The Cotton Club*, then Paul Bartel's comedy western, *Lust in the Dust* (1985). *Lust* reunited Strode again with Henry Silva. More TV roles came Strode's way in 1987, *On Fire* and *A Gathering of Old Men*.

Strode's last few roles were *Storyville*, 1992, Mario Van Peebles western, *Posse* in 1993, and Sam Rami's *The Quick and the Dead,* 1995. Strode had small roles in these last few films. Strode had lung cancer and died on December 31st, 1994, before *The Quick and the Dead* was released. Strode left a huge legacy of work behind him. He was the most recognizable black actor in the world with a career that spanned over 50 years. He was known for playing quiet, dignified men of action. Be it a leading role or a small part, when Strode was on screen, he captivated the audience. Strode's personal quote was, "If you're a nice guy, you can walk into any room in the world." Woody Strode was more than just a nice guy; he was a world-class athlete, a gifted actor and a role model. Strode opened the door for more black actors to get better roles in film and television. Woody Strode is an American treasure, no matter how good or how bad a film was, Woody's presence made it better.

42P's Top 20 American Grindhouse Westerns

1. ***Young Fury,*** 1965. Juvenile Delinquents out west terrorize a town. Could be the template for ***Young Guns***. Bloody and violent for it's time with brawls and spurting blood. With Rory Calhoun, Virgina Mayo, Lon Chaney and John Agar.

2. ***Rio Conchos,*** 1964. Vengeance. crazed Richard Boone is killing every Apache in sight after he finds his family massacred. Boone chews the scenery in the action packed film. Boone and a Union officer, Stuart Whitman, his sergeant, Jim Brown in his first film role, and Anthony Franciosa must find a wagon load of stolen rifles before they are sold to the Apaches.

3. ***Vera Cruz***, 1954. Western icons, Gary Cooper and Burt Lancaster, are upstage by their gang of hungry up &comers Ernest Borgnine, Charles Bronson, Jack Elam, Jack Lambert and others.

4. ***The Magnificent Seven***, 1960. Called the last great American western, this film launched the careers of Charles Bronson, James Coburn, Steve McQueen and Robert Vaughn. It spawned three sequels and a TV series plus countless imitations and rip offs.

5. ***Hang 'Em High***, 1968. Clint Eastwood's much anticipated return to the screen in his first starring role in an American western after his three Leone films. Co-starring a who's who of familiar faces including Ben Johnson, Dennis Hopper, Alan Hale, Bruce Dern, Bob Steele, LQ Jones, Pat Hingle and Ed Bagley.

6. ***Ride the High Country***, 1962. Sam Peckinpah's western was the swan song for two western icons, Randolph Scott and Joel McCrea. It also established Peckinpah's stock company of actors Warren Oats, LQ Jones, RG Armstrong. And John Davis Chandler

7. ***Major Dundee,*** 1965. Rendered an almost incoherent mess by Columbia Pictures, this was Sam Peckinpah's first epic production. Sam's fights with producers on this film were legendary as he went way over budget. The bloodshed here was a omen of things to come.

8. ***The Wild Bunch***, 1969. The film that set the bar for things to come. Peckinpah's depiction of violence flatlined a lot of audiences. Originally denounced as violent trash, it is now recognized as one of the greatest films ever made. The slow-motion "dance of death" has been used in hundreds of films both here and around the world. A true groundbreaker in American films.

9. ***Support Your Local Sheriff***, 1969. A comedy western that pre-dates ***Blazing Saddles***. Drifter James Garner is made sheriff of a mining boomtown. The cast is a who's who of familiar faces with Harry Morgan, Walter Brennan, Gene Evans, Dick Peabody, Bruce Dern, and Jack Elam.

10. ***El Condor***, 1970. An American western filmed in Spain and made to look like a spaghetti western. An unusual role for Lee Van Cleef as he is very manic and crazy in this film. It was the first of three times he would costar with Jim Brown. Brown is an escaped convict who wants to rob the fortress of El Condor of millions in gold bars. Great action sequences and a cast including Patrick O'Neal, Elisha Cook, Jr., Iron Eyes Cody, Mariana Hill and spaghetti western regular, Ricardo Palacios.

11. ***There was a Crooked Man***, 1970. Kirk Douglas robs $500,000 from a private citizen and winds up in a territorial prison with Warren Oates, Burgess Meredith, Michael Blodgett, Hume Cronyn, John Randolph and C.K. Yang. He offers the boys a split if they help him escape. Warden Henry Fonda has other ideas.

12. ***Chato's Land***, 1972. Charles Bronson as Pardon Chato an Indian who killed a marshal in self defense. When the

posse rapes his woman, Chato picks them off one by one. Jack Palance, Richard Basehart, James Whitmore, Victor French, and Simon Oakland are the doomed posse.

13. ***High Plains Drifter***, 1973. Eastwood's first shot at directing is either a western or a ghost story depending on your point of view. A stranger rides into town, stirs things up, rallies the town's people against 3 returning convicts, then leaves the town to it's fate before riding back for vengeance. Seems the town watched it's sheriff get whipped to death by the gang and did nothing to help.

14. ***Barquero!*** 1970. Lee Van Cleef returned to the states for this film. Warren Oats and his gang has wiped out and looted a town and needs Van Cleef's barge to escape. Of course he intends to burn the barge to avoid pursuit. Van Cleef isn't down with this. Aided by Forrest Tucker as Mountain Phil, they give Oats and company more than they bargained for. Co-starring Kerwin Matthews, John Davis Chandler, Brad Weston, Armando Silvestri, and Mariette Hartley.

15. ***Big Jake***, 1971. "The Duke" ups the ante in the violence department with this one. Richard Boone's gang raids a ranch, killing almost everyone and kidnapping Jake's grandson. They want a ransom, but Big Jake wants them dead. A lot more violent than any other of Wayne's westerns. With real life son Patrick Wayne, Chris Mitchum, Glenn Corbett, Bruce Cabott, and Harry Cary Jr.

16. ***Ride in the Whirlwind***, 1965. Jack Nicholson wrote this low budget western directed by Monte Hellman. Three cowboys are mistakenly pursued by a posse thinking they are outlaws. Cameron Mitchell and Harry Dean Stanton costar. Look for Gary Kent's 1st stunt as he get shots off a stagecoach in the first few minutes of the film.

17. ***The Hunting Party,*** 1971. Oliver Reed kidnaps Candice Bergen, wife of sadistic rancher, Gene Hackman. She is a teacher and Ollie wants to learn how to read. Hackman and his friends hunt down the gang with high powered rifles in a ***Wild Bunch.*** inspired bloodbath. Hackman's character here was the template for his roles in ***Unforgiven*** and ***The Quick and the Dead***. Brutal and unrelenting. Co-starring Mitchell Ryan, Simon Oakland, LQ Jones, and William Watson.

18. ***The Long Riders***, 1980. Brilliant casting of three sets of real life brothers as the James Gang. Stacy and James Keach are Frank and Jesse James, David, Keith, and Robert Carradine are the Younger Brothers, and Dennis and Randy Quaid are the Miller brothers. One of the last of the great westerns until their resurgence many years later.

19. ***Pat Garrett and Billy the Kid***, 1973, was to be Peckinpah's last western. James Coburn is Garrett, Kris Kristofferson is Billy. The best part of this film was that Peckinpah cast just about every living, at that time, western character actor in the film: LQ Jones, Slim Pickens, Elisha Cook, Chill Willis, Jason Robards, Jack Elam, Richard Jaeckel, Barry Sullivan, RG Armstrong, Matt Clark, Luke Askew, Emilio Fernandez, Paul Fix and others.

20. ***The Wrath of God***, 1972. Turn-of-the-century western as three con men face a firing squad only to get a reprieve if they can kill a local despot. Robert Mitchum is Father Van Horne, a priest or grifter? Victor Buono is Jenning, a crook, and Ken Hutchison is Emmett an Irish gunman. Frank Langella is the crazed despot who hates priests. Buono shamelessly chews the scenery and is pretty agile for a guy his size. Mitchum is great as usual. Co-starring Rita Hayworth, in her last role, Gregory Sierra, and John Colicos.

Growing Up Drive-In: Humble Beginnings

by Ken Kish

Growing up in Cleveland, Ohio, I was one of the lucky kids who had a slew of drive-in theaters and a couple of indoor theaters within close proximity of the house I grew up in. And like most of the kids in my neighborhood, I had a father who was, well, by most standards, thrifty. While my mom would take us to see the usual kiddie crap matinee in the indoor theaters to beat the summer heat on occasion, Dad's idea of a family night out was either two dollar car load night at the drive-in or the infrequent visit to the one restaurant near by that gave cops a discount on their meals.

As a kid of five or six years old, my fondest memories of those drive-in excursions was the fact that dad used to let me pick—or at least let me think I was picking—the movies we saw. And as a kid of five or six years old, most of the time I chose them by how cool the ad in the newspaper was. You see, this was the late 1960s. And back in those days, the independent movie scene was flourishing. Unlike today, where me and my wife get all kinds of free passes to see movies and still toss nine out of ten of them in the trash, back in the "good ol' days" you could see all kinds of movies in theaters and drive-in's that weren't stale, unimaginative turds made by the foreign investors who own what's left of Hollywood these days.

In Cleveland circa 1969, we had adult theaters that played X-Rated adult films 24-7 just like the big grind houses in New York and Chicago. We had neighborhood cinemas, repertory theaters that screened classic silent films, even the local libraries used to screen 16mm film in their basements for, get this, FREE. In essence, before Hollywood bought up their competition so your only choice is drizzling cinema diarrhea geared towards a two-digit I.Q. we had choices. And thanks to my dad, I was able to see a ton of films that most parents would say I was way too young to be seeing at the time.

While my mom preferred taking us to movies like *The Sound of Music*, I preferred *The Good, The Bad, and The Ugly*, and so did my father. So when mom wanted to see some Disney crap like *Bedknobs and Broomsticks*, *Bonnie and Clyde* won out. *The Love Bug*? Not when *The Illustrated Man* was playing at the same drive-in. If my mom complained that two boys under the age of seven or eight should not be watching stuff like *For A Few Dollars* more, dad always told her, "It's only a movie" and us guys won out. It never mattered much anyway as mom and my brother would always fall asleep in the back seat by the time the second movie rolled around, so it was usually just me and my dad who got to see the second feature before I dozed off on the way home.

In 1973 we moved from the city of Cleveland to the West side suburbs and that's when things really took off as far as my movie going went. I quickly found a movie loving friend in my buddy Tom that like myself, was bigger than the rest of our fourth grade classmates, and we rarely got stopped going to see any film we wanted to see no matter what actual rating it got. And when we did, his mom had the same "it's only a movie" thinking that my dad had, and she'd simply buy us a ticket and walk us to the guy who ripped the tickets in half and drop us off.

The little town we moved to in 1973 had it's own giant theatre that was built in the 1930s, and the suburbs had several independent theaters we could bus or bike to. And we did. Pretty much every weekend we caught a couple of films in air conditioned comfort, and since this was a time when as a kid, you pretty much left in the morning and came home when the street lights turned on without anybody actually wondering what you were up to, you could sit and watch movies all day if you wanted to. If it were a rainy day for instance, we'd just hop from theatre to theatre watching movies all day long. It was heaven for pre-teen B movie fans to say the least.

I also learned at an early age that you really didn't need a car to sneak into certain drive-ins with no troubles. Again, this was a time when you'd just tell you parents you were sleeping over a friend's house, or camping in the woods down the street, and nobody ever questioned us further about what we were planning to do. In hindsight, it was both a blessing and a curse, as I started pretty much every bad habit I've ever had by the age of thirteen and a few of them have taken me years to kick. But I digress. This isn't about the many "lost weekends" of my young adult life, but how I was able to watch so many incredibly cool films at an early age before Hollywood's collective autism shit all over anything people would consider even remotely original or worth paying to see these past twenty years.

We had a couple of single screen drive-in theaters around town, and I had friends that lived near them. As young teens, we'd simply ride our bikes to the back of the theaters, park, and sit on the back wall or back hill. Turn up all the speakers in the back two rows and instant free movie nights! And by the age of thirteen or fourteen, it wasn't any harder to score a six or twelve pack of beer to polish off while enjoying your free double features as it was to score a pack of Camels to smoke while drinking those beers. Beers made the bike ride home
more fun too. And other than occasionally being chased by a drive-in employee into the woods for a few minutes before we crept back to our favorite viewing point, nobody thought to ask what we were up to or where we disappeared to after dark.

While also in my early teens, I had a few friends that were a little older than I was who could drive. I could score beer and they could drive, so it was a match made in heaven as I no longer had to sit on the ground in the weather to watch B-movies at the drive-in. And unlike today, slowly cruising around with a case of beer in the back seat and a quarter pound of God's flowers under the driver's seat with a couple buddies was what we did to kill a night with nothing to do. We weren't hurting anything or looking for trouble. Just cruising around listening to the radio since this was also before companies like Clear Channel ruined radio from coast to coast. The world wasn't such a pussy ass uptight shit hole ruined by lawyers, deregulation, and right wing douche bags like it is today. These days I'd rather drive around in silence than turn on the radio.

My dad thought teaching your kid to drive as soon as he could look over the steering wheel was the thing a father and son did, so I knew how to drive long before most of the kids my age did. At the age of fifteen I had my temporary driving paper that allowed you to drive with a licensed driver in the car, but to my dad, it seemed silly to be with me since he knew I knew how to drive. He used to just give me the car keys and tell me "if you get busted, you'll never drive my car ever again…and put some fucking gas in it if you plan on just cruising around" and off I went. Got my driver's license as soon as I could and just like every other teenager, discovered girls. Nothing better than having your driver's license, being able to score beer, and hitting the drive-in with a girl next to you.

In the days between hitting up the drive-ins with friends that could drive, to the day I got my driver's license, I frequented every drive-in around Cleveland on a regular basis until the drive-ins started to slowly die off in the 1980s. By that time I accumulated quite a few drive-in adventures. Some good. Some bad. Some I didn't even remember until somebody told me what happened. I've had a handful of those "why is the car parked in the middle of the neighbor's front lawn" moments in my life. Shit, as they say, happens.

Next time I write up something for *Grindhouse Purgatory*, I'll revisit a few of my favorite drive-in stories. Or maybe I'll revisit stories centered around some of my favorite drive-ins? Since some of them are still around, I might even give a couple people a call so they can remind me exactly how I wound up forty miles from the drive-in passed out on a picnic table in a strangers back yard just to see if they can piece some of the shit I got into as a kid together for me? Then again, maybe they don't remember either. Acid was still pretty damn good back in the late '70s and early '80s.

Good, bad, or indifferent, I'm just going to call it growing up drive-in and leave it at that.

The Winged Serpent Rules

By Bill Adcock

Larry Cohen. Holy crow, you wanna talk about an underappreciated hero of horror cinema, let's talk Larry Cohen. For my money, Cohen has knocked it out of the park on more films then Wes Craven and Tobe Hooper put together. Even if he'd done nothing else besides *It's Alive* and *God Told Me To,* I think he'd still warrant a major spot in discussions of horror cinema. But Cohen didn't stop there; with two sequels to *It's Alive, Maniac Cop* and its two sequels, the amazing *The Stuff* (which is, in my eyes, a better satire on American consumerism then *Dawn Of The Dead*) and one of my personal favorites of the bunch, 1982's *Q: The Winged Serpent.* I've got a lot of love for this film, and not just because I'm a monster kid and a stop-motion animation geek. I think it's a very strong film overall, despite being overshadowed by the more overt social commentary in *It's Alive* and *The Stuff.*

Q weaves a number of individually-solid storylines into one very well-put together over-arcing tale. First, you have two cops, Detective Shepard and Sgt. Powell (David Carradine and Richard Roundtree, respectively—Kwai Chang Caine and Shaft, bitches!) investigating a series of unusual homicides around New York City in which the victim is found skinned, apparently while still alive. Secondly, another series of apparent homicides is going on simultaneously around the city, always in high places—a window—washer is decapitated, a rooftop sunbather snatched up by something unseen, etc.

Shepard begins to suspect these two killing sprees are related —he notes the religious significance of the skinned bodies in pre-Catholic Central American belief, and comes to the conclusion that some ancient god or monster (and he struggles to determine what the difference is between the two—something Cohen had previously explored in *God Told Me To*) has been awoken or summoned by the sacrifices offered, and is now feeding off of New Yorkers. Reading up on the subject of Mesoamerican mythology, Shepard settles on Quetzalcoatl, the Feathered Serpent God, as the likeliest culprit.

Meanwhile, the third plot arc weaves through all this, that of Jimmy Quinn (Michael Moriarty), a fumbling, paranoid jazz pianist-turned-thief who has just botched a diamond heist, losing $77,000 worth of diamonds under a truck. Fleeing from his enraged co-conspirators, he finds himself in the dome of the Chrysler building, where something has torn a very large hole in the side and, in a nest of twisted girders, laid a very large egg. Now Jimmy is trying to use the knowledge of where the creature is lairing to leverage amnesty and a big cash payout for himself, but he's getting chased down from two sides—from Shepard on one, and from Quetzalcoatl's skin-happy priest on the other.

As I get older, I find myself appreciating good writing and editing in a movie over anything else. I don't give a shit about blood and gore, and naked titties don't make a movie "good" in my estimation any more. But give me a writer/director who cares about telling a good story and telling it well, and I'll go to the ends of the earth to see it. While it's received a lot of crap from critics, for my money *Q: The Winged Serpent* is a damned good film. I really like the blending of the gritty police procedural elements with the monster-on-the-loose plot, I really like the interactions between the characters, the performances the actors give…everything on display here is, to me, top-notch, and this film should rightfully be a feather in Larry Cohen's cap.

The different plot – threads weave together organically here, forming a unified whole with nothing feeling shoehorned in or forced, which is more then I can say for any Hollywood release I've seen lately.

I thought the casting here was really top-notch as well. The three leads of Carradine, Roundtree and Moriarty have a really great rapport and having watched the film a number of times now, I can't think of anyone I'd rather see in these roles. David Carradine especially – he really excels here as the somewhat world-weary detective Shepard, and it makes me wish he'd had more opportunities to play **Dirty Harry**-style independent-minded cops. That's maybe a misnomer; while cynical and acid-tongued, Carradine's portrayal of Shepard lacks the bitterness of Eastwood's loose cannon cop, instead carrying a philosophical detachment that nobody but David Carradine could have brought to the role.

The animosity between Roundtree's character and Moriarty's character here was a real winner for me as well. There's clearly a racial element (Roundtree being black, of course, and being John Shaft above and beyond that) to their mutual antagonism but it's overlaid with a very 1970s-ish distrust for authority and rage directed towards "The Man," which Roundtree represents here (compare to Quetzalcoatl knows **how** many movies from the preceding decade pit a black protagonist against "The Man"!). When Quinn is brought in for questioning, Roundtree plays "bad cop" to the hilt, questioning Quinn's sexuality (suggesting Quinn might want to go back to prison as he misses the sodomy) and alternating between abusing – physically and mentally – and patronizing him. It's not hard to see why Quinn needs to be physically restrained from attacking Powell at one point, especially when Quinn notes that his first stint in jail was due to a crooked cop planting cocaine on him to get a conviction.

Completing the cast is David Allen's beautiful stop-motion Quetzalcoatl. For my money, Allen was second only to Harryhausen in his ability to bring stop-motion creatures to life, and Quetzalcoatl is one of his best. Eschewing more traditional Aztec designs of snakes covered in feathers, Allen's Quetzalcoatl more closely resembles a European dragon, albeit a stripped down one—no horns, no line of spikes down its back, no giant teeth, no giant armored scales, just giant wings and a deeply-keeled chest like a bird's; Quetzalcoatl here looks like something that could actually fly.

One last thing I love about this film and then I'll wrap this up—the fucking poster art has been preserved. In this miserable day and age of great poster art being a thing of the past and DVD/Blu-Ray covers being 2–minute hack Photoshop jobs completely lacking in inspiration or enthusiasm to entice the viewer to see the damn film, it's a miracle that Boris Vallejo's poster art for ***Q: The Winged Serpent*** was used for the 2003 Anchor Bay DVD release and the 2013 Scream Factory Blu-Ray. It's a beautiful piece, even if Vallejo's not my first choice of artists, and I love that I can take the DVD off my shelf and enjoy the poster art for a moment before I pop the DVD in the player. There's so many films I love that I can't say that about any more.

All in all, I think ***Q: The Winged Serpent*** is a damned fine piece of cinema and one more people should check out. Fusing gritty cop drama to monster rampage action in a way few films before or since can claim to have done, it's a smart, stylish film with a couple really solid performances, sharp writing, and a good looking monster. I can't ask for much more than that.

The Bloody Story of East Coast Indie Wrestling

The end of ECW came in the early 2000s. The niche promotion that started in the '90s was dead. Both the WWE and WCW not only copied ECW, but took most of its roster as well. The fabled ECW arena, on the corner of Swanson & Ricter in South Philly was empty, but it wouldn't be for long. There were a bunch of upstart indie companies that wanted to be the next ECW.

Jersey All Pro Wrestling started as ECW was still hot. Run out of Bayone, NJ, three money marks ran it. They also had a yearly convention in hotels were they would bring in a few big names like Stone Cold Steve Austin and Abdulla the Butcher. They would run a wrestling card the same night in the hotel. It was hard to stay in a hotel when you had Abdulla and his opponent bleeding all over a white-carpeted area. They were kicked out of that hotel.

They had another convention at The Crown Plaza in Secaucus, NJ. They had the Four Horsemen and Randy Savage signing autographs. Being I was a fan of the Horsemen, I wanted to go. I ran into a friend who asked me if I was coming back for the wrestling later that night. I had only been to one indie show in my life and it sucked. But I was talked into coming back. The show was held in the hotel ballroom. The main event was to be a cage match.

Before the show opened, a guy known as Fat Frank addressed the crowd. He screamed that if violence, blood and cursing offended anyone, they should get the fuck out of here now. Ok, now I was interested. These guys went out and really beat the crap out of each other. A wrestler called Homicide, who would go on to ROH and TNA, was wrestling a guy in the cage. ECW star and legit tough guy, New Jack stormed the ring and sliced up Homicide with the help of ECW stablemate, Jason Knight. The JAPW locker room ran in, but the two ECW guys escaped. Next match was a four way in the cage with barbed wire, mousetraps and other weapons. The finale was the debut of Low Life Louie Ramos, former Referee turned wrestler, against New Jack. The blood flowed like water.

JAPW ran a monthly show in Bayone at an abandon supermarket. Cultivating home grown talent and bringing in the occasional "name", the place was packed. Violence was the rule as chairs, bats, cheese graters, even a machete, were used by the wrestlers.

A Christmas Show featured a Xmas Tree Deathmatch where presents under the tree in the ring contained weapons. It was only a matter of time before the shit would hit the fan as this was brought to the attention of the authorities.

Someone talked to Senator Joseph Doria from Bayone about the carnage going on in his own backyard. Tapes were also sent to then NJ Govenor Christie Whitman. JAPW and another group, Combat Zone Wrestling, were singled out. Both groups lost the buildings they operated out of. CZW, which I will discuss here, moved to The ECW Arena in South Philly. JAPW moved from building to building. The stopped the blood letting and adopted a stronger style of wrestling, more hard hitting with the emphasis on athleticism and brawling. They had a huge and loyal fan

base, drawing close to 2000 to shows. They would eventually fuck that up.

Ian Rotten was one half of Bad Breed, a tag team with his "brother", Axel Rotton. In ECW, the Rottens had a falling out which led to a series of matches starting with the first barbed wire bat match and ending with a Taipei Death Match. Axel left ECW with hopes of getting into the WWE. Ian stayed, but shitty payoffs and heat with the owner of ECW made him decide to leave. Ian started his own promotion, the IWA. Low rent would describe it. Ian ran in areas with no state athletic commission to deal with. He also started using light tubes, barbed wire and even fire in his matches. About this time a wrestler calling himself Mad Man Pondo contacted Ian. Pondo was a fan of this violent stuff and offered Ian $300 to do a barbed wire bat match. Ian refused at first, then agreed to do a barbed wire strap match. Every time Pondo was hit with the strap, he would blade himself. Blading, getting 'color', juicing, gigging, all meant the same thing: one wrestler would cut himself, drawing blood, sometimes lots of it. Some wrestlers would take aspirins or liquor to thin the blood and make it flow more.

Ian finally said enough and agreed to train Pondo. Pondo and Rotten had a series of bloodbaths. One of them came up with a Four Corners of Pain Match. In each corner of the ring was something that could cut you: Light Tubes, staple guns, mouse traps and barbed wire. The first was held at a truckstop in NJ. Both men were bloody messes. The show was promoted by NWA promoter Dennis Corluzzo, who decided not to advertise it fearing it would get shutdown. Ian was really pissed at Corluzzo and, as far as I know, never dealt with him again. Rotten decided to have a King of the Death Match Tournament. Having seen the epic one held in Japan culminating with Terry Funk vs. Cactus Jack in an Exploding Ring Match, Rotten's would be more violent.

The first KOTDM was low rent at best. Using his local crew and bringing in Axel Rotten and Balls Mahoney, it was a two day blood feast. Light tubes, barbed wire boards, etc. were all part of the fun. But shit could go sour and it did. On one show, a wrestler was badly burned. During a Pondo vs. Mean Mitch Page match, Pondo hit Page with a clock he found at a garage sale. Half of Page's face was sliced open. During a fans bring the weapons match with Ian vs. Corporal Robinson, Robinson's head was cut so deep that it hit an artery and blood spewed into the crowd. Robinson almost died that night. During a light tube match between Pondo and Necro Butcher, Necro's arm was cut right down to the bone. The most infamous incident between Pondo and Rotten was on a CZW show. Pondo sliced Rotten's forehead down to the bone with a pair of scissors. Supposedly Pondo was given the wrong scissors and didn't know it wasn't the dulled pair. Rotten lost his shit and sliced Pondo's arm open with them. This incident created a problem between CZW owner, John Zandig and Rotten. Rotten said that Zandig made bank on that match, but never even called him to see if he was alright or chip in for medical bills. This would be used later as an angle that actually fooled the fans.

IWA had a loyal fan base and the gore fests kept them coming back. Ian would bring in talent like Jerry Lynn, Eddie Gurrero, Chris Candido and others to offset the violence. Ian came up with a Strong Style Tournament. This

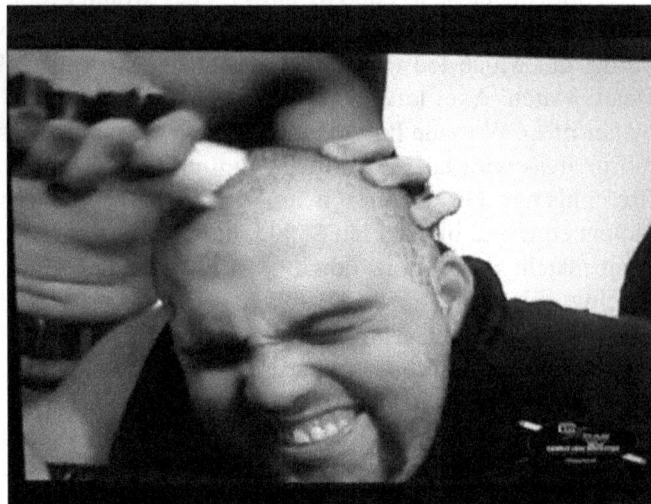

featured stiff, hard-hitting wrestling. Guys like Homicide, AJ Styles, B. Boy, Lo Ki, and others were brought in. The King of the Death Matches was their "wrestle mania" and the two day event started to feature real wrestling in between the bloodshed.

Combat Zone Wrestling was the brainchild of John Zandig. Zandig had been on the indie circuit as The Icon and, according to rumors, tried to get in ECW during the company's waning days. In 1999, Zandig and five of his students started running shows in South Jersey. The students were Lobo, Nick Gage, Justice Pain, TCK, and Ric Blade. Blade had a martial arts background and Lobo worked with Zandig outside of wrestling. Head trainer, Jon Dahmer was also on the roster as were local indie wrestlers Wifebeater, Rockin Rebel, The Backseat Boys, the SATs, the Brisco Brothers, Sick Nick Mondo and more.

Their brand of wrestling was called "Ultraviolence." Running out of The Champs Arena in South Jersey, CZW used barbed wire, glass, fire, cactus, light tubes, and even a weed whacker in their matches. Like IWA, CZW had some decent wrestling between the violence. But like JAPW, they incurred the wrath of NJ officials. Where JAPW toned it down, CZW said, "fuck you." They had "Fuck Christie Whitman" t-shirts printed up. They flipped off the state, but the state would contact the building and the towns. Rather than change, CZW moved to the ECW Arena in South Philly. JAPW's Fat Frank took a shot at Zandig during an interview. He came out with a weed whacker and said he didn't need this kind of shit to get over.

CZW's first arena show was ***Cage of Death 3***, their "Wrestlemania." The main event was Justice Pain vs. Wifebeater in a cage full of weapons. Wifebeater was one of the most popular wrestlers in CZW. He could take inhuman amounts of punishment, but could also dish it out. His weapon of choice was the weed whacker. There was a weird ending to this match. After taking a nasty bump off the top of the cage, which injured Wifebeater's shoulder, the lights went out. When they came on, ECW star The Sandman was in the ring. Obviously drunk, he couldn't remember the names of the two wrestlers who had just fought. Lights out again, then three other ECW alumni, Tod Gordon, Pitbull Gary Wolfe, and Rocko Rock were in the ring. They jumped The Sandman, then the CZW locker room ran them off. It was supposed to say ECW was out, CZW was in, but it was confusing and failed miserably.

CZW did have really good wrestling in between the violence. They ran a tournament called Best of the Best that featured junior heavy weights from all over the world. Each show was a great mix of brawling, gimmicks, and real wrestling. CZW cut a deal with a Japanese promotion called Big Japan. Big Japan specialized in Death Matches. From 2000 to 2001 they traded talent as Zandig, Wifebeater, Nick Gage, The Backseat Boys, Mad Man Pondo, Justice Pain, Ruckus and others had accompany vs. company feud. Japanese wrestler Jun Kasai joined the CZW team. In a match that would be called Un FN Believable in Delaware, Kasai was crucified, bombed into a pile of light tubes, slashing his elbow right down to the bone. He taped up the wound and continued the match.

During the Wifebeater vs. Ryuji Yamakawa match a spot was called for Wifebeater to put Yamakawa through a table at ringside. There were communication difficulties as Wifebeater pleaded that they shouldn't do the spot. Yamakawa insisted and the move ended his career. Unlike the tables used here, the Japanese tables were solid and hard to break. When Yamakawa hit the table, it slipped and his head hit the floor full force. He never wrestled again. After an "exploding panes of glass" match between Zandig and Japanese Death Match Legend, Mitsuhiro "Mr Danger" Matsunaga, the deal between the two companies imploded. No reason was given and the CZW crew left, except Mad Man Pondo. Pondo cut a deal to stay and was no longer welcome in CZW.

CZW ran a lot of different angles like takeovers from within as Lobo formed an army to oust Zandig and take over the company. But something else was going down that would change the face of wrestling in South Philly. At the time, three promotions were running out of The Arena: CZW, 3PW, and Ring of Honor. Occasionally JAPW would run a show there also. Ring of Honor was run by RF Video's Rob Feinstein and Doug Gentry with Gabe Sapolsky, who had worked for ECW. 3PW was run by former porn queen Jasmine Saint Clair and former ECW star, The Blue Meanie. The three groups co existed and used some of the same talent. Enter Rob Black's XPW.

Xtreme Professional Wrestling was a California company owned by porn czar, Rob Black. Black's Extreme Associates produced some of the most vile porn ever committed to video. His wrestling mirrored his porn as it took the worst elements of ECW, CZW, and Big Japan. Poorly trained wrestlers rolled around in broken glass, barbed wire, and raw sewerage. Ex ECW wrestlers, who had drug or other problems found work here. When ECW folded, Shane Douglas, Chris Candido, Sabu, New Jack, Chris Hammerick and others joined XPW. XPW wanted to run in South Philly. They also wanted to buy the Arena.

Rob Black offered to buy the building for $60K and was given the lease. CZW had made a counter offer, but it was turned down. CZW and ROH moved to building down the street. CZW mainstay, Justice Pain jumped to XPW. CZW and XPW ran shows on the same day. CZW had a packed house. XPW tanked. Even with former ECW stars on the card, the show only drew a couple hundred fans. Now here the big rumor I have heard from quite a few people who have inside information. Shane Douglas was to wrestle Terry Funk at the Arena. CZW, ROH, and 3PW wanted XPW gone. It seems the three groups paid Terry Funk to slice open his arm with a broken bottle on camera. This footage was sent to the PA State athletic Commission. Hearings were held. Shane Douglas was incensed by Funk's betrayal. After the hearings a ruling was made: No more light tubes, barbed wire, glass etc. To add more fuel to the fire, Jasmin St. Claire, who had done porn for Rob Black, spread a rumor that Black was using the Arena to warehouse porn.

XPW left and folded in 2003. The owners were indicted for sending obscene material through the mail by a federal prosecutor. Former XPW star, The Messiah, had joined CZW before this feud started. The Messiah was attacked in his home by two thugs who cut off one of his fingers. Messiah was said to have had an affair with Rob Black's wife, porn queen Lizzie Borden. This attack became national news. Messiah cut a promo at a CZW show, holding up his damaged hand and screaming "next time have the balls to do it yourself because your guys didn't get the job done." A huge "Fuck Rob Black!" chant started in the packed building.

CZW returned to the building, but didn't realize they had shot themselves in the foot. The ruling they used to get rid of XPW also applied to them and anyone else running shows in PA. Ironically Shane Douglas would be instrumental in getting the ban lifted. Shane promoted an ECW reunion show called Hardcore Homecoming. I attended this show, as I was huge ECW fan. The main event was to be a replay of the match that put ECW on the map. It was the original Three Way Dance with Douglas, Terry Funk and Sabu. Terry Funk came out before the match and said that we want to make tonight special, so give us a minute to get wired. I thought, "He can't mean what I think he means." The ring crew started taking down the ropes and stringing up barbed wire. The official from the PA State Athletic Commission stopped them. Story was the Douglas walked up to him with checkbook in hand and said how much is the fine because this match will happen either way. Rather than risk the over 2000 fans in attendance rioting, they backed off.

CZW ran several take over angles where Zandig would lose control of the company. Zandig decided to have his own Death Match show. The Tournament of Death was held in a bar's parking lot some place in Delaware. Barbed wire boards, staple guns, and mousetraps, light tubes, etc. Nate Hatred, Adam Flash Wife Beater, Homeless Jimmy, Sick Nick Mondo, Zandig and The Necro Butcher spilled the sauce. A highlight was Sick Nick Mondo power bombing Homeless Jimmy off the back of a truck through a pyramid of light tubes and tables. Wife Beater won over Sick Nick in a 200 light tube match.

One of the best angles was an invasion by IWA. Booker Mike Burns set the angle up using the real life animosity between Ian Rotten and John Zandig. Rotten, Corporal Robinson, and JC Bailey stormed the ring at a CZW show. They tied up Zandig and stapled dollar bills to him. The CZW locker room was locked, so the wrestlers couldn't come to his aid. They honestly weren't alerted to the angle. The fans rioted, pelting the IWA wrestlers with everything, including chairs. The stage was set for the summer of 2003. The two groups would exchange talent. CZW's Tournament of Death had five IWA wrestlers and three CZW wrestlers. In the semi finals, Zandig and Sick Nick were on the roof of the bar, swinging light tubes at each other. The finish was that Zandig would power bomb Mondo through a stack of tables from the roof. It was a forty. foot drop. They overshot their mark and Mondo not only broke his wrist in three places, but cut an artery in his back. He was taped up and finished the tournament, beating Ian Rotten in the finals. Mondo credited Rotten for walking him though the match.

IWA's King of the Death Matches had CZW stars and other wrestlers on the card. It was a 2-day fan's wet dream as Indie stars Homicide, Sonjay Dutt, Jimmy Jacobs, Balls Mahoney, Toby Klein, Matt Cross, and others were featured. In the semi finals, Mad Man Pondo beat Nick Gage in what Balls Mahoney called "the sickest bump I have ever seen." Pondo won, beating JC Baily in a Steel Cage House of Horrors Death Match. The feud ended at a CZW outdoor show where Zandig beat Ian Rotten in an electrified steel cage match.

Things went well for CZW until Cage of Death 7. Wrestler Chris Hero cut a promo challenging Ring of Honor star, Bryan Danielson to a match. Zandig was furious backstage as he wasn't told about the deal. Zandig didn't not want to work with Ring of Honor. A shouting match with Mike Pancoast, who's company was responsible for logos and production, ended with Zandig throwing Pancoast down a flight of stairs. Zandig was really pissed at his booker, Mike Burns, for not coming to him with the ROH deal, which never happened. CZW continued to thrive, running monthly show at the arena. With the ban on weapons lifted, except for light tubes, The Cage of Death Shows became more elaborate.

The team of Justice Pain and Nick Gage were out of control for real. They started really hurting guys. Management wanted to teach then a lesson. They brought in Necro Butcher and Mr. Insanity Toby Klein, known as the Tough, Crazy Bastards. They were told not to holdback on Pain & Gage. Necro had wrestled Samoa Joe on the afternoon card and was pretty banged up. But the TCB beat the living shit out of Pain & Gage. Gage was having a run of real bad luck. During a Tournament of Death Match, he was set on fire and badly burned. A huge weapons match between him and Justice Pain was stopped when Gage broke his collarbone two minutes into the match. The Psycho Shooter, Drake Younger took his place. During another TOD Match, 200 light tubes around the ring against Thumbtack Jack, Gage crashed though the tubes and severed an artery under his arm. He had to be air lifted out for medical treatment. A drugged out Gage robbed a bank in South Jersey for $3000. Fans actually turned him in after seeing his face on the security camera. Nick is currently serving a five-year sentence.

Zandig, however, was not doing well. One of the shows, where he was booked in the main event, had him substitute Trent Acid as he had to go work a part time job to pay his bills. In 2009 he announced he was stepping down due to financial reasons and injuries. He sold the company to wrestler DJ Hyde. One of the main problems wrestling the hardcore style was that it shortened careers. Most of the guys who started with CZW, Ric Blade, Mondo, Wife Beater, Lobo and others were long gone before the sale of the company. CZW is still viable today but with an entirely different roster.

My involvement with wrestling was accidental. Crowbar, a local wrestler who had worked for ECW, WCW, TNA and others, was having a benefit for wrestler Sabu, who had been hospitalized for months with no insurance. I bought a ticket, then noticed they were having an auction to raise money for Sabu. I contacted Crowbar and volunteered to do the auction as I had experience doing them for a couple of conventions. He took me up on the offer. I got there early and much to my surprise, Sabu was there. I talked to him for quite a bit and he was super cool. I did the auction, putting a lot of humor in it. The wrestlers seemed to appreciate what I did. It was the last time I paid to get into a show.

I had become friendly with the guys at RF Video. I was a long time customer. After Rob Feinstein and Doug Gentry lost Ring of Honor, they started or fronted for another promotion, Pro Wrestling Elite. They asked me to work security, which I did. Doug had a real flair for booking matches. They brought in talent like AJ Styles, Homicide, Steve 'Monsta' Mack, EC Negro, Sabu, Mana, and others. But there were problems. The first show, the building was called. Someone didn't want the show to run and told a bunch of lies. When we got to the building, we were told we couldn't run there. A deal was cut with a run down movie theater around the corner. We ran the show there. A couple of hundred fans showed up.

The main event was Sabu vs. Mana, but Sabu missed his flight. Tommy Dreamer, former ECW star was called up and agreed to substitute. During that match, Doug grabbed me and told me Sabu had just showed up and was changing in his car. We had to hold the crowd, so the Tomeselli Brothers attacked Harry Smith and were beating him down until Sabu ran in. Mana, bloodied from his match with Dreamer, threw a chair from a balcony at Sabu. The two brawled all over the building. The fans loved it.

The 2nd show, although loaded with talent, flopped. Two other shows were running within 50 miles the same night. It killed attendance and the backer pulled out after that show. I wound up driving the 350 lb. Samoan, Mana to get some Gator Aid. Mana was from New Zealand and was a humble guy. He could really wrestle, but fell into the trap of doing hardcore matches. He was really pissed when the WWE took his face paint gimmick and put it on one of their guys. He was a super nice guy, but is now paralyzed from the sternum down from all the punishment he took.

Doug and Rob were offered a booking job for another group, Pro Wrestling Xplosion. Run by former Atlas Security head, Ronnie Lang, who struck me as an arrogant prick, the first show was to be at The Arena. Lang had a problem: he wanted some of his old ECW friends on it, specifically The Dudley Boyz. The Dudleys were big stars at this point and wanted big $$. Rob told Lang not to do it, but it was done despite Rob's warning that it wasn't worth the price. That and the fact the show was run on an off night, lost money.

Lang ran a 2nd show, somewhere in East Buttfuck, Long Island. It took us three hours to find the place. We arrived to find Doug puking his guts out in the parking lot. He thought he had the flu. He even called me up to apologize for not socializing. The card was ok, but Doug wasn't. Doug was hospitalized with endocarditis, bacteria in the heart. Doug passed away at age 33. I went to the funeral. For all Doug had done for the business and for the wrestlers, maybe twenty guys showed up. I realized something after this, the mentality of a lot of people is "it's not what you have done for me in the past, it's what are you going to do for me today." In my estimation, that kind of thinking sucks.

Cyberspace Wrestling was former wrestler Billy Firehawk's promotion. It ran out of a PAL building in Wayne NJ. Firehawk would book big names like Jeff Jarrett, America's Most Wanted, Chris Candido, Rhyno, April Hunter, Lex Luger, Abyss, Sonjay Dutt and others on the card. Firehawk had a build like Abdulla the Butcher and would get involved in matches. People crapped on him all over the Internet for that. But he seemed to be having fun and always asked the fans what they would like to see.

He did, however, push the envelope. A series of Abyss vs. Mana matches spun out of control. They brawled though the crowd, using chairs, chains, staple guns and thumbtacks. Abyss hit Mana so hard with a chair that it actually shattered. They did a sick spot on a scaffold where Mana went though a pile of tables. Someone started calling the town about the goings on at Cyberspace Shows. During a feud between Slick Wagoner Brown and Rodney Mack, Mack's real life wife, ECW wrestler Jazz, hit Slick with her car in the parking lot. After this, and a couple of brawls that wound up outside the building, Firehawk lost the venue. He tried two other buildings, but someone from a rival promotion, National Wrestling Superstars, kept calling the towns about how out of control Cyberspace shows were. They didn't help themselves when they tried to use fire during an angle. Firehawk's goal was to go national. It would never happen. In 2006 he was hospitalized for pancreatitis. He died from complications arising from diabetes at age 40.

3PW was owned by Jasmin St. Claire and The Blue Meanie who were a couple at that point. They used former ECW talent and brought in big names like Bam Ban Bigelow, Abdulla, X. Pac, Terry Funk, Jerry Lawler and others. The shows were good; they even had Zandig and Wife Beater vs. Sandman and Raven. Raven never even got in the ring, he had Jack Victory 2nd him and he stayed on the mike though out the match. It was entertaining to say the least. True to form, Jasmin disappeared, leaving The Blue Meanie to deal with the fallout. The Rockin Rebel and Jack Victory rallied the locker room to save the show. That was the last show 3PW would run.

Lots of one-shot promotions would pop up. UXW ran on Long Island and had cards that ran 8 hours. Reason for that was the first few matches were "ticket sellers", untrained guys who sold tickets for the promotion so they could appear in the ring. After a few nasty accidents and a near death, UXW relocated to Florida. WSU, Wrestling Superstars Unleashed, was run by Jack Sabbott, not his real name. Jack had a habit of building up shows, then canceling them when the money wasn't coming in. He used a guy, Sean "The MiC" Macaffery to book his shows. The MiC ran one of the most out of control Indy wrestling websites, The DOI. He learned how to book matches from running UXW shows.

When Sabbott bailed on an all women's show, The MiC stepped in and took over. It was supposed to be a one shot deal, but impressed with the hard work the girls did, he decided to keep it going. I knew The MiC from hanging out at JAPW and other shows. He asked me to work security. I said doesn't women's wrestling suck in general? He said give this one a chance. So I agreed to do it and the show was held at Gino Caruso's Wrestling School in Lake Hiawatha NJ. Little did I know that show would be a pivotal moment for the company.

Some of the wrestlers with WSU were Mercedes Martinez, Cindy Rodgers, Angel Orsini, Pryme Tyme Amy Lee, Jana, Nikki Roxx, and Champion Alicia. Luna Vachon came in to team with Amy Lee as Satan's Sisters. They were to face a very green team, The Diva Killazs. Luna and Amy laid the match out to The Diva Killers. Luna told them do not go near my neck. The two didn't listen and went right for Luna's neck. Luna beat the crap out of one of them and was really pissed. Amy tagged in and told them to take it down a notch. She got kicked in her bad ear and that was that. Amy & Luna beat the shit out of them and their manager, Liz Savage. The two locked themselves in the bathroom, then climbed out the window. Luna and Amy cut a promo, screaming at The MiC never to put us in with fuckin' greenhorns again. Of course this wound up on the Internet and people got curious about the promotion. Alicia was the heel champ and defended the title every show. TNA star Awesome Kong was brought in and a feud started with her and Amy Lee. They brawled all over the building and out to the street.

WSU started drawing decent crowds, but with success comes problems. Former JAPW booker, Ray Sager, joined WSU. Sager was responsible for some great angles with JAPW, drawing their biggest crowds. Originally, Sager was part of a tag team called The Sickness with Fat Frank from JAPW. Strangely, Frank was not happy with Ray going to work for WSU. At several shows, right in front of The MiC, he said he was going to form a JAPW Women's Division. Now up until this point, JAPW was drawing huge crowds to it's monthly shows in Rahway NJ. Bringing in wrestlers like Abyss, Rhyno, Sabu, Teddy Hart, Necro Butcher and their home grown stars, Jay Lethal, Lo Ki, Homicide, Danny Demanto, and Monsta Mack, they had great shows.

The mood soured, however, with Fat Frank starting problems. The MiC got fed up and stopped going to JAPW shows. I was helping the RF Video table and shit was said loud enough that I would over hear it. It wasn't a good atmosphere to be in. Someone circulated phony flyers in Lake Hiawatha that WSU would be running a no rope barbed wire match with light tubes and thumbtacks. This was brought to the town and Gino got heat for it. The town made a ruling that no more shows could be run out of his building. WSU moved to the old movie theater in Boonton that PWE used. Some guys who were loyal to JAPW had been moonlighting for WSU. Monsta Mack, had been doing commentary on WSU DVDS. He quit with no notice. The company that filmed JAPW shows also was filming WSU shows. A crazy Amy Lee vs. Awesome Kong match went all over and even outside the building. That footage got "lost."

Now when your company depends on DVD sales, this really hit hard. That company was replaced. I didn't realize how deep this shit was until there was a WSU match on a PWL show. Alicia vs. Velvet Skye was the match and, for some reason, I was asked to tape it. Not a problem for me, but something else would be a problem. The main event was supposed to have Samoa Joe in it. Joe couldn't make it, so JAPW star Lo Ki substituted. Lo Ki had issues with RF Video going back to his ROH days. Lo Ki went bat shit during a match and kicked his opponent, Dan Maff, in the back of the head, knocking him out. When Doug Gentry went to check on Maff, Lo Ki hit him too. Feinstein fired Lo Ki on the spot.

Lo Ki told the promoter that if RF Video was filming, he wouldn't do the main event. They now asked me to film it. I said, "Wait a minute, he saw me sitting with you guys." I had no doubt this guy would take a cheap shot at me. They said they would have a hard camera in the balcony. I said OK, because if this fucker tried something, we'd have it on tape. Being that this was a four. way match with Lo Ki, Necro Butcher, Eddie Kingston, and Danny Demanto, I said I would shoot as little as possible of Lo Ki. When Kingston and Necro brawled out of the ring, I stayed with them. Lo Ki shot me some dirty looks, but I stayed far away from him.

WSU was thriving. Mercedes Martinez won the title and had great matches against Angel Orsini. A cage match, a bull rope match and a historic Iron Women Match that went 67 minutes. Anything male wrestlers had done, they would do. It was a class act and Amy Lee became a regular on my radio show. I would have a lot of the girls on the show to promote WSU. The building was great and the owner let us do anything we wanted, but it was out in the middle of nowhere. The MiC cut a deal with Mike Morgan to run shows at his ACE school in Union City NJ. It was a great venue, holding about 400 people. But the JAPW bullshit continued. They ran their first "Women's Division" show in front of 20 people. Some WSU stars were on the card. I honestly don't know if they were told by WSU management not to appear, but a few girls didn't come back. One girl, Roxie Cotton, started talking shit about Angel Orsini using drugs. During an indie show, Angel took her out for real with a rear naked chokehold that left Roxie laid out cold.

Someone from JAPW called the town and said liquor was being served. Morgan was furious and being he ran his own promotion out of the building, he had a few JAPW wresters there who he had trained. They weren't happy either as they would lose a payday if Morgan folded. The town eventually condemned the building. The MiC was getting burnt out and had health problems. They moved to another venue in NY. I didn't follow as it was just too hard to get to. They had been doing Internet Pay Per View Shows which were very successful. The MiC sold the company. I watched one of the new PPVs and it wasn't the same. Cindy Rogers retired due to injuries. Amy Lee also retired. Mercedes Martinez was a great champ, but was moving to Florida and trying to get into law enforcement. She dropped the title to killer heel, Jessika Havoc. The company still exists, but Women Superstars Uncensored, became Women Superstars Unlimited. More family friendly I would guess. I just heard that CZW owner, DJ Hyde just bought the company.

JAPW, a company that was drawing close to 2000 fans per show, got stupider. Maybe as a result of fucking with WSU and other promotions, attendance dropped off. Where John Zandig wouldn't deal with them, new CZW owner DJ Hyde would. They ran an invasion angle with Nick Gage and Nate Hatred attacking the JAPW tag team champs. CZW's Cage of Death and JAPW's Anniversary show were on the same day, so DJ Hyde invited them to do a co show at The Arena. JAPW would run in the afternoon, CZW would run that evening. This had been successful with an IWA afternoon show and a CZW show months ago. It wasn't successful this time. JAPW drew about 200 fans, CZW sold out with SRO. JAPW started bad mouthing CZW. That ended that. JAPW shows rapidly got out of control with brawling in the stands, breaking vendor's tables, and bringing in

strippers and pole dancers. They spent huge money on outside talent. A Jushin "Thunder" Liger vs. Homicide main event, drew less that 200 fans. Considering Liger was a flight in from Japan, they lost money. The atmosphere

at the last few shows I attended was tense. The booking sucked too. One show, right before intermission, had Hailey Hatred in street clothes attack Sara Del Ray. The two brawled from one end of the building to the other, breaking tables, chairs and the JAPW merchandise booth. After the match, I left as there were three matches left on the card and they couldn't top what I had just seen. That match was so intense that it killed the rest of the show. It should have been the 2nd to the last match. It just showed me how little effort was being put into these shows.

The last show I was at, a fight erupted in the crowd as someone threw a punch at a wrestler. The ring crew got drunk and started threatening the RF Video guys and myself. Fuck this, it wasn't fun anymore. JAPW stopped running shows, Seems the IRS may have been auditing one of the owners. I lost interest and was moving out of Jersey at that point. After I left, other groups like Evolve, Dragon Gate and others were running shows. CZW is still viable but the legendary Arena was sold and hasn't been reopened.

Any entertainment business is shitty at best. Wrestling was no different. Wrestlers feeding off a rabid crowd's energy would push their limits. Injuries were common, and so were deaths. JC Bailey, Trent Acid, and Brain Damage, young, gifted workers, passed away. Drug overdoses were common, so were suicides. Ian rotten was accused of stealing the proceeds for charity shows. He also admitted on a radio show that he gave JC Bailey painkillers. He was ostracized on the air by Mad Man Pondo, Joe Bailey, Bull Pain, Mickie Knuckles and others. IWA folded and, as of this writing, is still not operating.

Indie wrestling is the training ground for future stars. JAPW stars Homicide, Lo Ki and Jay Lethal were hired by TNA which is national. Several CZW stars, like John Moxley and Sami Callahan are now in the WWE. I know CZW still has some deathmatches at shows. The only other ones that I'm aware of are the clusterfucks run by The Insane Clown Posse. After awhile you get desensitized to this stuff. The hardcore style shortens careers and lives. I enjoyed my time working with WSU, PWE, and others. It was an experience I'll never forget. I met some incredibly talented people during those years and I wish them the best.

Dedicated to JC Bailey, Mike Graham, Matt Borne, Hangman Bobby Jaggers, Brain Damage, Trent Acid, and Doug Gentry. RIP.

"He Ain't Freaky. He's My Brother."

Frank Henenlotter's *Basket Case*
by Robert Morgan

It was a Saturday evening in early February 1989. I was a few weeks from turning 10 years old. My mom and I were hunkered down in the den of my late grandmother Betty's house, toasty warm as the air outside turned to bitter cold. That afternoon I had bought the new issue of *Starlog* magazine and was engrossed in an article about the impending release of *The Fly II*. Mom had the television on and was flipping channels in a desperate attempt to find something worth watching. The networks were no good (and still aren't if you ask me) so she tried the few basic cable channels we had at our disposal.

She came upon the USA Network—back in the days when they aired all manners of crazy flicks and reruns of cheeseball TV action shows from the past few decades—and my attention was briefly torn away from the magazine when I glanced up at the screen and saw an elderly man getting his face torn to shreds by a misshapen monstrosity that dwelled inside of a brown wicker basket. You know, the kind an adult might use to cart around dirty laundry or store priceless family heirlooms. There wasn't much blood shown since it was still considered the family hour (it was close to nine in the evening, if memory serves correctly) and censorship standards for basic cable channels were stricter than they are now, but what I had seen was enough to completely capture my interest. I was hooked into this movie's spell, whatever the fuck it was, and was ready and willing to drink in the rest of its gruesome lunacy as if it was an oasis in a desert of boring and disposable TV programming.

Mom promptly changed the channel.

I never forgot that night. Most of my childhood memories have been permanently suppressed because they weren't worth remembering anyhow, but from that evening on I knew that one day I would have another shot at seeing Frank Henenlotter's *Basket Case* from beginning to end.

"What is the secret Duane is hiding in the basket?" So went the ominous-sounding narrator from the *Basket Case* trailer.

I won't bother with spoiler warnings because the movie is more than three decades old and if you still haven't seen it, fuck you. As you can now tell, I am oblivious to your needs and happily so. In my never. ending to build the greatest Blu-ray collection known to civilized mankind a visit to Ebay resulted in my purchase of a steelbook edition of *Basket Case* and its two inferior (but great fun in their own way) sequels released by a U.K. company called Second Sight Films. Ever since I invested in a region free Blu-ray player over a year ago I've been picking up imported releases of some of my favorite films that were either still unavailable in the States or available on subpar discs with shit video and audio quality and almost nothing in the way of bonus features. The cineaste in me just has to own the best version of a film I love on home video, regardless of the nation from which I have to import the title. It's amazing how some titles that get treated like complete garbage here in the home of the brave are treated with reverence and honor in other countries, particularly the ones we love to boast about saving their asses in World War II.

Watching the first **Basket Case** for the first time in several times I was impressed by how well it has held up over the 32 years since it first jolted the hell out of cynical horror fans. The original remains the best of the trilogy and one of the finest and startlingly original horror films to reach audiences in a dark decade where visionary filmmakers were being waterboarded into unblinking submission by the purse holders of Tinseltown. Director Henenlotter, who also wrote the script, personally supervised the film's high. definition restoration knowing that it would never look as good as its slicker, bigger-budgeted competition. It didn't need to though. One of the film's greatest strengths is its distinctive texture and atmosphere and the authentic New York locations where production mostly took place. The characters live in grungy motels, work in seedy offices, and spend their free time getting plastered in low. rent bars and dozing off in grindhouse movie palaces while dubbed Hong Kong chop-socky flicks spool away on the theater screen. There is a dark, grimy beauty to these locales (captured in full bloody color by cinematographer Bruce Torbet, who also shot Henenlotter's Brain Damage and Brian DePalma's early feature **Murder a la Mod**) and Henenlotter knew them well because he had lived most of his life in NYC and considered those rundown no-tell motels and exploitation movie houses a part of his own cultural identity.

He was a student of the cinema as his fellow New Yorkers Martin Scorsese and William Lustig had been before him, and after having briefly worked in advertising Henenlotter set out to make the sort of unhinged, balls. out exploitation flicks he loved to watch on the sleazy screens of 42nd Street growing up. Prior to making his feature directorial debut he had made some short films on 8mm and graduated to 16mm as his filmmaking ambitions grew. His 1972 black & white short **Slash of the Knife** was shown at a 42nd Street movie theater in New York City alongside John Waters' breakthrough film **Pink Flamingos**. **Basket Case** was shot on 16mm film stock with only $30,000 or so in the bank to keep the cameras rolling. Even in those days most independent horror films were made on budgets of six figures at least; the original **Night of the Living Dead** cost $114,000 to make more than a decade before **Basket Case**, an amount that increased quite a bit when you factor in inflation.

Like the majority of low. budget independent horror films that came before and after, **Basket Case** didn't require a lot of money for Henenlotter to realize his vision without having to compromise—an opportunity that would not present itself much in the years that followed the film's release. He wisely confined the story to a handful of locations and limited the characters to those of the greatest importance, with a few random eccentrics left in to ground everything in a warped reality like Joe Clarke's boozing Irish schemer Brian "Mickey" O'Donovan. They were a far cry from the vapid parade of sex-starved teen dullards that only existed to be sacrificial lambs to the latest slaughter spree of Michael Myers of Jason Voorhees. In comparison, the characters of **Basket Case** could have emerged virtually unaltered from the plays of William Inge.

Basket Case is, at its core, about the futility of honoring family obligations. The story begins with wide. eyed young Duane (Kevin Van Hentenryck) traveling to the Big Apple from the small town upstate where he had lived until now. He seems pleasant enough as an individual, but ask him what he's got in the wicker basket he carts with him all over town and chances are you'll get a vague response, an averted gaze, and a hasty exit. The basket contains his brother Belial, a misshapen lump of pulsating flesh that can't possibly pass for human but was once a part of Duane's body. They were born joined together and the birthing killed their mother, a tragedy that would forever infect their relationship with their bitter, enraged father (Richard Pierce). The brothers' only source of non-judgmental love was their kindly aunt (Ruth Neuman), but she couldn't save them from being forcefully separated surgically by a trio of surgeons secretly hired by the father. Duane was finally free to live a normal life and yet he was doomed from the start to spend that life taking care of Belial—now perpetually pissed and quick to be pushed into brutal murder—and seeking revenge on those who literally tore them apart against their will, thus prompting their journey into the steel and concrete canyons of the big city.

Duane's as amazed by New York's limitless promise and pleasures as any fresh. faced farm boy just off the bus from Bumfuck, Kansas. He probably could make it there, and if the Chairman of the Board knew what he was talking about the kid could then make it anywhere. Then there's Belial, just as human on the inside as his normal. looking brother but imprisoned forever in a body that deprives him of unassisted movement or speech. Even when the little "squashed octopus" (Duane's words) begins his bloody killing spree you can't help but empathize with the predicament he and his brother share. The two of them share a telepathic bond they use to communicate—mostly because Henenlotter couldn't afford a more functional Belial puppet until he made the sequels—but you have to wonder if Belial isn't also using that special connection to influence his brother's behavior at times. Duane doesn't seem to have a murderous bone in his body, so when he assists Belial in the murders of the three surgeons who separated them it almost feels like he's being carefully coerced into doing so, as if he were more of a hostage overcome by Stockholm Syndrome than a dutiful sibling just trying to do right by the only family he has left. Anyone who has ever been saddled with the responsibility of providing care for a relative unable to do so for themselves could empathize.

Speaking of those surgeons, they certainly are a fun bunch. Lifflander (Bill Freeman) was the doctor who delivered Duane and Belial into a world that had no need for their kind and then delivered into the hands of his colleagues Needleman (Lloyd Pace) and Kutter (Diana Browne). Kutter functions as the trio's unofficial leader, both Lifflander and Needleman seemingly consumed by massive guilt and not very effective adversaries. Neither is Kutter for that matter, but her death scene is the natural conclusion to the brothers' mission of retribution because it's given an actual build-up. Plus she's a downright despicable person who isn't afraid to dismiss Duane offhand even though she has no idea why he would seek her out after so many years, other than to thank her (the suggestion of which appears to offend him almost as much as her blasé attitude towards Belial's livelihood in a crucial flashback scene). When Belial finally gets his clawed mitts on her smug, unsympathetic face even Jesus Christ would cheer for her demise. Afterwards we would immediately forgive him.

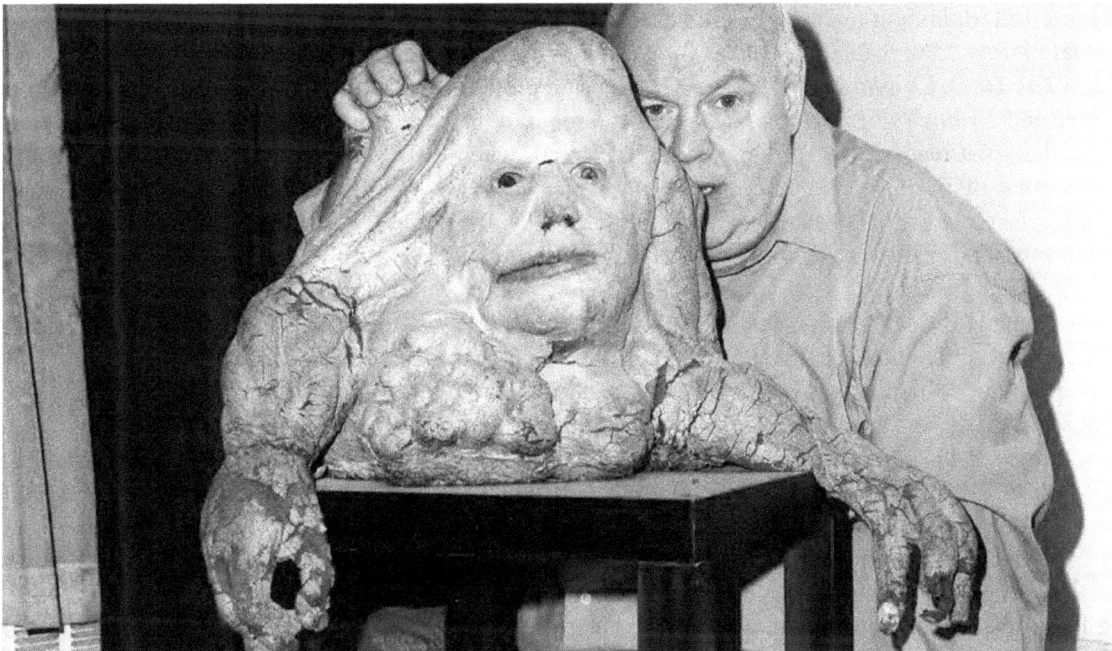

There may not be much story in **Basket Case** but it has enough of a plot to make it stand head and shoulders above the glut of independently. produced horror films of the time, most of which believed that a psycho with an axe terrorizing scantily. clad ingénues in a sorority house was enough to justify a 90. minute running time. It's a crafty revenge tale with some interesting complexities in its so. called heroes and villains and some invaluable supporting players that elevate **Basket Case** into a true one-of-the-kind feature without breaking a sweat. As much as I enjoyed the two sequels Henenlotter made nearly a decade after the release of the original I always felt that he made a mistake taking Duane and Belial away from the unsentimental and honest city streets and placing them in a heightened setting with a cast of comical freak characters that made them seem perfectly normal. The Hotel Broslin is one of the best locations ever established for a horror film, the modern day equivalent of the country inns and taverns from countless Universal and Hammer monster movie classics. The hotel itself was actually several locations given the film's miniscule funding, but you can hardly tell the difference in changing sets.

Henenlotter chose the right actors to give them a sense of life, my favorites being Beverly Bonner's friendly hooker Casey and the cantankerous hotel manager played by the late Robert Vogel. Terri Susan Smith's love interest Sharon comes across as flighty and eccentric so it's no wonder why she would find a kindred spirit in Duane. If her blonde hair looks ill fitting it's because it was a wig; Smith had been in a punk band at the time she won the role of Sharon and had to conceal her shaven scalp. If you ask me, they should've junked the wig. Browne makes Kutter into a perfectly apathetic adversary worthy of nothing but hatred (unlike the other two surgeons Lifflander and Needleman, guilt. ridden shells of humanity searching for an end to their psychological suffering).

Belial himself (itself?) is brought to life through a combination of puppetry, stop. motion animation, and putting a pair of clawed gloves on anyone willing to play the monster's hands for a scene—a task usually fulfilled by the director. The low. fi effects get the job done and Henenlotter is wise to not linger on them long enough for the illusion to be spoiled. The sequence where Belial becomes furious at Duane's newfound happiness with Sharon and proceeds to go on a rampage of hotel room destruction that would earn him much respect from your average British heavy metal band is hilarious as it's accomplished with painstaking stop. motion animation, possibly the most arduous stretch of the production and achieved entirely by Henenlotter. Belial's herky-jerky movements recall the clay animation of cartoons like Gumby and the self. righteous religious pander Davey and Goliath—but if they were created under the influence of Psilocybin mushrooms—but the effect never takes the viewer out of the film. You have no choice but to accept the crudity of the poorly funded animation because if it was as professional and fluid as Ray Harryhausen's mythical beasts it would've appeared out of place.

Basket Case spawned few prolific careers after managing to find great success as a readily. embraced cult oddity on the midnight movie circuit and later on home video during the rise of VHS rentals and sales, the latter due to Media Home Entertainment releasing a priced. to. own tape for $20 that soon became one of their biggest sellers. But the special effects crew featured a pair of future heavy hitters in the industry including one Oscar-winner in John Caglione, Jr. (*The Dark Knight, Dick Tracy*). After having plied his trade on the bigger-budgeted studio productions *Quest for Fire* and *Friday the 13th Part II*, Caglione came in to provide some relief work for Kevin Haney (*Cocoon, Iron Man 3*), the artist responsible for the creation of Belial, when Haney was compelled to take a better paying job on the effects crew of *Wolfen*. The gore effects of *Basket Case* are plentiful but are accomplished mostly through suggestion and protracted shots of the juicy aftermath; we never see guts getting ripped out and used for upholstery, though Henenlotter and company happily provide us with some mangled faces, a body torn in half, and the crowning grace for the moment when Dr. Kutter meets Belial. Henenlotter would unfortunately have to tone down the gore content when he made the sequels for Shapiro. Glickenhaus Entertainment in the early '90s in a hopeless bid to find a wider and more profitable audience, and thus their compromised nature couldn't be concealed.

I've given up hope that the cackling apoplectic music score by Gus Russo will ever be released on CD, though I doubt I would like it even more if I heard it isolated from the rest of *Basket Case*. It plays like a soap opera soundtrack composed by a mental institution. Guess what? That makes it the perfect musical accompaniment to Henenlotter's dirty, deranged horror comedy playing out before our eyes. Maybe it will be made available one of these days, but I doubt it. Yet it doesn't make me feel disappointed. It would be impossible to listen to Russo's music on its own without imagining the scenes that went them, so perhaps it's for the best that an official soundtrack album has never existed (bootlegs are a different story).

Much like its iconic mutant Belial, *Basket Case* was never meant to be contained. Henenlotter figured his first movie would only play 42nd Street grindhouses and then fade into obscurity. Far from it. Films that dare to be different and are made with intelligence, skill, and a depraved but fertile imagination don't deserve such a miserable fate. More than three decades after it enthralled horror fans and made the notoriously prickly (but mostly just a prick) Rex Reed proclaim it "the sickest movie I've ever seen", Frank Henenlotter's gloriously gory and intimate creature feature remains his magnum opus and one of my most personal favorite genre films of the 1980s. You can dismiss it, bury or burn it alive, or throw it from the rooftop of the highest building imaginable, but you will not be able to kill this beast.

Belial will not be denied.

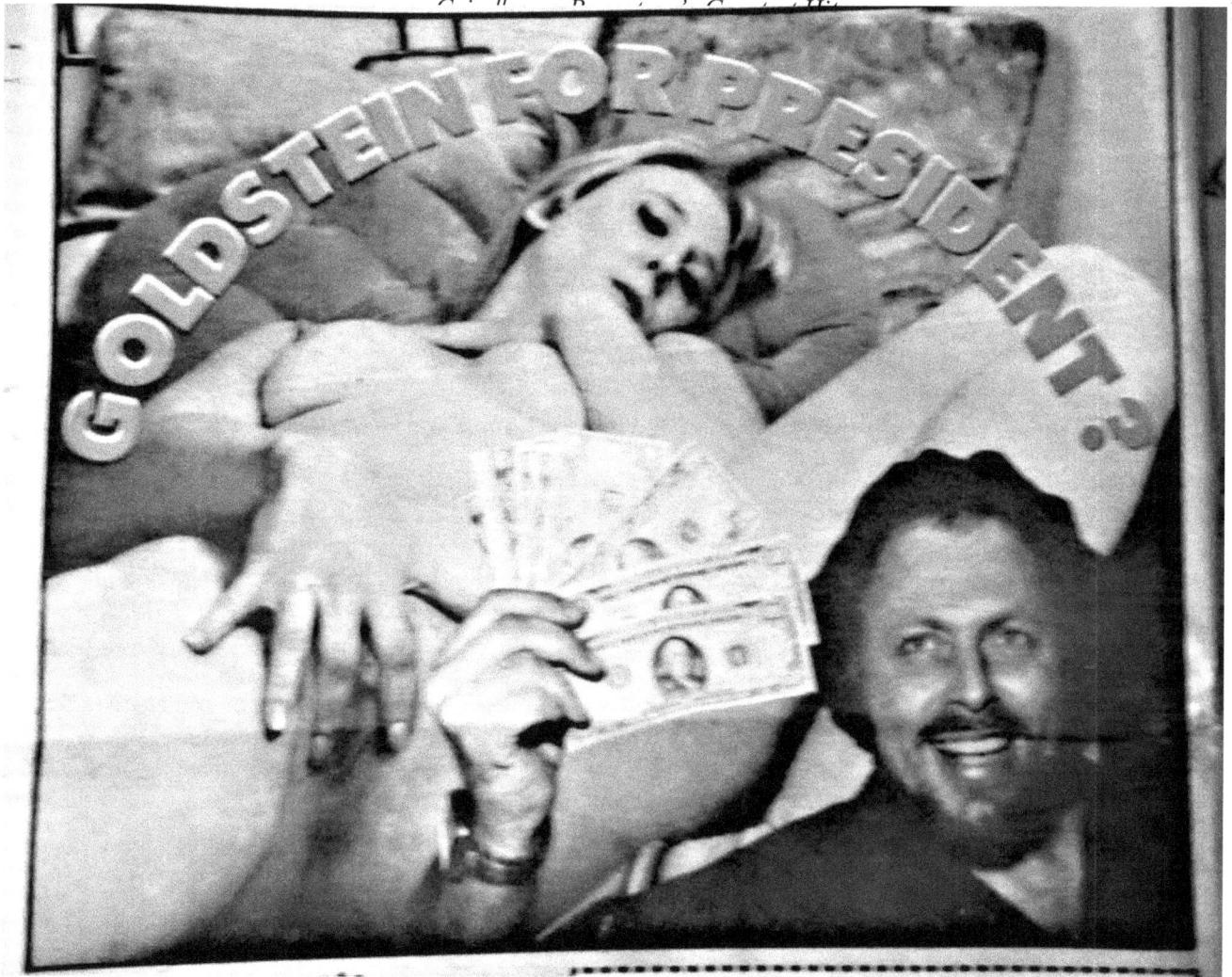

Goodnight Sweaty Prince

Remembering Al Goldstein
1936—2013

Back in '68 the porn was working it's way into the mainstream like a noxious bubble of gas surfacing in a septic tank. Porn was raw and dirty back then, but would soon be injected into the consciousness of mainstream America. Two men, Al Goldstein and Jim Buckley, created a guide to all the sex related businesses in NYC and surrounding areas. It was called *Screw* and was cheaply printed on newspaper. It covered XXX films, peepshows, Dime–A–Dance Parlors, Massage Parlors, Strip Bars, Whore Houses and more.

I discovered *Screw* because it made the 6 o'clock news. It was the anti-porn crusaders that thrust *Screw* into the spotlight. As a teen with raging hormones, I had to see what all the uproar was about. I went into the city and picked up an issue. Being conditioned to rub one out over color mags like *Playboy, Gent, Nugget*, etc., *Screw*'s black-and-white pics were a let down. But later I realized that most guys had zero chance of screwing *Playboy* type models, but they did stand a chance scoring the type of women pictured in *Screw*. With their saggy tits, hairy bushes and armpits, these were the women of *Screw*.

For me, it was a quick graduation from rubbing one out to porn to finding hookers. *Screw* helped by listing massage parlors, houses, and the best locations to find streetwalkers. If a place was good, *Screw* raved about it. If something sucked, was a bait & switch, or just a rip off, *Screw* would demolish it in print. By the time Al took over the entire operation, *Screw* was an extension of Al's personality. Al would make a lot of enemies, enemies that he would take on in print. Mayors Abe Beam, John Lindsey, Ed Koch, Rudy Giuliani would all feel Al's wrath. Al created the "Goldstein Curse" to use on his enemies. It actually worked. Savior of Times Square and rabid anti-porn crusader, Father Bruce Ritter, crashed and burned when it was discovered he was using donations to pay for trysts with male hustlers. American Airlines, Pillsbury, Mercedes Benz and others all became targets of Al's wrath when he perceived that they fucked him over. When Al was screwed by Florida appliance dealer, Brandsmart, Al ran a full-page ad that said, "If You Like A Huge Cock in Your Ass, Shop at Brandsmart."

Al had said that *Screw* was fueled by hate, not love. Al made a fortune on "phone sex." Phone sex was an 800 number that you called and talked to a hot lady who talked dirty to you while you jerked off. At $3 per minute, the trick was to keep you on the phone. The success of these led to more diverse phone sex with gays, mistresses, and trannies. Al made enough coin to be able to lash out at his critics and enemies. If they took Al to court, he would win. Pillsbury took him to task over the depiction of the Pillsbury Doughboy fucking the Dough Girl. Al won that battle as the ad was a "parody." This court ruling open the door for more parody ads, not only from *Screw*, but from *Hustler* and other mags.

My first actual encounter with Al was at the late, lamented Harmony Burlesque. While watching strippers, Al burst in with the entire Midnight Blue camera crew. Most of the patrons pulled their coats over their heads and hit the exits. Not me—I sat there while Al's crew was shooting footage of a hot black stripper whose every move threw a bucket of sweat into the dwindling crowd as the camera lights were that hot. After the shoot, I was one of the few remaining patrons. Al invited me to join the crew at the bar around the corner. I had a few drinks and just watched the antics of "The Pied Piper of Porn." I left at closing time. Little did I know that Al would become a pivotal force as I became a writer.

I was hired by **Something Weird Video** to write liner notes for their 8mm collections and for *The SWV Blue Book*. I did need to do some research and find some graphics. SWV arranged for me to visit the offices of *Screw*. It was a cramped building in the west 20s. I elbowed my way past the hookers and trannies paying for their weekly ads. Al and editor, Eric Danville graciously let me sift though the archives, photocopying ad mats and the like for *The Blue Book*.

The years rolled on and I wound up working in NYC for NYC Liquidators. I read every weekly issue of *Screw* for the five years I was there. Sadly these were the waning days for that old Times Square squalor. Al vented his spleen on law & order mayor, Rudi Giuliani who was rabidly anti porn. Rudy was using the AIDS epidemic to close any sex related business he could. He really incurred Al's wrath when "free" papers like The *Village* Voice and *The New York Press* began running the same hooker and trannie ads, plus phone sex ads. Al' s argument, and it was a good one, was that any kid could grab one of these papers and see these ads. You had to buy *Screw* and if you weren't 18 or older, no dice. Giuliani did nothing to stop this, he wanted Al out of business.

The next time I saw Al was the day after the Chiller Theatre convention. He was waiting for a bus back to the city as he had spent the night with his new girlfriend, Linnea Quigley. We shot the shit for an hour or so, then he gave me a card with his private number and told me that if I ever needed anything, just call. While working at Liquidators, an event was scheduled at The Javits Center right under Giuliani's nose. I believe it was called Eroticon, but it was a multimedia event dedicated to sex. All the major players in NYC were there. Candida Royal Feme Video, Troma, writers like Jack Ketchum, performers like Menage, and others. NYC Liquidators took a spot and advertised that Menage and 42nd Street Pete would be there. We sold $25,000 worth of porn vids in two days.

Wandering around the place, I had a couple of drinks with Jack Ketchum, which wound me up and got me into a selling mood. I went back to the Liquidators booth, pretty buzzed, and proceeded to go full tilt bozo, loudly hawking product. Norman looked at me and said, "If I knew all I had to do is liquor you up, I would have bought you a bottle." I sold a shitload of tapes. On my next break, I saw Al holding court. I sat down next to him and we had a laugh about putting one over on Giuliani. "Fuck that cocksucker," Al said, "This is a classy event. The only thing sleazy here is me and you." I took that as a compliment.

In 2003 Norm passed away and Liquidators closed. The last peepshow on 42nd street closed and *Screw* folded up. Al was having physical and mental problems. He left a death threat on an employee's answering machine and was hauled into court. Al, quite simply, was fucked over by the system he fought. He was incarcerated for a bit, then he was homeless. He lost everything. He got a couple of jobs, but when you are used to being in charge, it's hard to take orders. Al was in a homeless shelter, a long hard fall for a guy who once had millions of $$.

Al had a savior in comedian and magician, Penn Gillette. Penn got al an apartment and paid the rent. Al had a stroke and wound up in the VA Hospital as Al had served his country. I believe he also had other ailments including being a diabetic. In December a post on Facebook said Al had died. I called former *Screw* editor, Eric Danville, and he told me that Al was alive and his "death" was a misinterpreted tweet. Sadly, two days later, Al passed away peacefully in his sleep.

Al Goldstein, love him or hate him, was a tireless anti censorship crusader, and an advocate for free speech. He was a true product of NYC, a lager than life character, who took on the system and beat them at their own game. Mayors John Lindsey, Abe Beam, David Dinkins, Ed Koch and Rudy Giuliani all fought Al and lost. Al even survived a hit put out on him by John Gotti. Al did something to incur the Teflon Don's Wrath, but then someone pointed out to Gotti that Al was good for business as he endorsed mob controlled bordellos, massage parlors, and porn films. The hit was called off.

Thank you, Al, for everything you have done for the industry. You were a one of a kind, a groundbreaker, a fighter, and a clown all rolled into one. RIP my friend and I hope you're eating prime pussy in the endless Grindhouse beyond the veil.

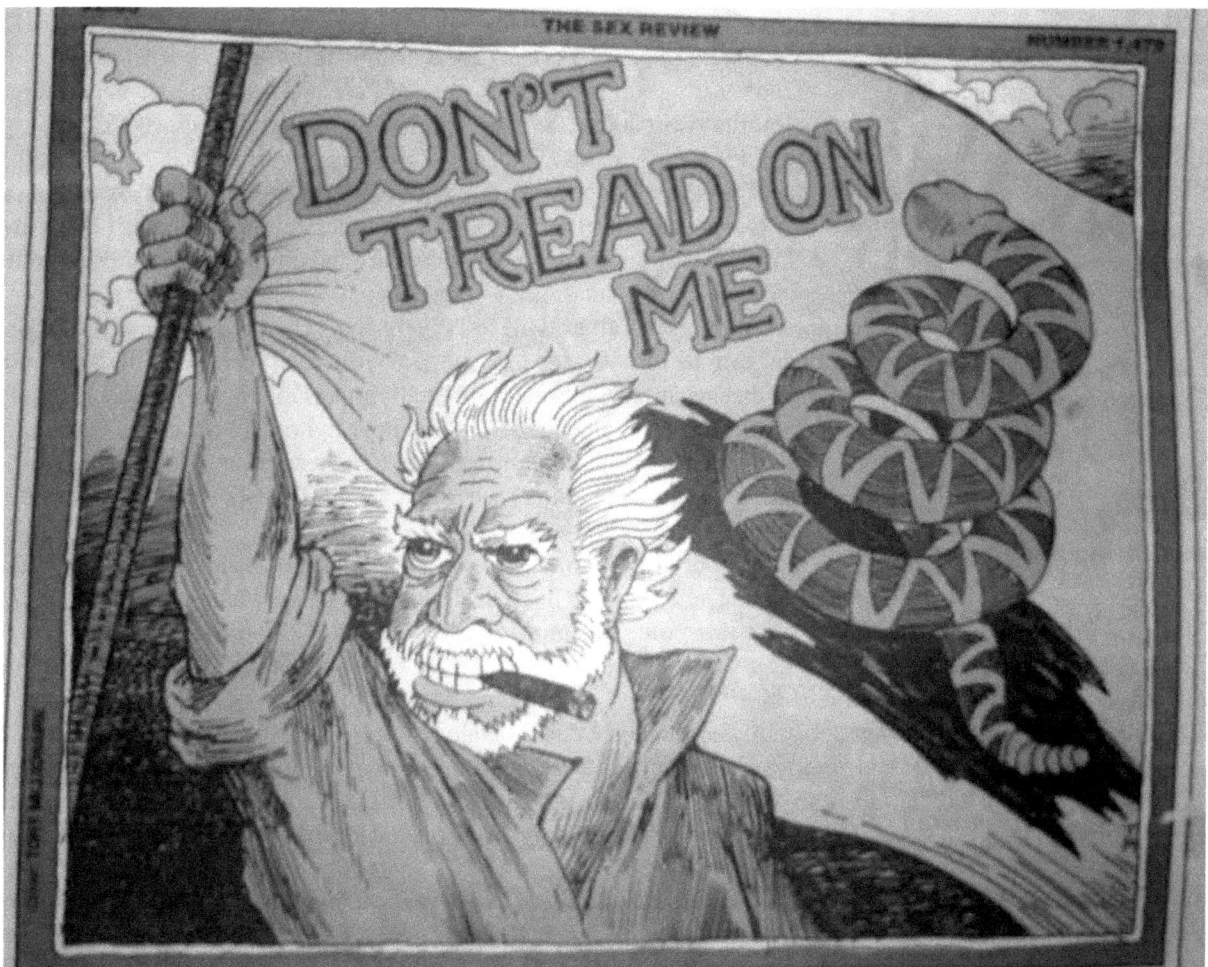

ROOTS OF EXPLOITATION: JUNGLE JITTERS

Film is a wonderful medium to create with. Back in the '30s, there was no Hayes Code or rating system, so almost anything went. Certain things you couldn't show but you could allude to. The concept of getting lost in a South American jungle would eventually give birth to the most horrific sub genre ever made, the cannibal film. Everything has a beginning. *Five Came Back* (1939) was the beginning. Of course I didn't see this film in a theater. I saw it as a kid as older films were used as filler for a new medium, television.

Twelve people are on a plane when a storm forces a crash landing in a South American jungle. Pilot and copilot, Bill and Joe (Chester Morris and Kent Taylor); a mobster, Pete (Allen Jenkins) escorting his boss's son, Tommy; a "fallen" woman, Peggy (Lucille Ball); Crimp (John Carradine), a bounty hunter bringing a political prisoner, Vasquez (Joseph Calleia) to his execution; and eloping couple Judson and Alice (Patrick Knowles and Wendy Barrie); and an older couple, the Spenglers (C. Aubery Smith and Elisabeth Risdon).

Tommy is put on the flight in care of Pete. Seems someone is gunning for his father. A radio broadcast announces that Tommy's father was killed by rivals. Pete tries to cover this up. The rest of the passengers all have issues and will be tested. Crimp is an alcoholic with a bad temper. The Spenglers are having marital problems. Now they have crashed in headhunter country and don't know it yet.

Now they all have to cooperate as they have to build a makeshift runway to take off. The other situation is fuel. They don't have enough. They have one weapon: Crimp's revolver. Bill tells them that when the plane is ready, only five of them can be on it. Vasquez bonds with the Spenglers. Judson and Alice become disenchanted with each other. Crimp wanders off, drunk. Tommy finds him and thinks he is sleeping. He gets Pete, who find an arrow in Crump. Pete sends Tommy back, but is shot himself. Vasquez palms Crimps revolver. Drums are beating as the headhunters surround them. The plane is ready, but only five will be going.

When Judson tries to take over, Vasquez shoots him. Vasquez tells Bill, Joe, Peggy, Alice, and Tommy to get on the plane. The Spenglers have decided to stay. The plane takes off. Mr. Spengler asks Vasquez if he has enough bullets to take them out. Vasquez looks at the gun and it has only two bullets left. He tells him yes. Spengler asks Vasquez to do it when she is not looking. As they embrace, Vasquez shoots them. Then he waits for the headhunters to come for him.

The film was a big hit and ran constantly in the early days of television. John Farrow was the director. Lucille Ball was quite the hottie back then before she became Lucy Ricardo and had a hit TV show. Kent Taylor was a popular actor in B. films of the '30s and '40s. In his later years, he appeared in a ton of Grindhouse films like *The Crawling Hand, Brides of Blood, Brain of Blood, Hells Bloody Devils, Satan Sadists*, and others. He died in 1987 at age 80.

Chester Morris appeared in thirteen *Boston Blackie* movies. After that, he claimed no producer would put him in an "A" picture. He was the lead in 1956's *The She Creature*, as Doctor Carlo Lombardi. He did mostly TV appearances until 1970, when he appeared in *The Great White Hope*. He died in 1970 at age 69.

Seventeen years later, Farrow would remake the film with a different name and a different cast, *Back from Eternity* (1956). Guess they figured no one would remember the other one. But this one wound up on TV pretty quick. It is better written and updated. Now we have a commercial airline piloted by a hard drinking Bill (Robert Ryan), Rena (Anita Ekberg) is a hustler that was just run out of Vegas. She is destined for a whorehouse in Boca something called the Blue Moon. Joe (Keith Andes) is the copilot. The Spanglers are more combative than in the other film. A couple, Louise and Jud (Phyllis Kirk and Gene Barry), are getting married. Pete (Jesse White) is a mobster taking mob kingpin's son, Tommy (Jon Provost), to the Blue Moon to hide out. Pete doesn't want to go. He

puts Tommy in the care of the stewardess, Maria. But after he reads that his boss was just gunned down, he changes his mind. They have one stop before Boca. They are held up as they have to take on two more passengers. A murderer, Vasquel (Rod Steiger), and the bounty hunter bringing him in, Crimp (Fred Clark). This Crimp is a real scumbag. He has the only gun and he drinks a lot.

Bill tries to get Rena not to go to The Blue Moon. Being that her passports have all been revoked, she says she has no choice but to go "work for Aunt Sophie." The plane hits a storm and is battered around. The stewardess is sucked out when a door breaks open. They crash-land in a valley. Vasquel and Mr. Spangler know they are in head. hunter country.

Now they all have to work together. Crimp tries to take over the plane in a drunken rage. Joe knocked him out and Vasquel palmed the gun. He gives the gun to Bill. They build a forge to repair parts of the plane. Jud keeps getting drunker and says they'll never get out. Bill gives Pete the gun as he is standing guard. Crimp knocks Pete out, then takes the gun and some supplies before running off in the jungle.

Tommy is following a monkey and finds Crimp. He tells Pete and Rena that Crimp is sleeping. He leads them to Crimp's body. Pete tells Rena to take Tommy back to the plane. Pete searches Crimp's body for the gun. Pete staggers into camp with an arrow in his back. They try to take off, but an oil line bursts. Bill gives them the bad news. Four of them will have to stay behind. They argue who will stay and who will go. Vasquez pulls the gun out and tells them that being he is going to die either way, he is the most qualified to make that choice.

The Spanglers tell Vasquel that they will stay. Vasquel says that Bill, Joe, Rena, Louise, and Tommy should get on the plane. Jud rushes Vasquel and is shot. The plane takes off, but the savages are moving in for the kill. Vasquel has only two bullets left. He uses them on the Spanglers. Something he really didn't want to do.

Even though considered a "B" movie, the film is very good. Add in a catfight in the water between Rena and Louise to spice things up.

Robert Ryan had a long career until his death from lung cancer in 1973. He was 63 years old. He was Deke Thorton in **The Wild Bunch**. Anita Ekberg did a lot of grindhouse films like **Fangs of the Living Dead, Killer Nun, The Cobra, Deadly Trackers**, and others. She died in 2015 in Italy at age 83. Keith Andes looked and sounded a lot like Peter Graves. He was in **Blackbeard the Pirate** and did a lot of TV. He died in 2005 at age 85. Phyllis Kirk was in **House of Wax** and a lot of TV. She died in 2006 at age 79. Rod Steiger was in over 100 films, from **Al Capone** to Sergio Leone's **Duck, You Sucker**. His last film was **Pool Hall Junkies** in 2002. He died in 2002 at age 77.

Gene Barry was in **War of the Worlds** and was TV's **Bat Masterson**. He died in 2009 at age 90. Jesse White became the beloved Maytag Man from 1968 to 1989 on TV commercials. His last film was **Matinee**. He died in 1997 at age 80. Jon Provost played Timmy on TV's **Lassie** from 1957 to 1964. Fred Clark always played a guy you loved to hate. He did a lot of TV and was in **Curse of the Mummy's Tomb**. He died in 1968 at age 54.

Jivaro! (1954) Was another lost-in-the-jungle/attacked-by-headhunters film in full color and 3D. Rio (Fernando Lamas) has a trading post in a South American jungle. It is infested with lowlifes. Rio is trading goods with a tribe of natives. When he opens crates to show them his goods, a couple are full of rocks. All these came from Pedro (Lon Chaney, Jr.). Rio confronts Pedro, who says, "Who'da thought those savages would open all the crates?" Rio had to give up his watch and ring to walk away alive. He helps himself to a ring and a watch in Pedro's store, then beats the crap out of him.

Chaney is fourth billed here, but this is his only scene in the entire film. Jerry Russell (Richard Denning) is a drunk looking for a treasure. Denning could play a drunk with a great deal of conviction. He played one in **Unknown Island**. He is also shacked up with a local girl, Maria (Rita Moreno). Jerry's fiancée, Alice (Rhonda Fleming), comes looking for him. He has told her he's a plantation owner. Rio takes her to find Jerry passed out in the bar. Tony (Brian Keith) is one of the barflies in Rio's place. Tony and another hanger-oner, Vinny (Morgan Farley) are convinced this treasure is real.

Tony sets Alice up for what is an attempted rape. Rio intervenes and brawls with Tony. Lots of two-fisted action in this film. Jerry, Tony and Vinny go into headhunter country looking for the treasure. Alice convinces Rio to help her find them. They find their bodies riddled with arrows. Grim scene with Jerry's body stuck in a tree swaying in the wind. Rio and Alice find cover and hold off the savages until help arrives.

By the time *Jivaro!* was released, the 3D craze was over, so it was released flat. It was shown regularly on WOR's **Million Dollar Movie** when I was a kid. Lamas was a big star back then and played just about every scene with his shirt open to his naval. Even a tux would be open to his naval. All of these films hinted at the savagery of jungle natives. Even the first two **Tarzan** movies had excessive brutality concerning natives and what they did with their captives.

In 1972 the lost. in. the. jungle genre would reach horrific new heights with Umberto Lenzi's **Deep River Savages**, aka **The Man from Deep River**, a grisly film that featured cannibalism as a selling point. Nastier films, **Jungle Holocaust, Trap Them and Kill Them**, and **Cannibal Holocaust** would follow. Lenzi would have the last word on the genre he created with **Make Them Die Slowly** which ran an astounding ten weeks straight at The Liberty Theater on 42nd Street.

Eli Roth tried to capitalize on this with his **Green Inferno**. Sorry, Eli, the only reason this short. lived genre worked was because no one had done it before. These were different times and you could push the envelope. **Cannibal Holocaust** was called "The Mother of all Cannibal Movies," but even though it's hugely popular now, it only ran a week at the Harris Theater on 42nd Street. People just couldn't handle how grim it was. It got a new lease on life when Grindhouse Releasing put it back out theatrically in a restored version.

GOD'S GUN

GOD DAMN AWFUL LAST WESTERN

A spaghetti western shot in Israel, a pre-Cannon Golan-Globus Production. Directed by Frank Kramer (Gianfranco Parolini), who directed *Sabata*. Starring Lee Van Cleef, Jack Palance, Richard Boone, Leif Garrett, and Sybil Danning. This would be Van Cleef's last western. Here he plays twin brothers. One is a priest, the other a gunfighter.

Lee has a ridiculous, longhaired toupee and a fake mustache and goatee. Father John has Johnny (Leif Garrett) help him in the church. Johnny discovers a gun left by Father John's brother, Lewis. Johnny wants to learn how to shoot. The Clayton gang has hit the town, led by Sam Clayton (an overacting Jack Palance) Palance's actual son, Cody, plays his son Zeke, a rapist. Richard Boone, in sort of a cameo, is the Sherriff.

After the gang kills a local man in a saloon, Father John tricks them and takes the killer in. The gang swears revenge. Father John is gunned down in front of his church. Johnny takes the gun and goes looking for Lewis. Somewhere along the way, Johnny becomes a mute. This is fine because he couldn't act in the first place. He finds Lewis living with his daughter. Instead of making Lewis look a little different, he has the same shitty wig and fake facial hair.

Lewis goes back with Johnny and dresses as his dead brother. All involved in Father John's murder are killed— In a stupid plot twist, it is revealed that Johnny is actually Sam Clayton's son. Ironic that his real son is playing his character's son. Sam has delusions about taking Johnny with him. Johnny mother is Jenny (Sybil Danning) who was raped by Clayton years ago.

Clayton ends up getting shot in the local graveyard and does an exaggerated death scene. The Sheriff arrests Zeke and takes him to hang. The film was shot on the cheap and shows it. There is some violence, mostly headshots. Palance shamelessly chews the scenery. Boone seems completely wasted and lost. Part of the reason was his distinctive voice wasn't used.

Boone was in poor health and drunk on the set. He told people in an interview that he just did "the worst picture ever made." Boone got into an argument and stormed off the set without looping his dialog. In some versions of the film, Van Cleef, Palance, and Boone are all dubbed by other actors. The film went straight to video. A film Lee did prior to this one, ***Kid Vengeance*** or just ***Vengeance***, was released after ***God's Gun***.

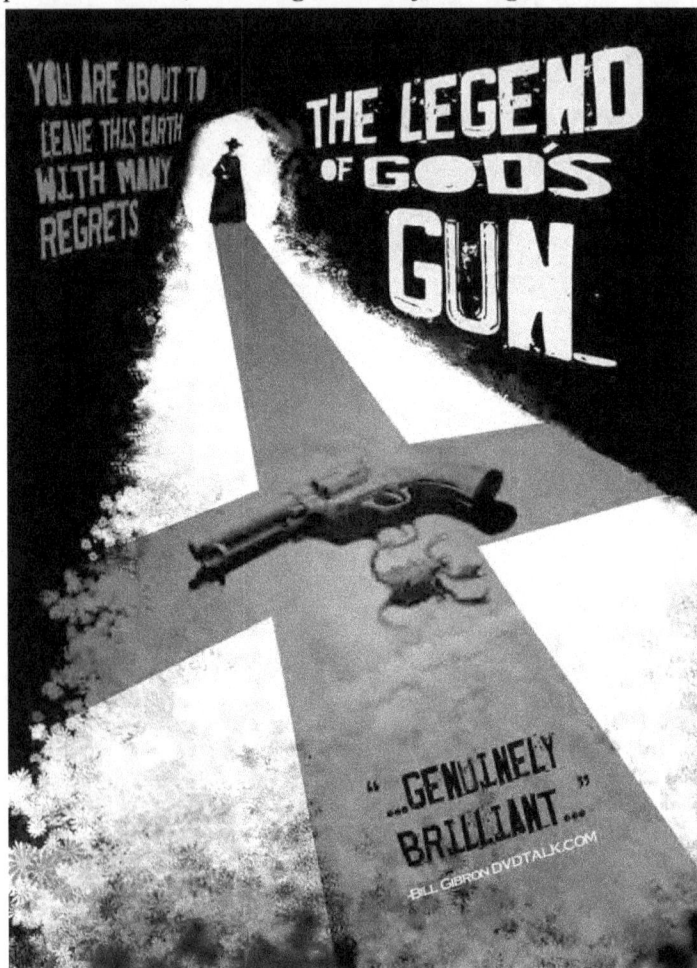

Vengeance or ***Kid Vengeance*** was another turd shot in in New Mexico. Another Golan Globus Production. I read these guys were complete marks for American actors.—It would have gone straight to video if Leif Garrett's hadn't become a teen idol with the release of an album. The director did mostly TV shows and ***Cornbread, Earl and Me***.

Van Cleef is McClain, a bandit with what looks like a fake beard. John Marley is Jesus, his 2nd in command. Jim Brown is Isaac, a prospector who struck it rich. Matt Clark is one of four brothers trying to rob Isaac's gold. Leif Garrett can't act. Being I'm a huge fan of Van Cleef, I decided to see this film as it was playing at a grindhouse, The Hollywood Theater, in the ghetto of East Orange NJ.

The place reeked of pot. In fact there was a haze of pot smoke in the lobby. No one cared. I lit a joint as the film started.

Dad is teaching Tommy (Garrett) to shoot. "There is hunting, then there is killing," he explains. McClain and his gang are in town getting supplies. The sheriff wants them gone in an hour. Isaac comes in with a bag of gold dust to be appraised. He is confronted by Grover (Matt Clark) and his three brothers.

They tell Isaac they are now his partners. A fight breaks out and one brother accidentally shoots another. Jesus sees the fight and finds out about the gold. They follow Isaac. Isaac runs into Tommy and family. Later so does the gang. McClain kills the father, rapes the mother, then kills her. Weird scene for Lee as he refused to hit the prostitute in The Good, the Bad and the Ugly. Guess he really needed the money. Now Tommy is tracking the gang as they have his sister, Lisa (Glynnis O'Connor), a captive.

Tommy starts killing gang members using snakes and scorpions. As an "avenger" he looks really out of place dressed like a Little Lord Fauntleroy. Grover and his brothers find Isaac's mine. They stake him out and take the gold, but McClain and his gang show up. They shoot it out. One brother is killed, the other two hide in the mine. McClain leaves Isaac to die. Tommy frees Isaac and the two join forces.

They track the gang to their hide out. McClain has a woman and a son there. He's going to 'retire" after they split the gold. The two idiot brothers try to grab it first and are gunned down. Isaac throws a bundle of dynamite into the building. McClain gives him back the gold, but isn't giving up that easily. Isaac throws more dynamite, killing Jesus and most of the gang. Isaac is killed freeing Lisa. McClain tries to make peace with Tommy, but Tommy empties a rifle into him. These scenes are poorly lit. McClain's son gets the drop on Tommy, but lets him ride away. The end.

So now I'm stoned and pissed off that I wasted 90 minutes of my life watching this. I was going to leave, then the co feature came on, ***Assault on Precinct 13***. Intrigued, I stayed and became a John Carpenter fan. It really sucks that Lee's last two westerns were so bad. Not knowing what was going on in real life, Tom Atkins told us during a Q&A that he worked with Lee on ***Escape from New York*** and Lee was dying of throat cancer. That was 1981. Lee died of heart failure in 1989. He either beat the cancer or it went into remission because he didn't do another film, ***The Killing Machine***, until 1984. Then he had a TV series, ***The Master***, and did six more films before he died.

Forgotten Horrors: The Manster

Here we have a film that created the dreaded two headed monster sub genre. An American production shot in Japan around 1959. It opens in a bathhouse with Japanese ladies bathing. A hairy creature bursts in and blood splatters across the screen as the credits roll. Doctor Suzuki is the resident mad scientist whose laboratory is built in the side of a volcano. Guess that's prerequisite for '50s and '60s mad doctors, having labs in dangerous places. She Demons mad doctor had a volcano too. *Mad Doctor of Blood Island* had a cave laboratory. And so on.

Anyway the rampaging creature is Suzuki's brother. The brother and Suzuki's wife volunteered to test his new serum. Genji Suzuki is disfigured and kept in a cage. She makes Sarah Sanders Huckabee look cute. The brother is a hairy monster that Suzuki shoots. He disposes of the body via a sliding door that opens into the volcano, how cool is that? A reporter, Larry Stanford, visit's the Doctor to get a story.

The doctor slips a drug into his drink. Over the objections of his henchwoman, Tara, he injects his new improved serum into Larry's neck. Larry wakes up and apologizes for falling asleep. Suzuki asks Larry to join him in Tokyo for some fun. Larry is supposed to return to New York to see his wife. Suzuki takes him to a " house of pleasure' to get laid. Suzuki also fixes him up with Tara who is "available." Not-so-subtle hints of rampant sexual activity.

Larry's wife, Linda, arrives un announced. Larry leaves with Tara then goes on a bender. He sees a patch of his skin turn weird on his shoulder. Then his hand turns into a claw. He wanders into a temple, then kills the priest he encounters. He starts killing random women he finds walking the streets. His boss visits him, bringing a psychiatrist. Larry goes ballistic and chases them out. Larry pulls off his shirt to find an eye growing out of his shoulder.

Larry goes to the psychiatrist's office and breaks in. The doctor calls the police. Larry starts moaning and grows a second head. Picture a balloon inflating.

Larry strangles the doctor and the cops chase him. The Larry thing kills a lot of cops, bashing their heads in with rocks. He throws a couple off of a building. He heads back to the lab. Suzuki shoots his former wife and is about to commit *hara-kiri* when Larry arrives. Suzuki injects Larry with another serum. Larry kills the doctor with his own knife. He knocks out Tara and carries her to the volcano. The new serum makes Larry split into two beings; one is Larry, the other a hairy beast. The split is done behind a tree as the two pull apart.

The hairy thing tries to throw Tara into the volcano. Larry stops him and they brawl. When Hairy gets the upper hand, Tara attacks him. Hairy throws Tara into the volcano. Larry pushes Hairy over the edge as the police arrive. Larry's boss and Linda ruminate on the good in Larry versus the evil in him.

The Manster was originally released as *The Split* and put on a double bill with *Horror Chamber of Doctor Faustus,* the retitled *Eyes Without a Face*. It was sold to TV as *The Manster* and became fodder for horror host on shows like Chiller and Supernatural theater.

There was never a two-headed monster craze, but some other two headed monster movies were made. *The Thing with Two Heads* (1972) featured the head of a racist doctor (Ray Milland) being transplanted on a death row inmate (Rosey Grier). Written by the team of Lee Frost and Wes Bishop and directed by Lee Frost. The head to head dialog is pretty funny.

The Incredible Two-Headed Transplant (1971) had Bruce Dern doing what he does best, acting crazy. He is Doctor Girard, a rich mad scientist. He grafts the head of a psychopath (Albert Cole) on to a hulking, retarded man (John Bloom). It escapes and terrorizes the local populace. Look for Gary Kent as a biker trying to fight the monster.

The Man With Two Heads (1972) didn't have two heads. It's Andy Milligan's take on *Dr. Jekyll and Mr Hyde*. Distributor William Mishkin changed the title from *Dr. Jekyll and Mr Blood* to capitalize on the aforementioned films. If two heads were actually called for, Andy would have glues a paper mache` one on the actor's shoulder.

Obviously director Sam Rami had seen *The Manster.* In his *Army of Darkness*, Ash grows an eye on his shoulder, then a head, then splits into two people. *The Manster* fell into public domain, but recently was restored on a new Blu Ray. Trust me, it's worth a look.